THE
MINAMATA STORY

An EcoTragedy

SEÁN MICHAEL WILSON
ILLUSTRATIONS BY AKIKO SHIMOJIMA
FOREWORD BY BRIAN SMALL

STONE BRIDGE PRESS • *BERKELEY, CALIFORNIA*

Published by
Stone Bridge Press
P. O. Box 8208, Berkeley, CA 94707
TEL 510-524-8732 • sbp@stonebridge.com • www.stonebridge.com

Text © 2021 Seán Michael Wilson.
Illustrations © 2021 Akiko Shimojima.

Thanks to Hiro Babaguchi for art assistance.

Printed in the United States of America.

p-ISBN 978-1-61172-056-3
e-ISBN 978-1-61172-940-5

FOREWORD

Minamata's sacrifice to industry demands greater international recognition. In the 1970s Eugene Smith's documentary photographs[1] iconized Tomoko Kamimura and her mother. The art critic John Berger,[2] with a comprehension strengthened by long thought about peasant losses,[3] tells us that Smith's iconic photos take the form of Mary embracing Jesus. The long-suffering mourner embraces the tortured and sacrificed victim. We worry about authoritarian abuses of religion, but some experiences are beyond our ability to comprehend verbally, so we work with sacred images. The sacrificial victims of Minamata help us grasp the industrial destruction of life.

Minamata should be a place of sacred contemplation. Just as dioxins in the breast milk of mothers the world over are invasive,[4] methylmercury compounds in the brain and uterus are invasive. Industrially produced methylmercury combines with cysteine to mimic methionine, an essential amino acid. People and cats, living organisms in general, are defenseless, taking in mercury-based poison while mistaking it for methionine.

Chisso's factory poured effluent into an enclosed portion of the Shiranui Sea until it came to be suspected of causing the strange disease. But instead of rethinking its chemical processes and trying to remove harmful products, the corporation diverted the effluent to a river mouth for wider dispersal.

The Minamata Story: An EcoTragedy shows us the human damage of factory effluent in the Shiranui Sea. We have to apply this real-world example to better understand the ecologies of our earth and our bodies, and to better inform our search for remedies.

Brian Small
Activist and teacher

1   Eugene Smith and Aileen M. Smith, *Minamata* (Holt, Rinehart, and Winston, 1975).
2   John Berger, *Understanding a Photograph* (Penguin Classics, 2013).
3   ———, *Pig Earth*, vol. 1 of *Into Their Labours* (Vintage Books, 1979).
4   https://storyofstuff.org/wp-content/uploads/2020/01 StoryofStuff_AnnotatedScript.pdf (accessed 2019/12/17).

PAST AND PRESENT

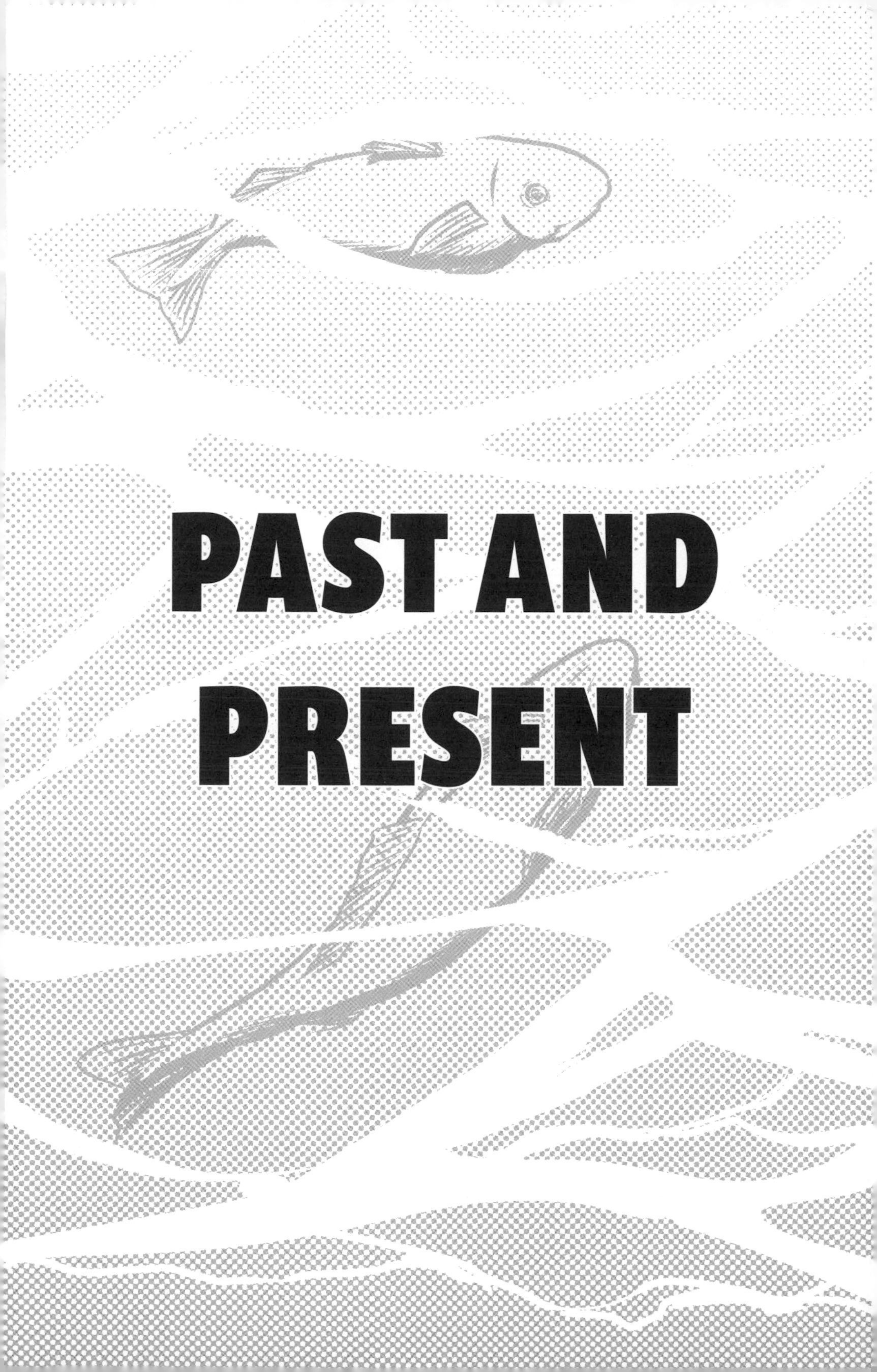

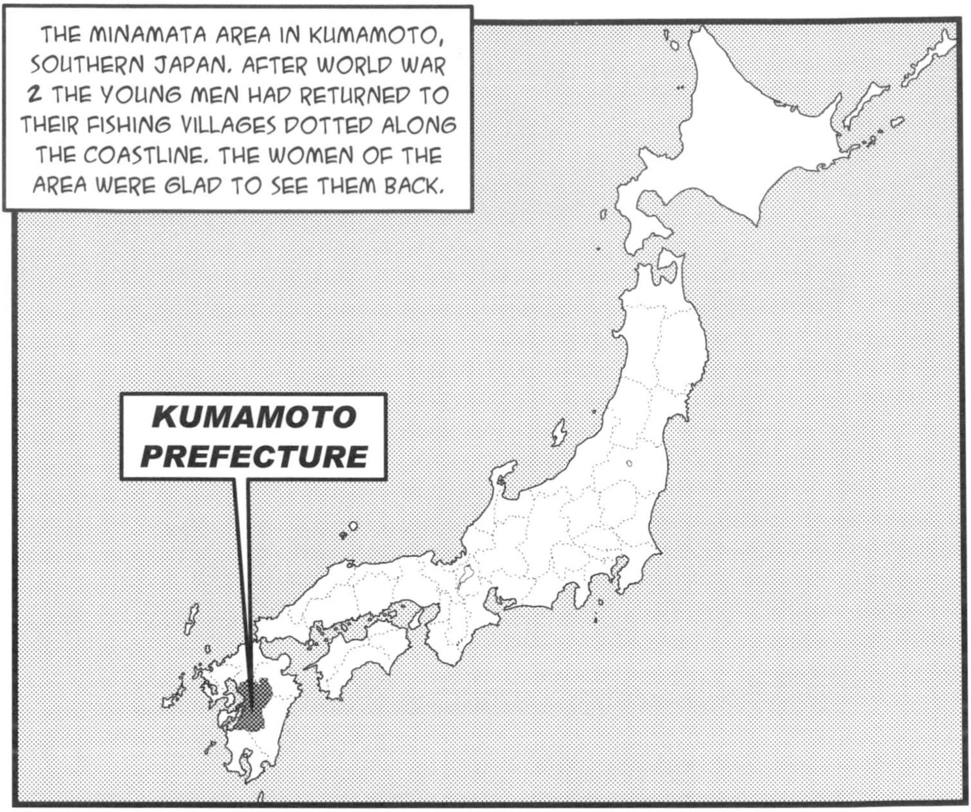
THE MINAMATA AREA IN KUMAMOTO, SOUTHERN JAPAN. AFTER WORLD WAR 2 THE YOUNG MEN HAD RETURNED TO THEIR FISHING VILLAGES DOTTED ALONG THE COASTLINE. THE WOMEN OF THE AREA WERE GLAD TO SEE THEM BACK.
KUMAMOTO PREFECTURE

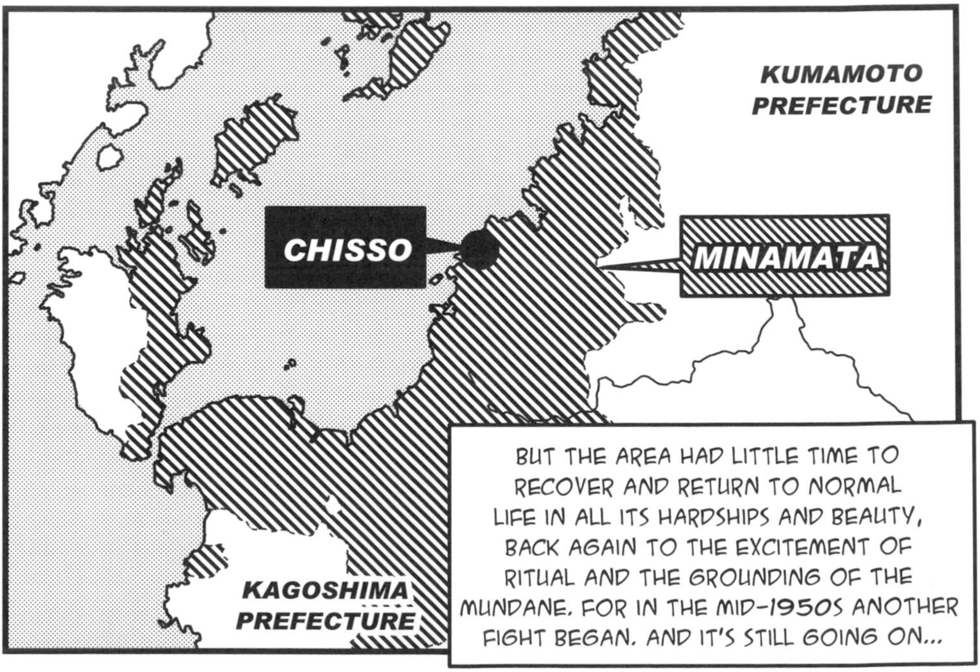
KUMAMOTO PREFECTURE
CHISSO
MINAMATA
KAGOSHIMA PREFECTURE
BUT THE AREA HAD LITTLE TIME TO RECOVER AND RETURN TO NORMAL LIFE IN ALL ITS HARDSHIPS AND BEAUTY, BACK AGAIN TO THE EXCITEMENT OF RITUAL AND THE GROUNDING OF THE MUNDANE. FOR IN THE MID-1950S ANOTHER FIGHT BEGAN. AND IT'S STILL GOING ON...

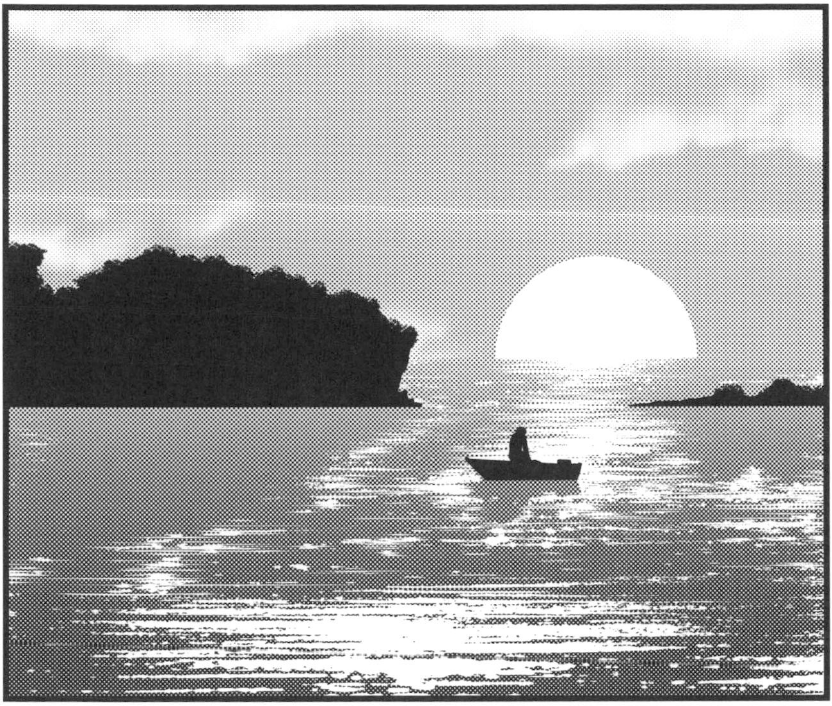

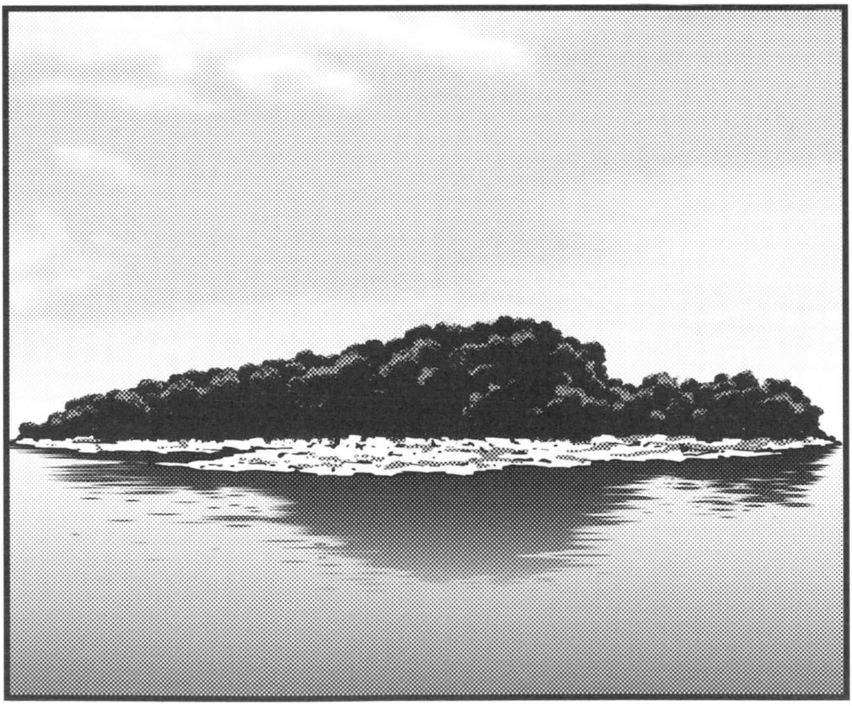

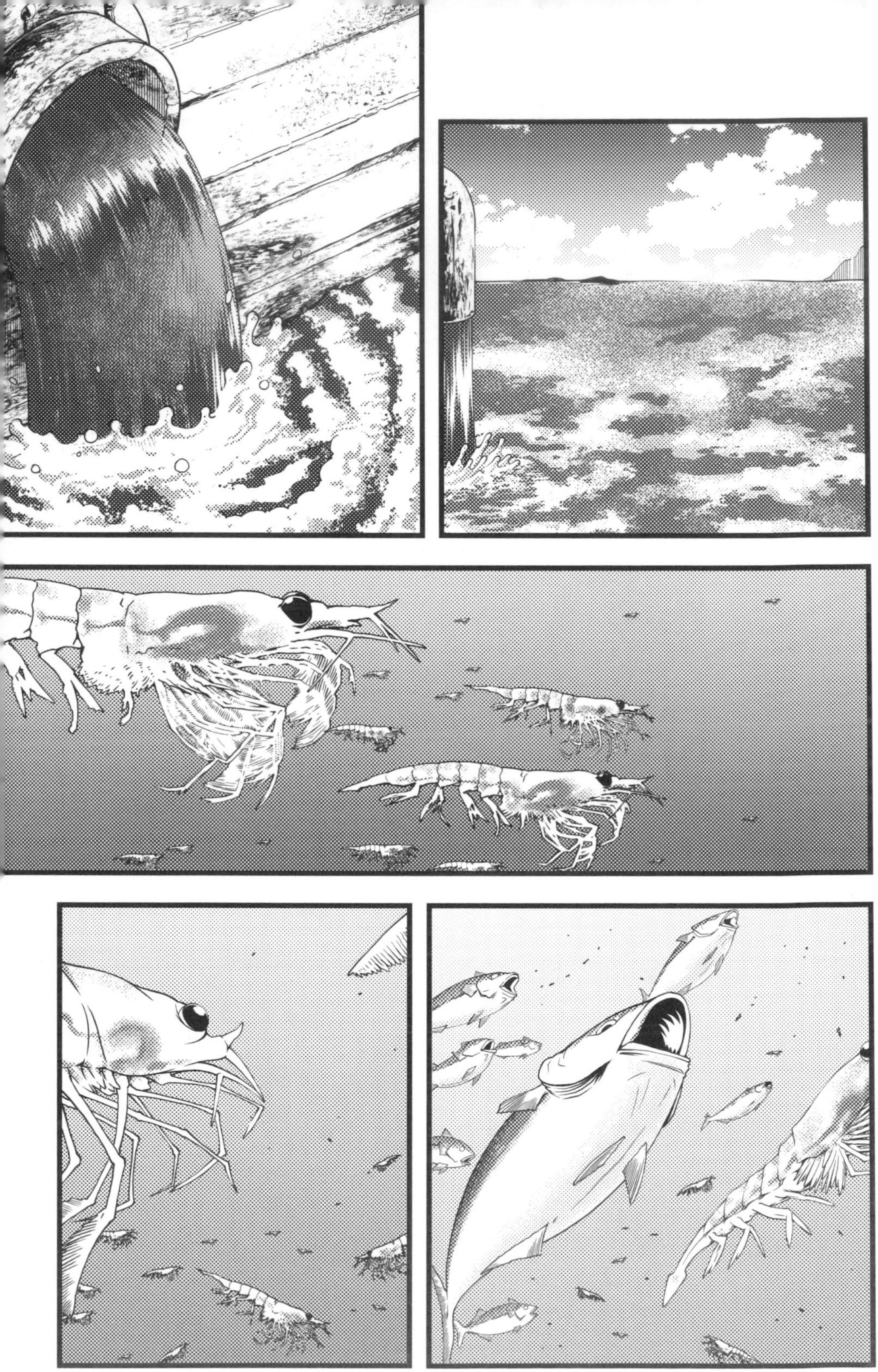

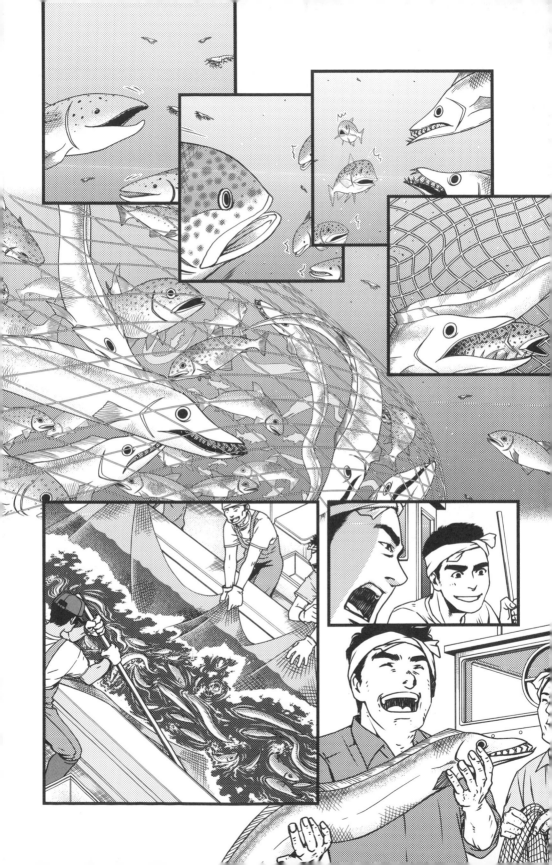

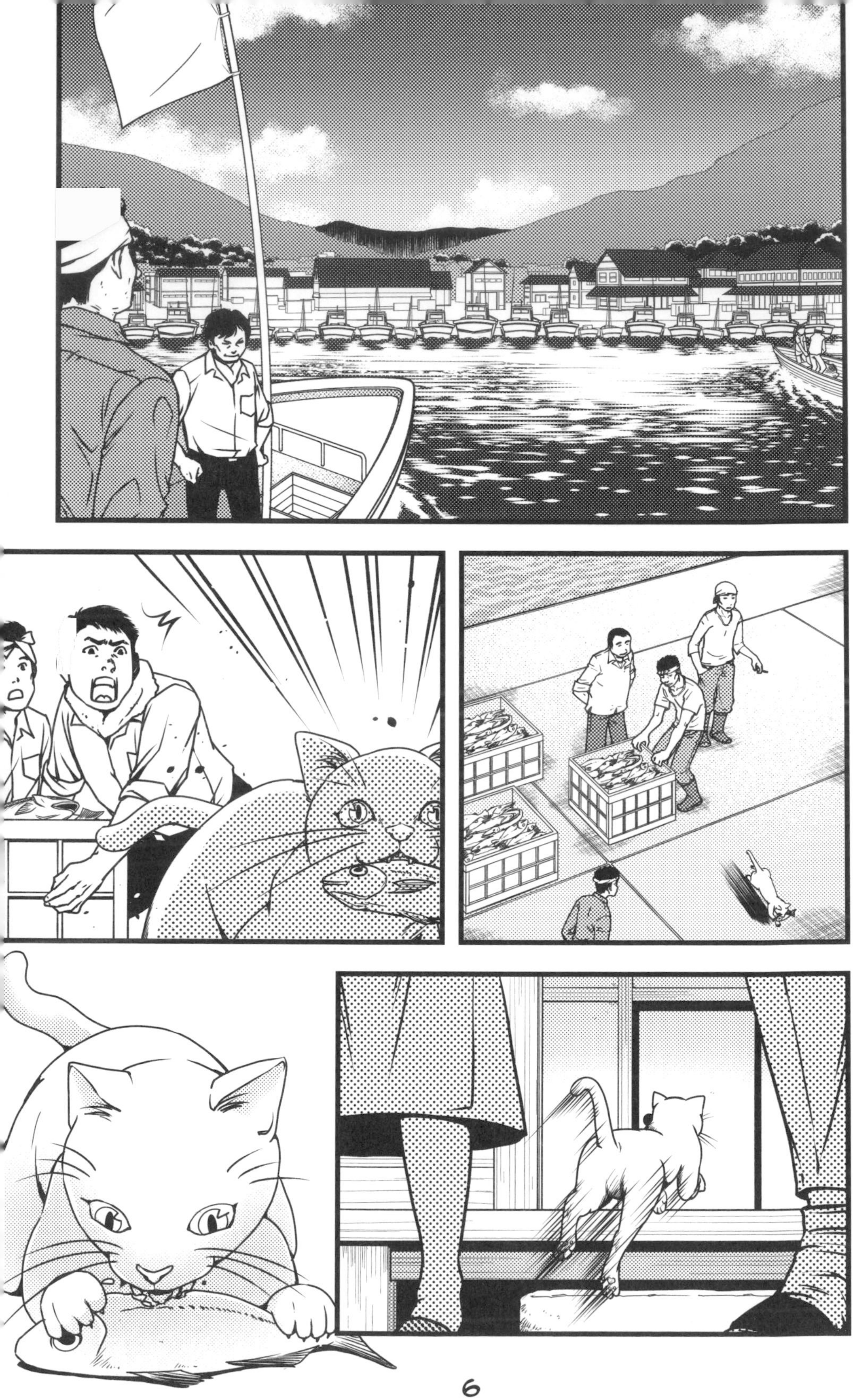

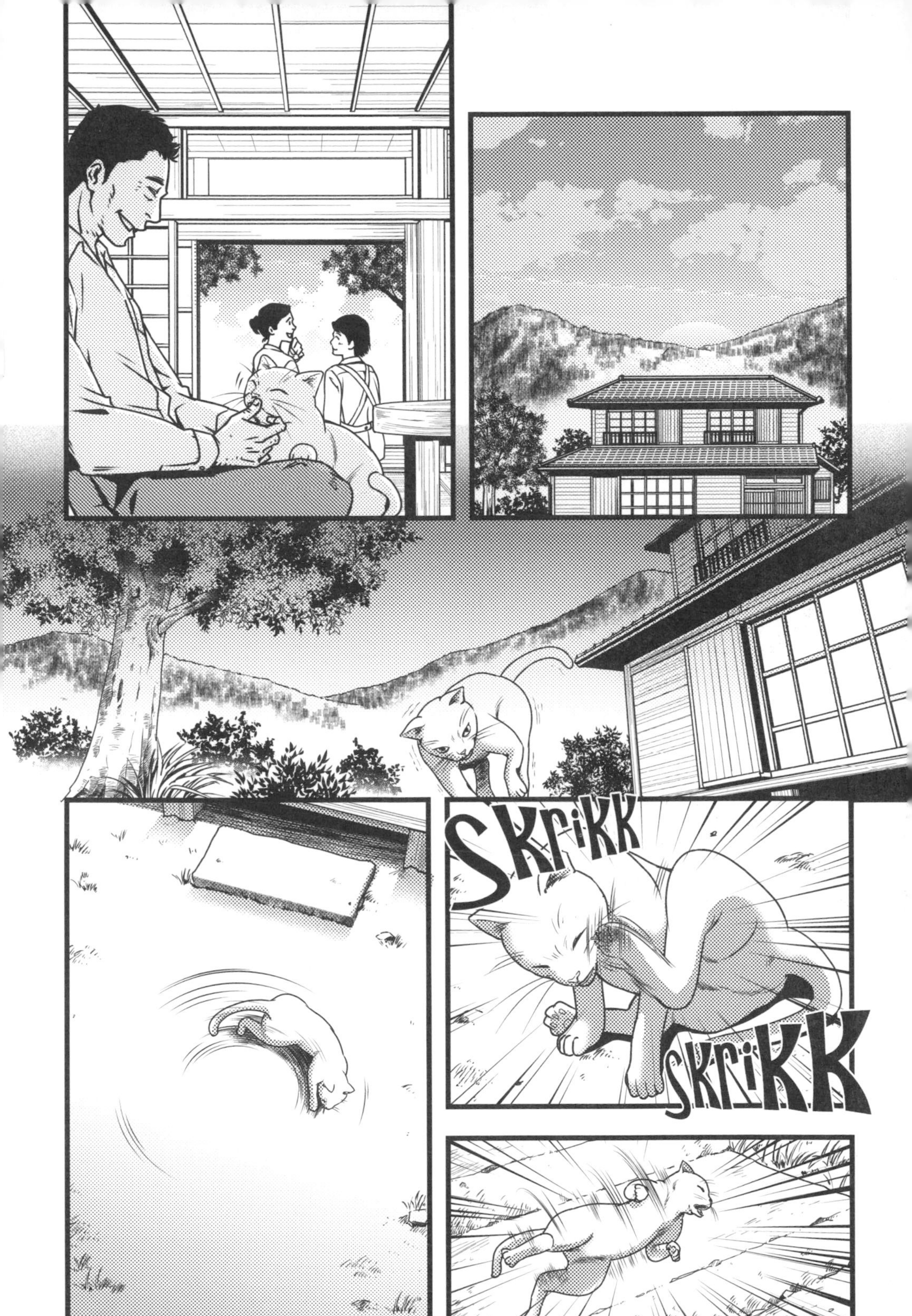
SKRIKK
SKRIKK

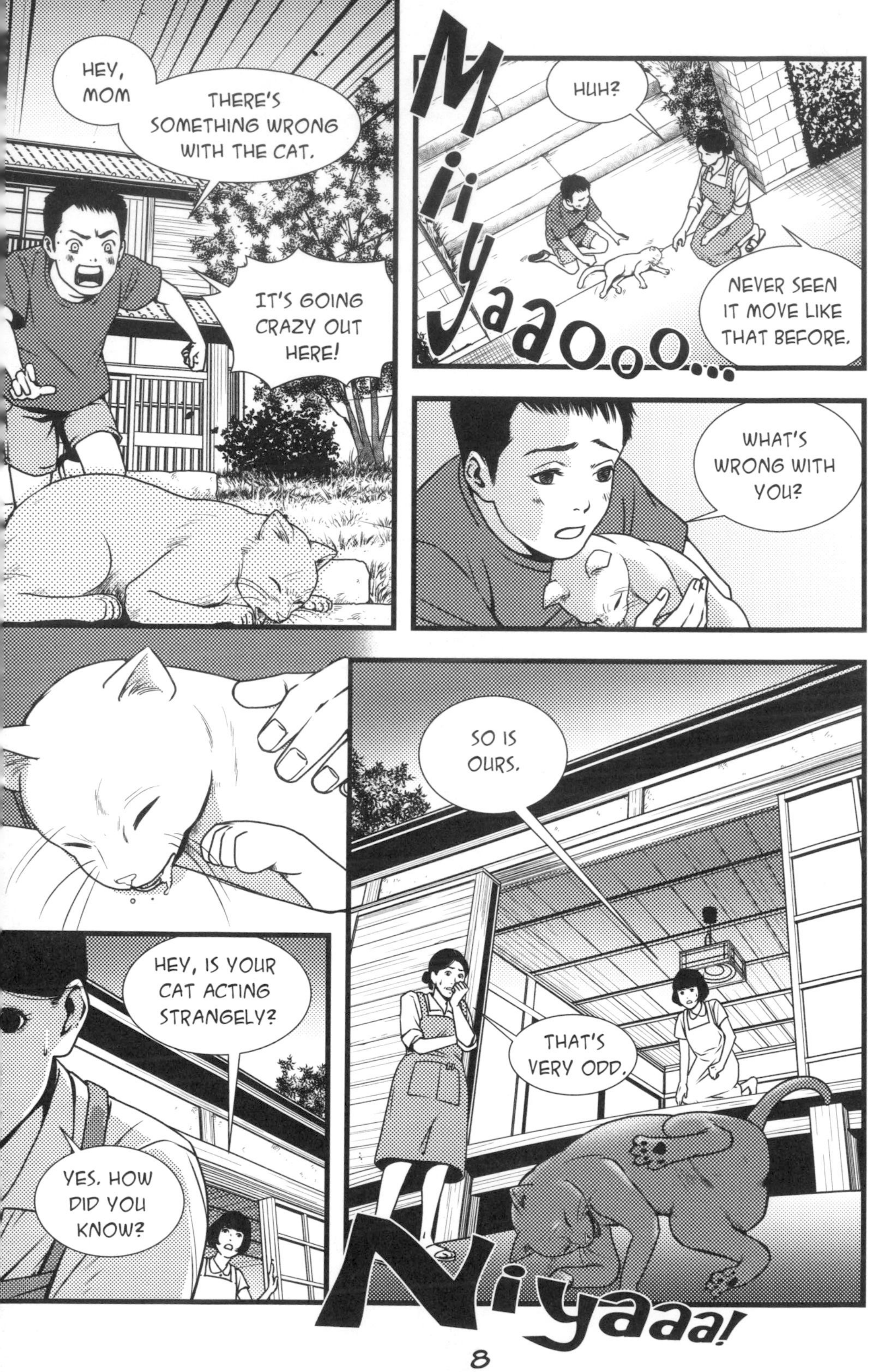
HEY, MOM
THERE'S SOMETHING WRONG WITH THE CAT.
IT'S GOING CRAZY OUT HERE!
Miiyaaooo...
HUH?
NEVER SEEN IT MOVE LIKE THAT BEFORE.
WHAT'S WRONG WITH YOU?
HEY, IS YOUR CAT ACTING STRANGELY?
YES. HOW DID YOU KNOW?
SO IS OURS.
THAT'S VERY ODD.
Niyaaa!

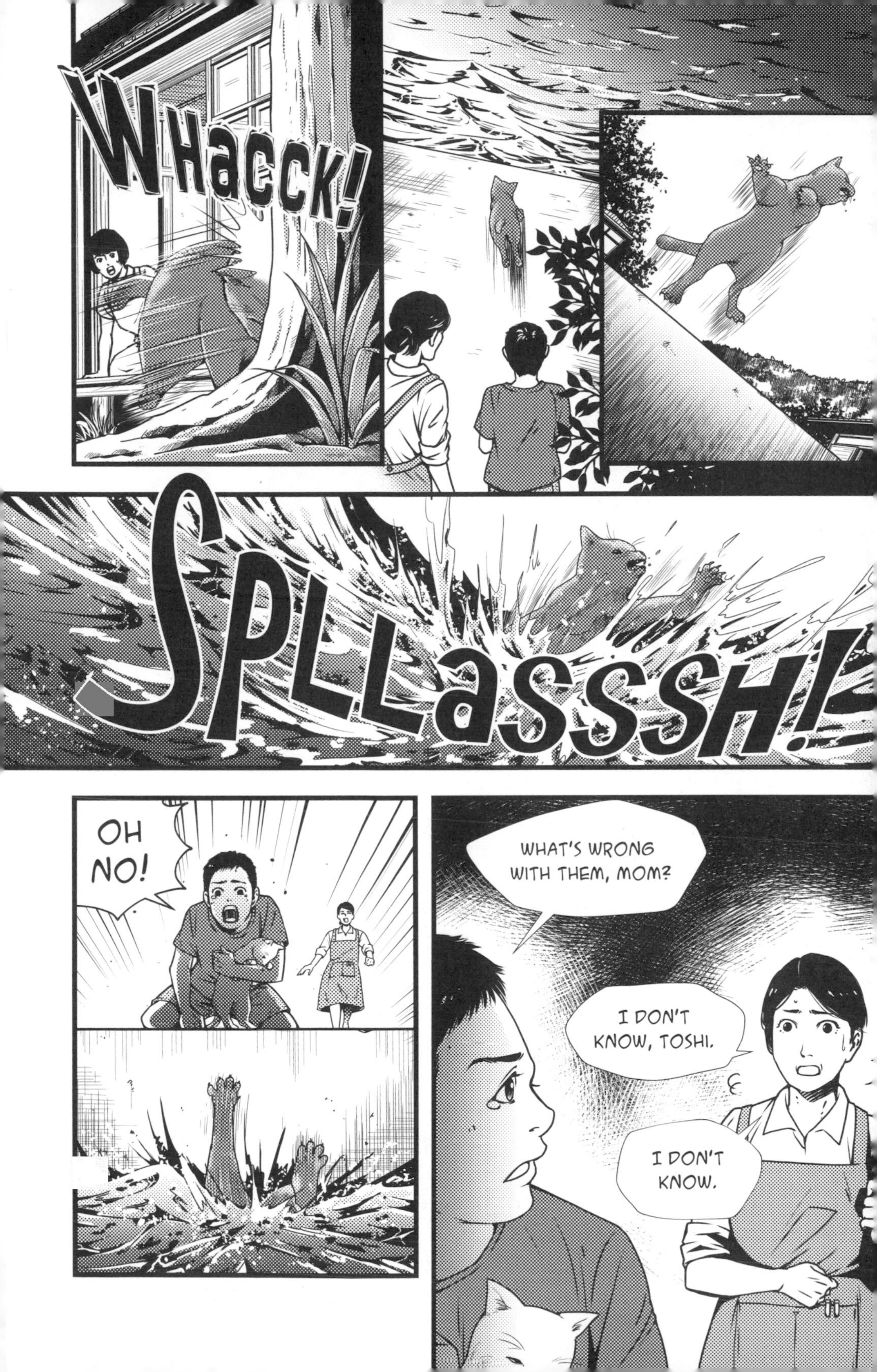
WHACCK!
SPLLASSSH!
OH NO!
WHAT'S WRONG WITH THEM, MOM?
I DON'T KNOW, TOSHI.
I DON'T KNOW.

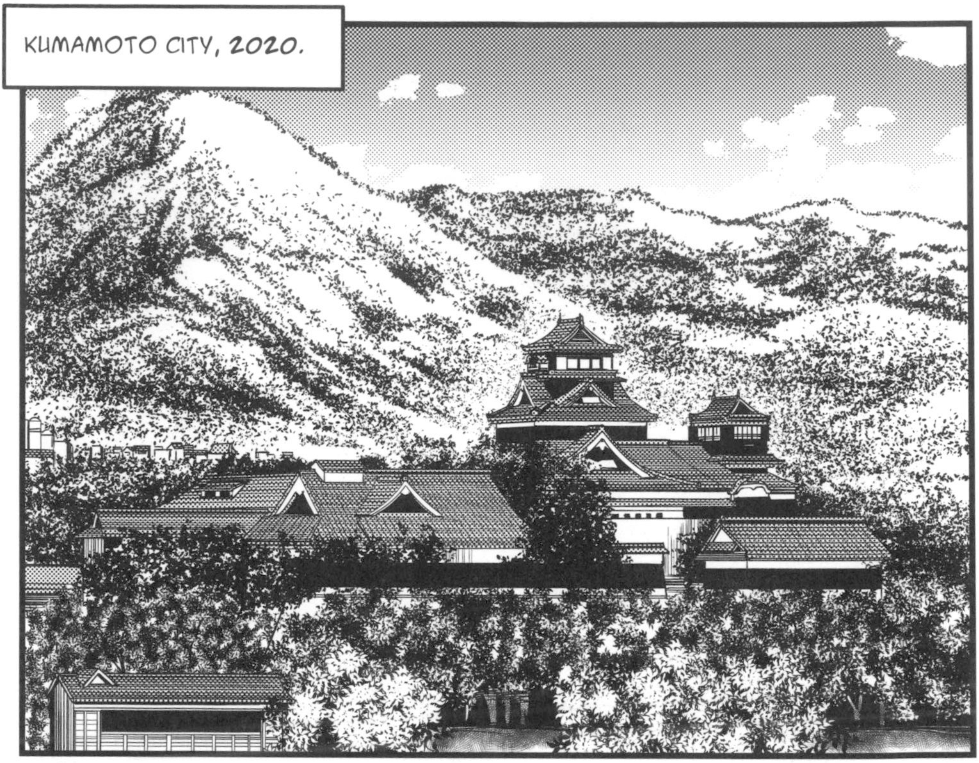
KUMAMOTO CITY, 2020.

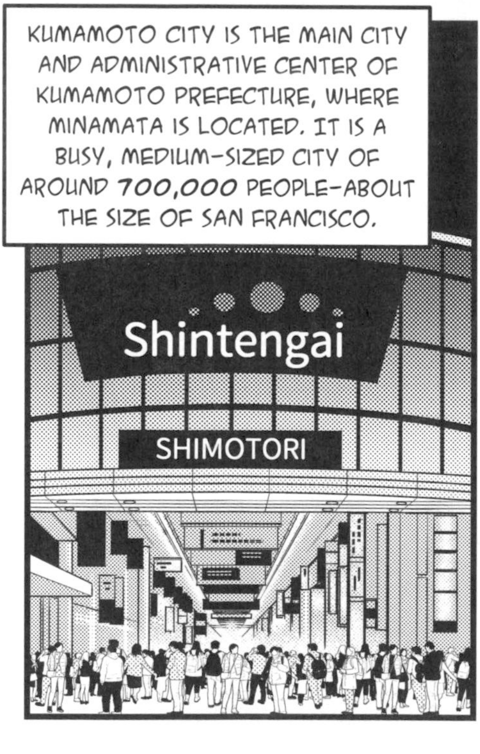
KUMAMOTO CITY IS THE MAIN CITY AND ADMINISTRATIVE CENTER OF KUMAMOTO PREFECTURE, WHERE MINAMATA IS LOCATED. IT IS A BUSY, MEDIUM-SIZED CITY OF AROUND 700,000 PEOPLE-ABOUT THE SIZE OF SAN FRANCISCO.
Shintengai
SHIMOTORI

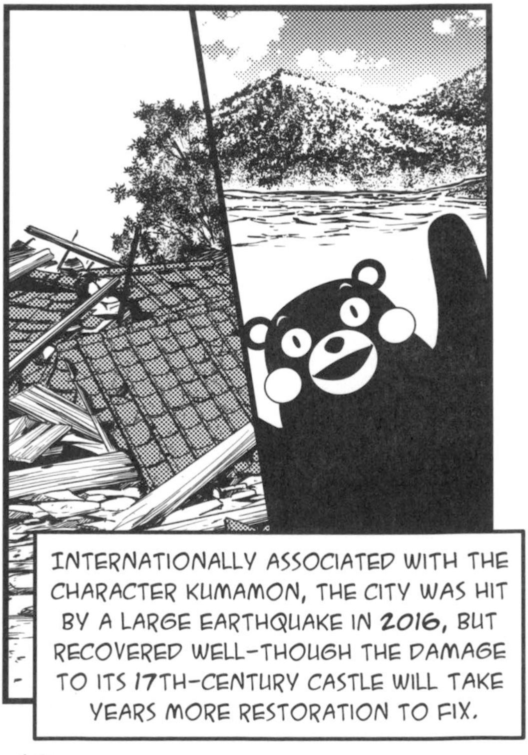
INTERNATIONALLY ASSOCIATED WITH THE CHARACTER KUMAMON, THE CITY WAS HIT BY A LARGE EARTHQUAKE IN 2016, BUT RECOVERED WELL-THOUGH THE DAMAGE TO ITS 17TH-CENTURY CASTLE WILL TAKE YEARS MORE RESTORATION TO FIX.

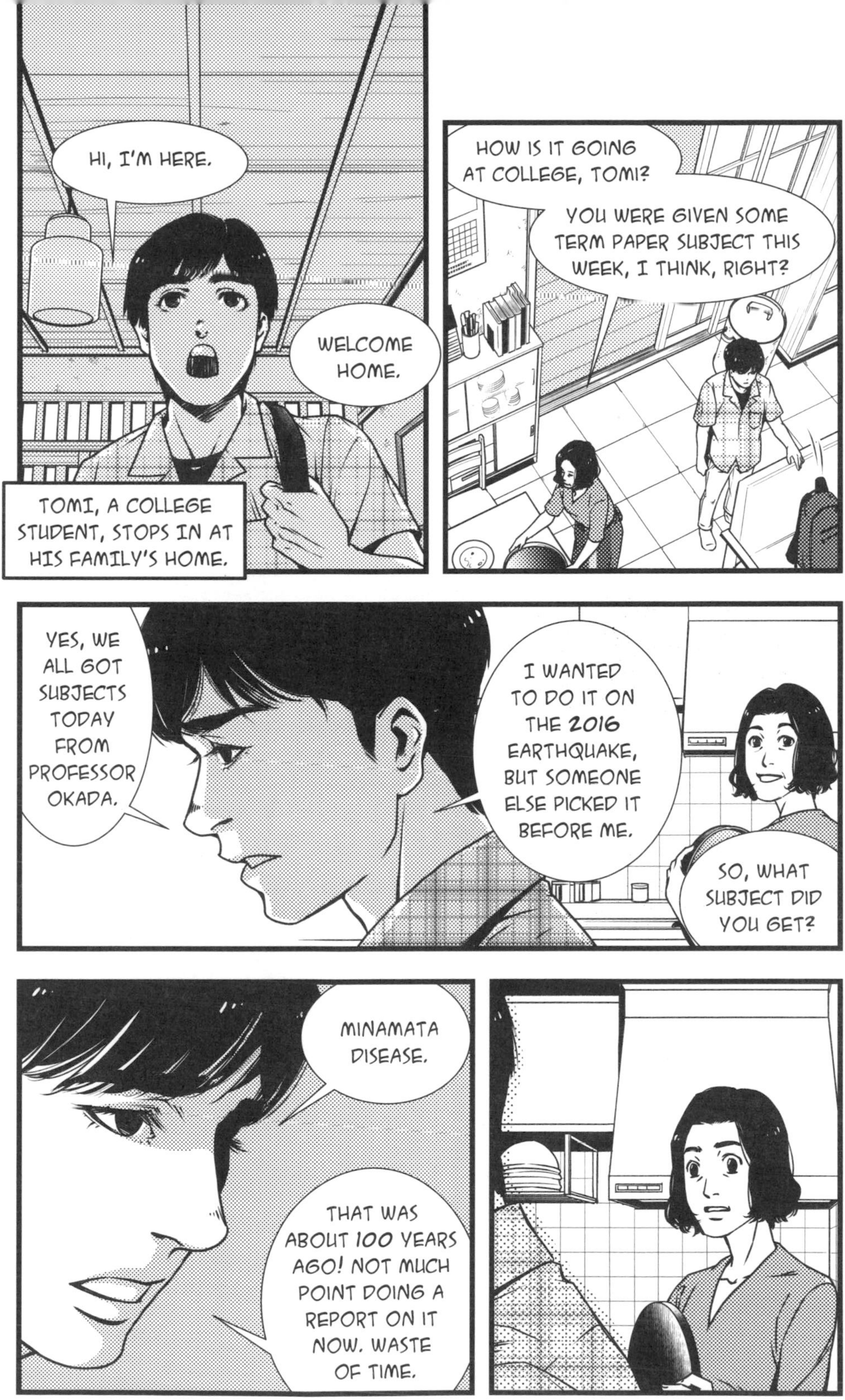
HI, I'M HERE.
WELCOME HOME.
TOMI, A COLLEGE STUDENT, STOPS IN AT HIS FAMILY'S HOME.
HOW IS IT GOING AT COLLEGE, TOMI?
YOU WERE GIVEN SOME TERM PAPER SUBJECT THIS WEEK, I THINK, RIGHT?
YES, WE ALL GOT SUBJECTS TODAY FROM PROFESSOR OKADA.
I WANTED TO DO IT ON THE 2016 EARTHQUAKE, BUT SOMEONE ELSE PICKED IT BEFORE ME.
SO, WHAT SUBJECT DID YOU GET?
MINAMATA DISEASE.
THAT WAS ABOUT 100 YEARS AGO! NOT MUCH POINT DOING A REPORT ON IT NOW. WASTE OF TIME.

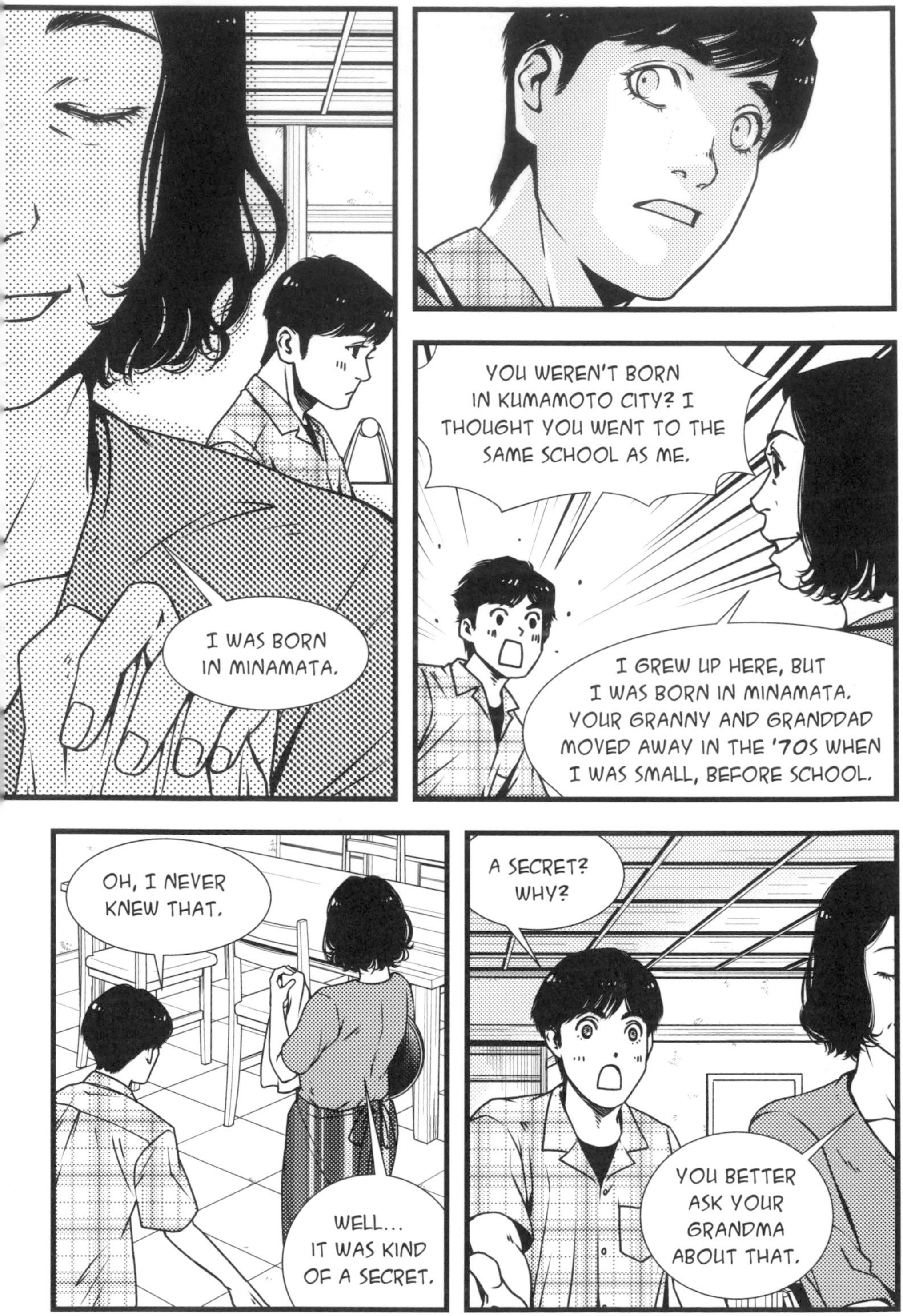
I WAS BORN IN MINAMATA.
YOU WEREN'T BORN IN KUMAMOTO CITY? I THOUGHT YOU WENT TO THE SAME SCHOOL AS ME.
I GREW UP HERE, BUT I WAS BORN IN MINAMATA. YOUR GRANNY AND GRANDDAD MOVED AWAY IN THE '70S WHEN I WAS SMALL, BEFORE SCHOOL.
OH, I NEVER KNEW THAT.
WELL... IT WAS KIND OF A SECRET.
A SECRET? WHY?
YOU BETTER ASK YOUR GRANDMA ABOUT THAT.

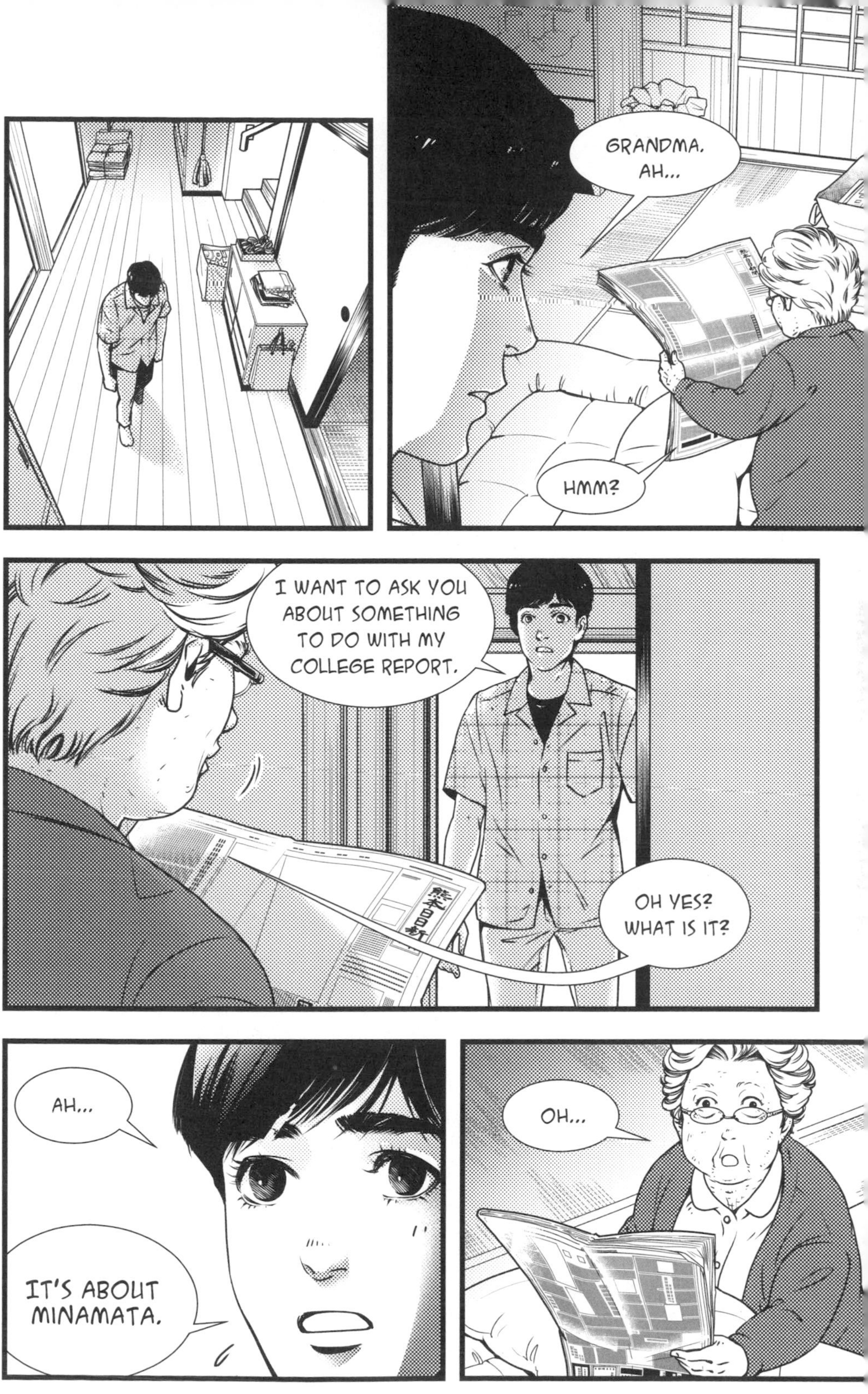
GRANDMA, AH...
HMM?
I WANT TO ASK YOU ABOUT SOMETHING TO DO WITH MY COLLEGE REPORT.
OH YES? WHAT IS IT?
AH...
IT'S ABOUT MINAMATA.
OH...

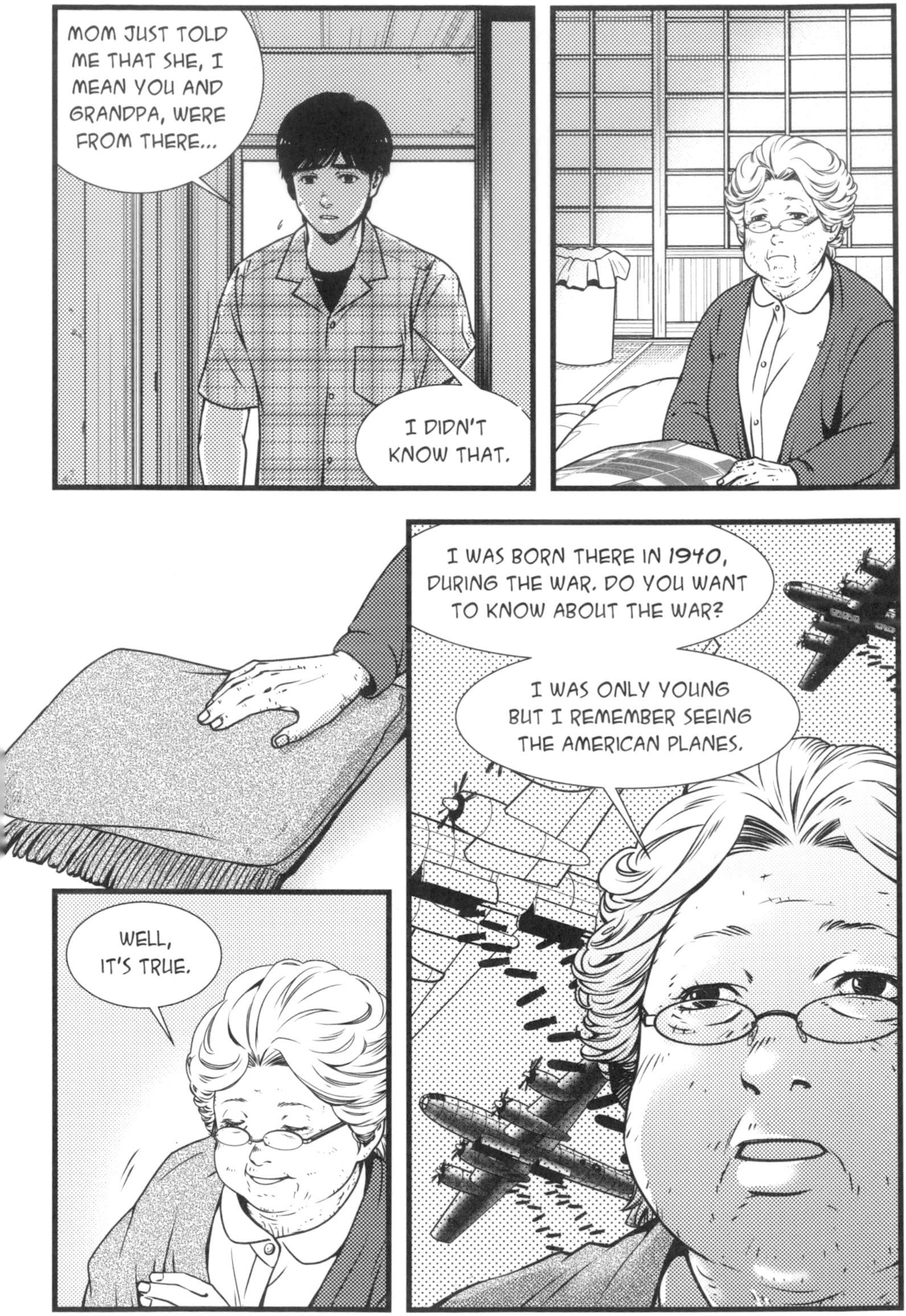
MOM JUST TOLD ME THAT SHE, I MEAN YOU AND GRANDPA, WERE FROM THERE...
I DIDN'T KNOW THAT.
WELL, IT'S TRUE.
I WAS BORN THERE IN 1940, DURING THE WAR. DO YOU WANT TO KNOW ABOUT THE WAR?
I WAS ONLY YOUNG BUT I REMEMBER SEEING THE AMERICAN PLANES.

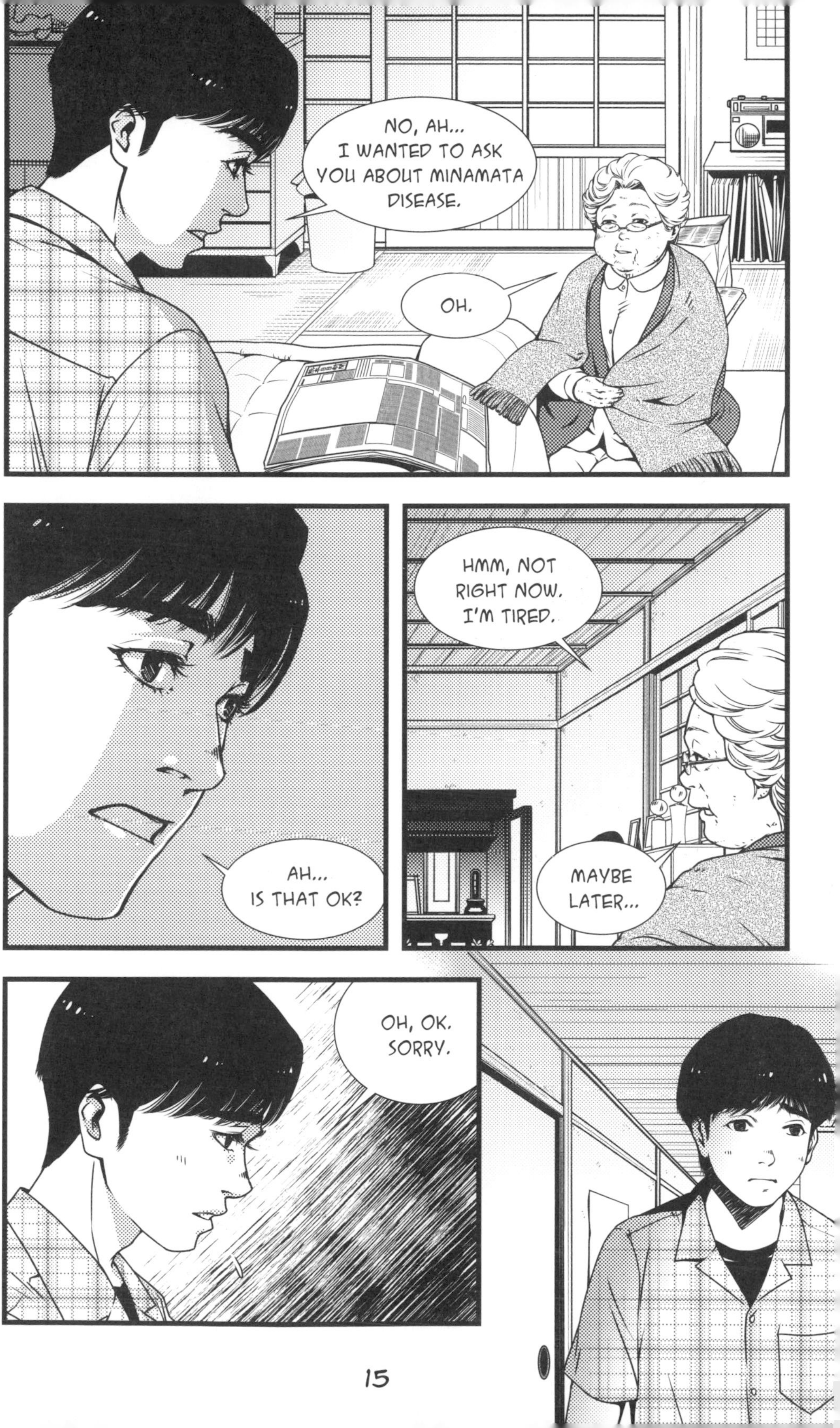
NO, AH...
I WANTED TO ASK
YOU ABOUT MINAMATA
DISEASE.
OH.
AH...
IS THAT OK?
HMM, NOT
RIGHT NOW.
I'M TIRED.
MAYBE
LATER...
OH, OK.
SORRY.

LATER...

METHYLMERCURY WAS RELEASED FROM THE FACTORY INTO THE SEA, THEN ACCUMULATED IN AQUATIC ORGANISMS VIA THEIR GILLS OR INTESTINES DIRECTLY, OR THROUGH THE FOOD CHAIN OF BIGGER FISH EATING SMALLER FISH.

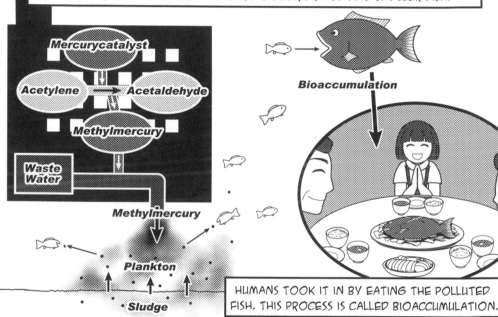

Mercurycatalyst

Acetylene → *Acetaldehyde*

Methylmercury

Waste Water

Methylmercury

Plankton

Sludge

Bioaccumulation

HUMANS TOOK IT IN BY EATING THE POLLUTED FISH. THIS PROCESS IS CALLED BIOACCUMULATION.

TOMI, YOUR GRANNY SPOKE TO ME.

OH, I THINK I UPSET HER MAYBE.

NO, NO, SHE SAID IT'S OK. SHE'LL TALK TO YOU TOMORROW ABOUT IT. SHE'S JUST TIRED NOW.

OH, OK... GOOD.

水俣病

HOMECOMING

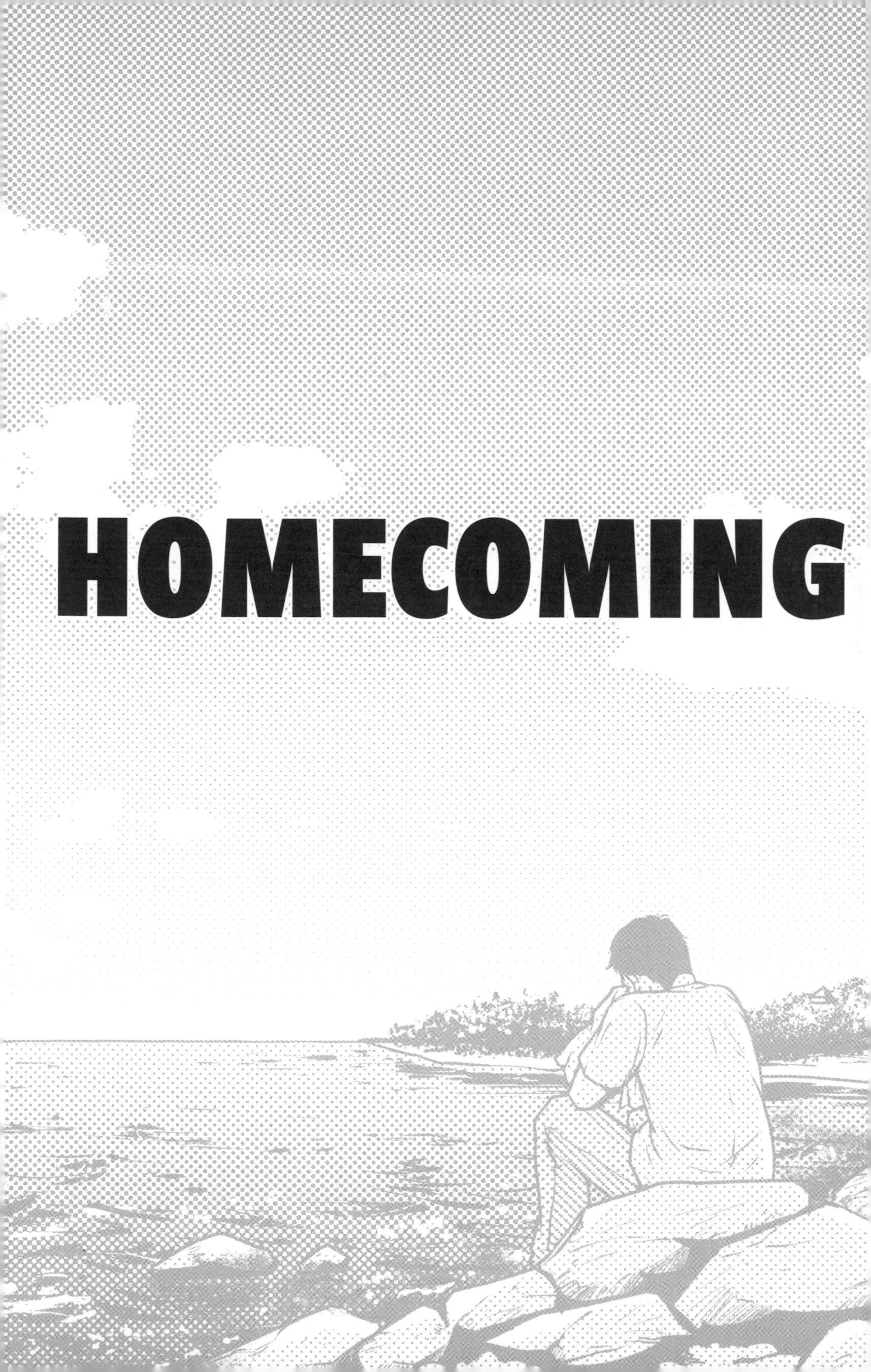

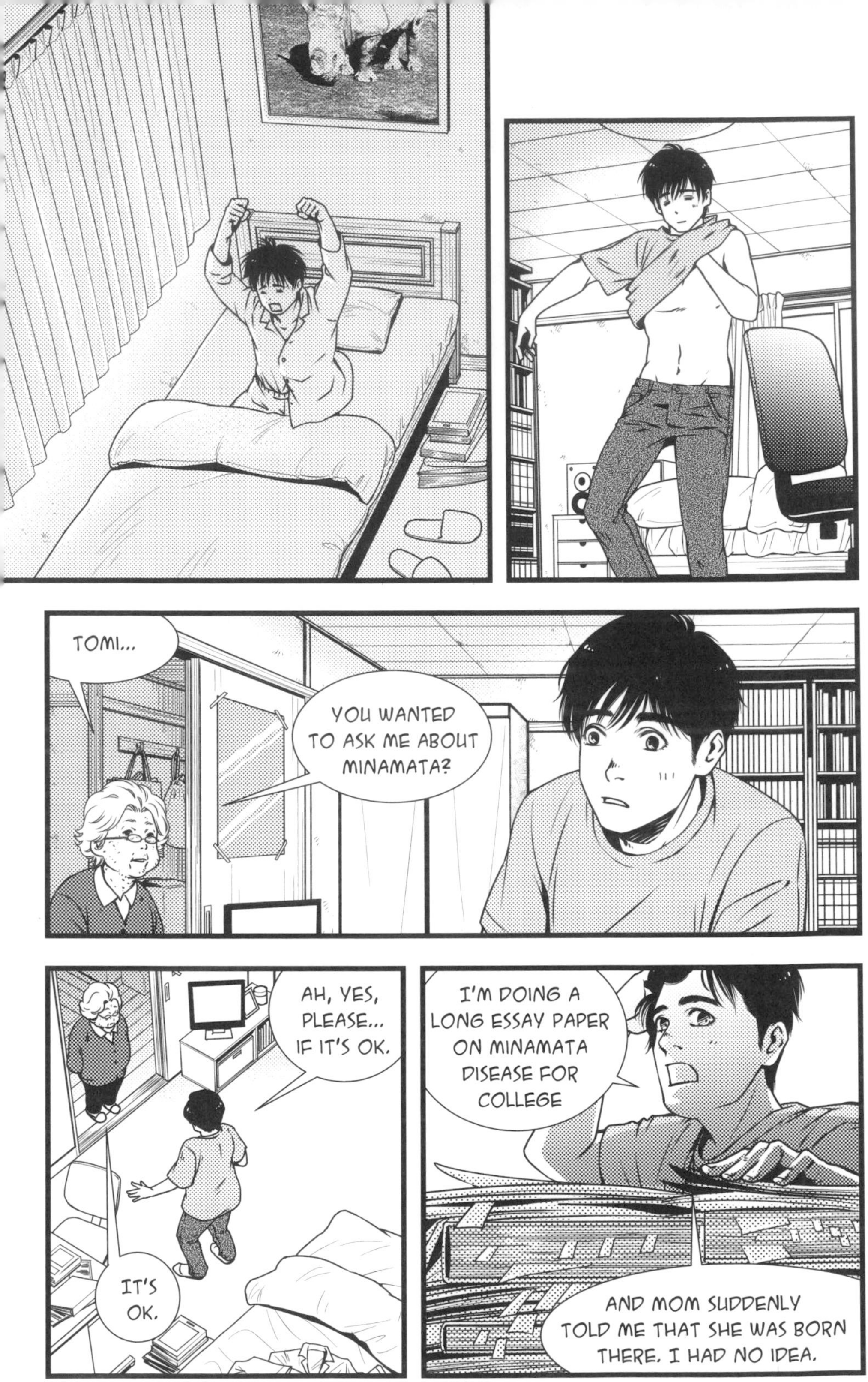
TOMI...
YOU WANTED TO ASK ME ABOUT MINAMATA?
AH, YES, PLEASE... IF IT'S OK.
IT'S OK.
I'M DOING A LONG ESSAY PAPER ON MINAMATA DISEASE FOR COLLEGE
AND MOM SUDDENLY TOLD ME THAT SHE WAS BORN THERE. I HAD NO IDEA.

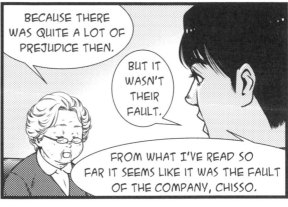

WELL, LET ME TELL YOU SOMETHING SERIOUS. A LOT OF PEOPLE LEFT MINAMATA IN THE '60S AND '70S WHEN THE DISEASE PROBLEM WAS THE MOST WIDELY KNOWN. AND MOST OF THEM FELT IT WAS A SHAMEFUL THING AND KEPT IT A SECRET.
WHY WAS THAT?
BECAUSE THERE WAS QUITE A LOT OF PREJUDICE THEN.
BUT IT WASN'T THEIR FAULT.
FROM WHAT I'VE READ SO FAR IT SEEMS LIKE IT WAS THE FAULT OF THE COMPANY, CHISSO.
YES. BUT THINGS ARE RARELY SO BLACK AND WHITE, SO CLEAR CUT. LIFE IS COMPLICATED.
LET ME TELL YOU SOMETHING ABOUT WHAT HAPPENED THEN.
"NOWADAYS ALMOST EVERYONE SAYS WHAT A PITY IT WAS FOR THE MINAMATA DISEASE SUFFERERS, BUT BACK THEN IT WAS DIFFERENT. I REMEMBER ONE PARTICULAR SIGN FROM WHEN I WAS ABOUT 17 OR 18."
魚屋
売られている魚はすべて遠洋でとられたものです
SIGN: "ALL THE FISH WE SELL ARE CAUGHT IN THE DEEP SEA."

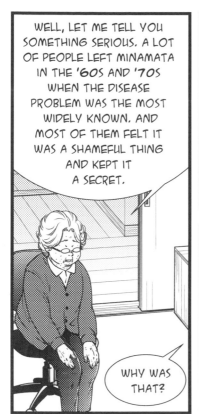

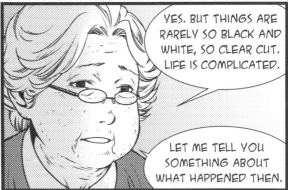

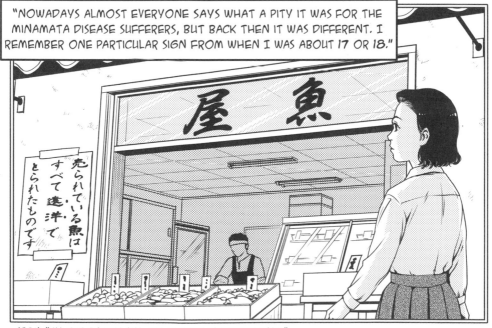

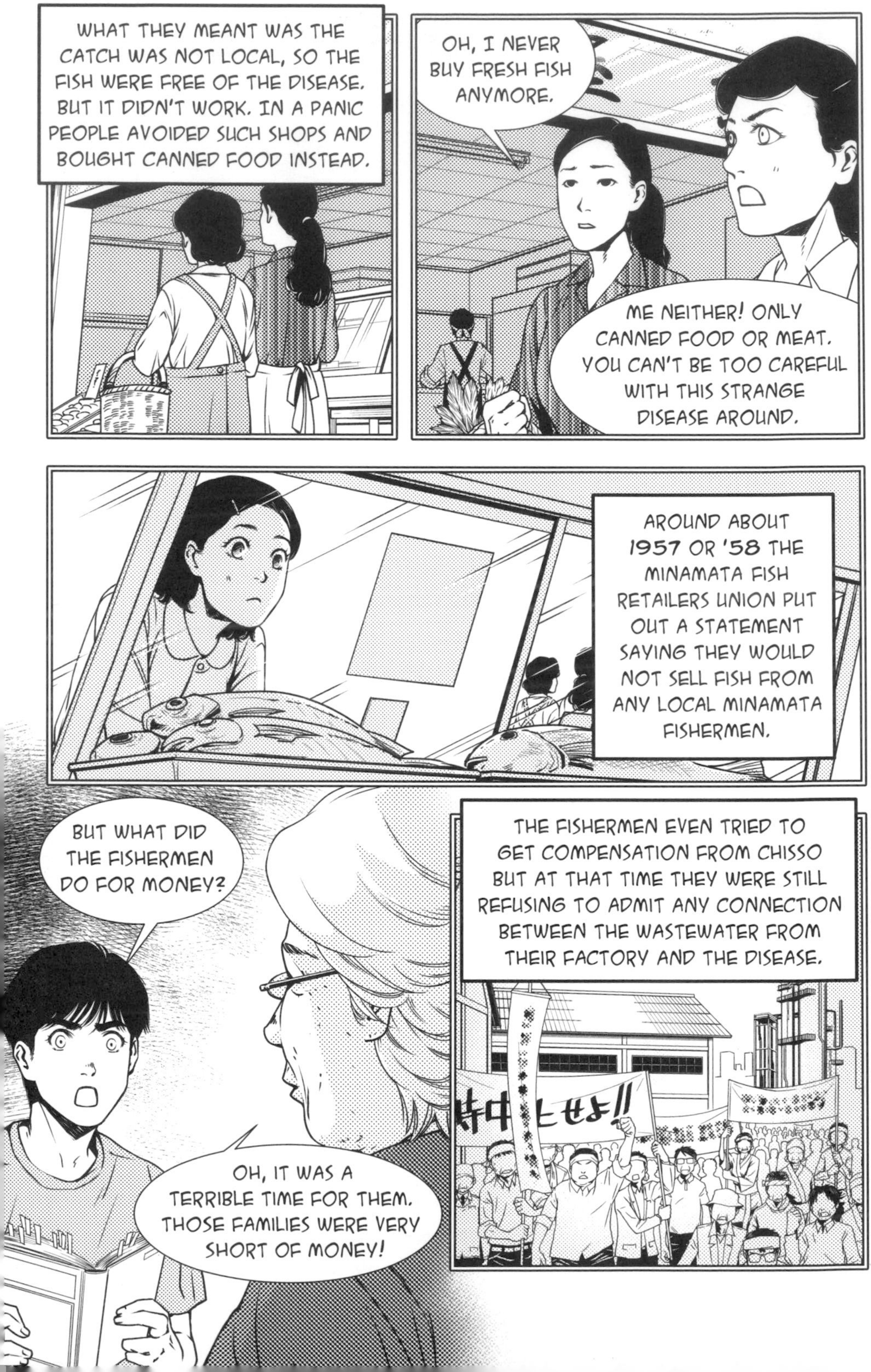
WHAT THEY MEANT WAS THE CATCH WAS NOT LOCAL, SO THE FISH WERE FREE OF THE DISEASE. BUT IT DIDN'T WORK. IN A PANIC PEOPLE AVOIDED SUCH SHOPS AND BOUGHT CANNED FOOD INSTEAD.
OH, I NEVER BUY FRESH FISH ANYMORE.
ME NEITHER! ONLY CANNED FOOD OR MEAT. YOU CAN'T BE TOO CAREFUL WITH THIS STRANGE DISEASE AROUND.
AROUND ABOUT 1957 OR '58 THE MINAMATA FISH RETAILERS UNION PUT OUT A STATEMENT SAYING THEY WOULD NOT SELL FISH FROM ANY LOCAL MINAMATA FISHERMEN.
BUT WHAT DID THE FISHERMEN DO FOR MONEY?
OH, IT WAS A TERRIBLE TIME FOR THEM. THOSE FAMILIES WERE VERY SHORT OF MONEY!
THE FISHERMEN EVEN TRIED TO GET COMPENSATION FROM CHISSO BUT AT THAT TIME THEY WERE STILL REFUSING TO ADMIT ANY CONNECTION BETWEEN THE WASTEWATER FROM THEIR FACTORY AND THE DISEASE.

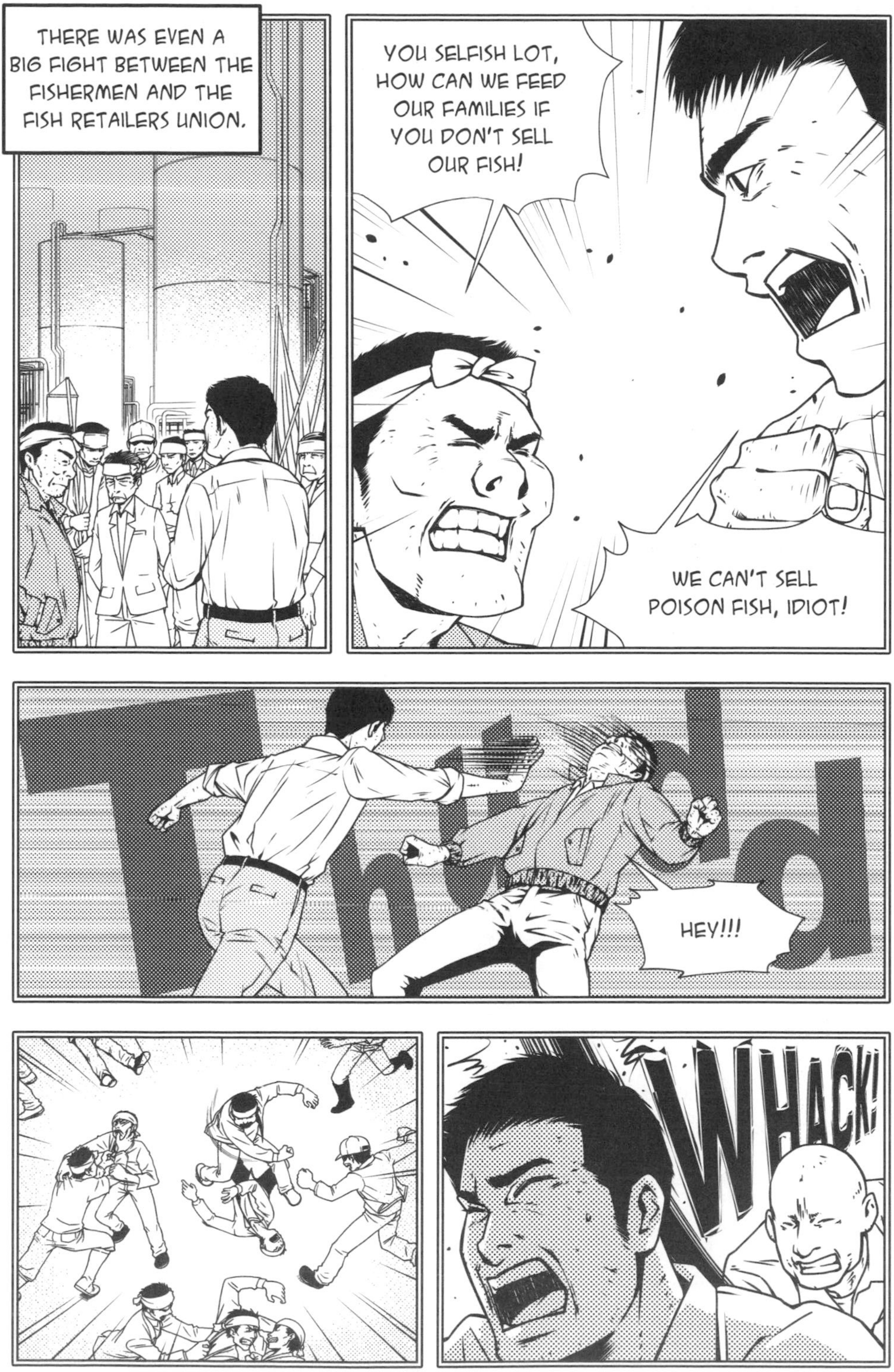
THERE WAS EVEN A BIG FIGHT BETWEEN THE FISHERMEN AND THE FISH RETAILERS UNION.
YOU SELFISH LOT, HOW CAN WE FEED OUR FAMILIES IF YOU DON'T SELL OUR FISH!
WE CAN'T SELL POISON FISH, IDIOT!
Thud
HEY!!!
WHACK!

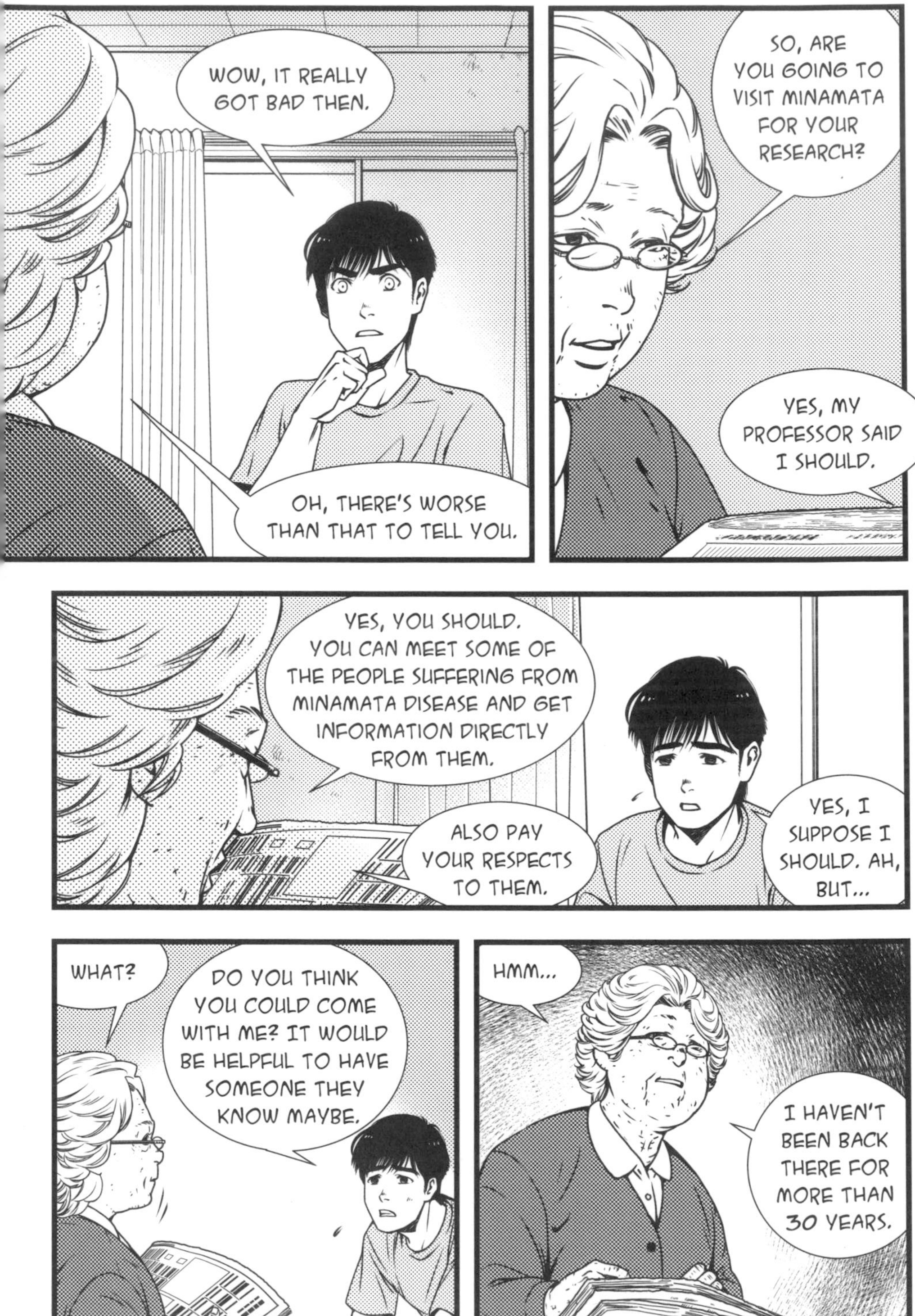
WOW, IT REALLY GOT BAD THEN.
OH, THERE'S WORSE THAN THAT TO TELL YOU.
SO, ARE YOU GOING TO VISIT MINAMATA FOR YOUR RESEARCH?
YES, MY PROFESSOR SAID I SHOULD.
YES, YOU SHOULD. YOU CAN MEET SOME OF THE PEOPLE SUFFERING FROM MINAMATA DISEASE AND GET INFORMATION DIRECTLY FROM THEM.
ALSO PAY YOUR RESPECTS TO THEM.
YES, I SUPPOSE I SHOULD. AH, BUT...
WHAT?
DO YOU THINK YOU COULD COME WITH ME? IT WOULD BE HELPFUL TO HAVE SOMEONE THEY KNOW MAYBE.
HMM...
I HAVEN'T BEEN BACK THERE FOR MORE THAN 30 YEARS.

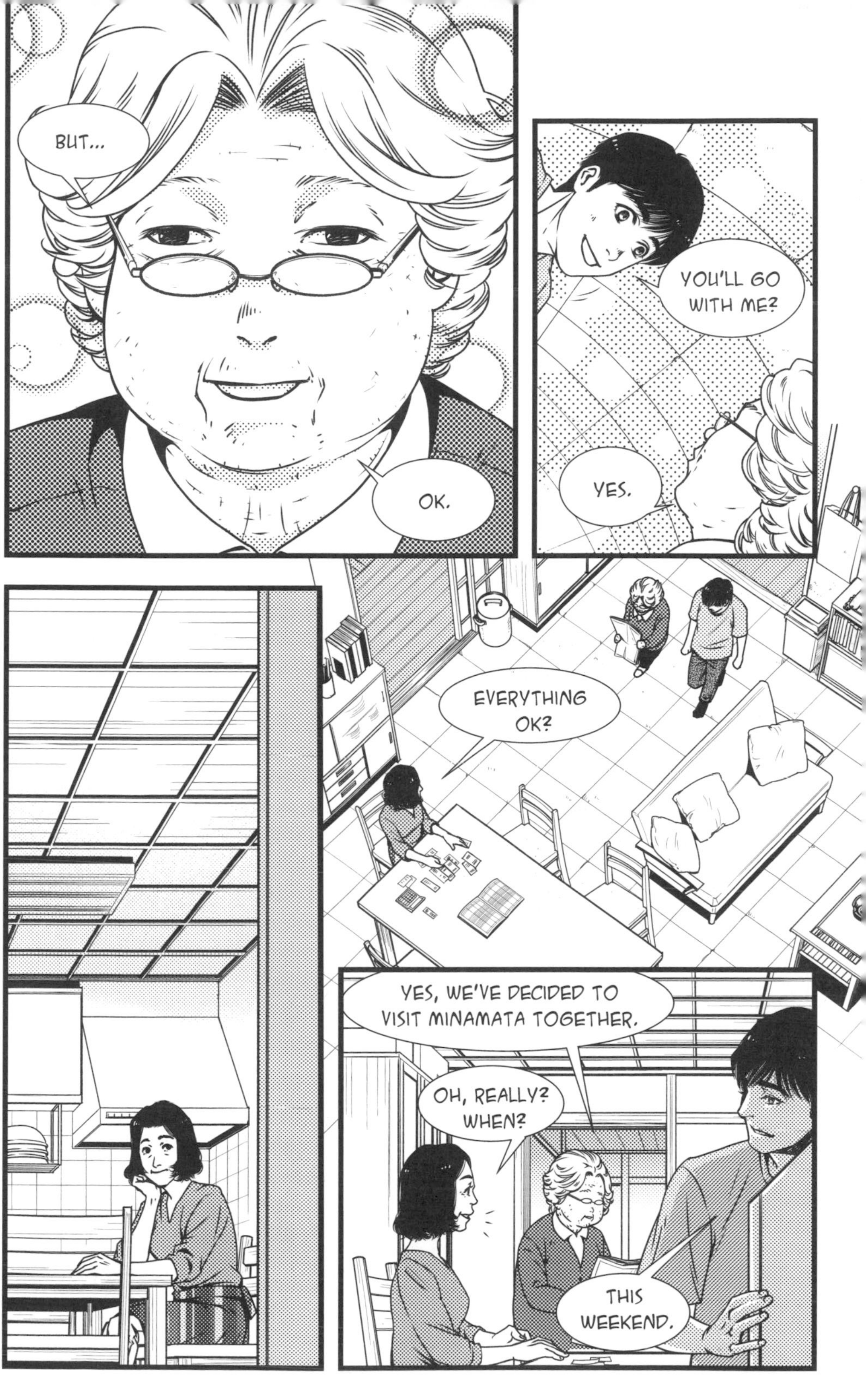
BUT...
OK.
YOU'LL GO WITH ME?
YES.
EVERYTHING OK?
YES, WE'VE DECIDED TO VISIT MINAMATA TOGETHER.
OH, REALLY? WHEN?
THIS WEEKEND.

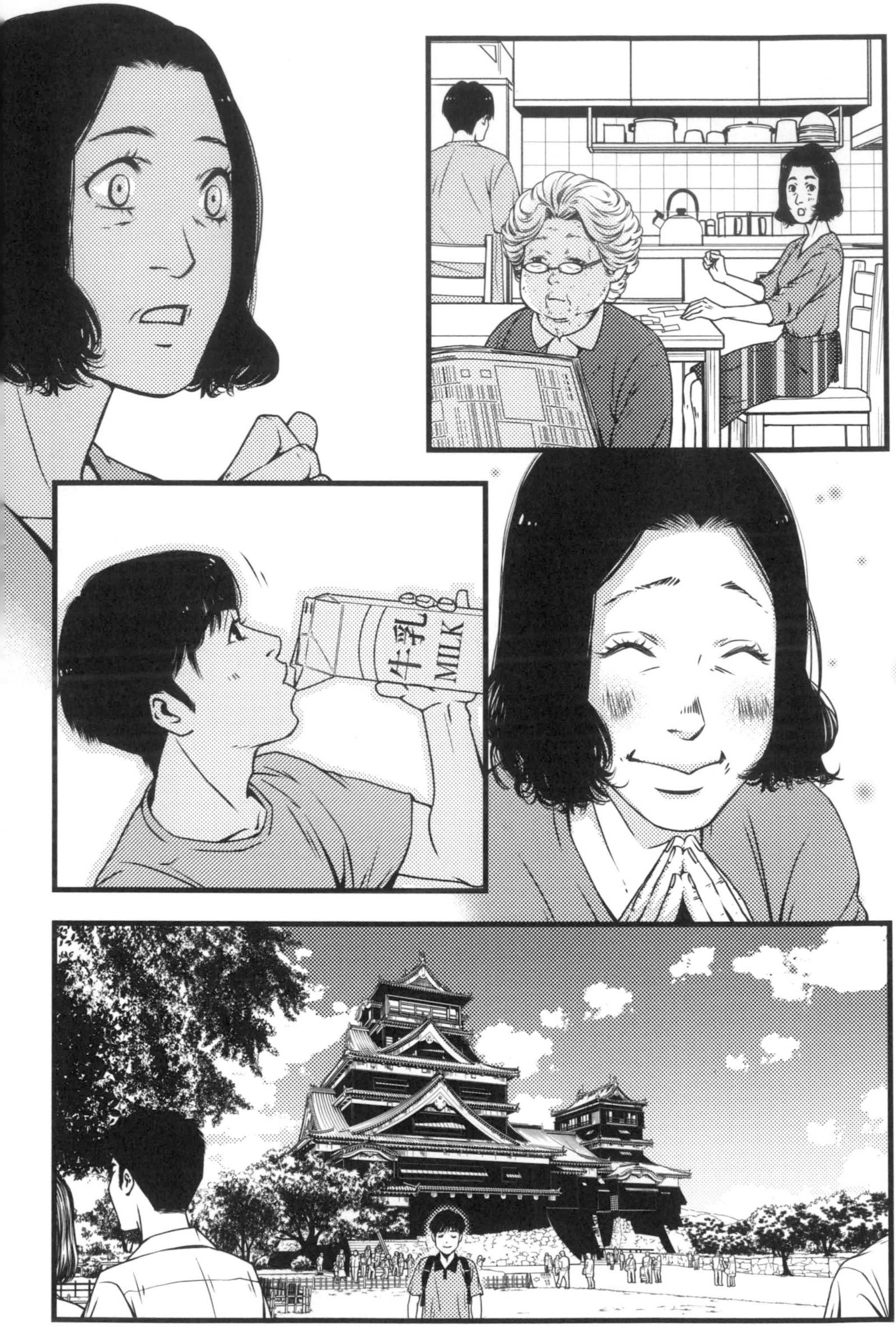
牛乳
MILK

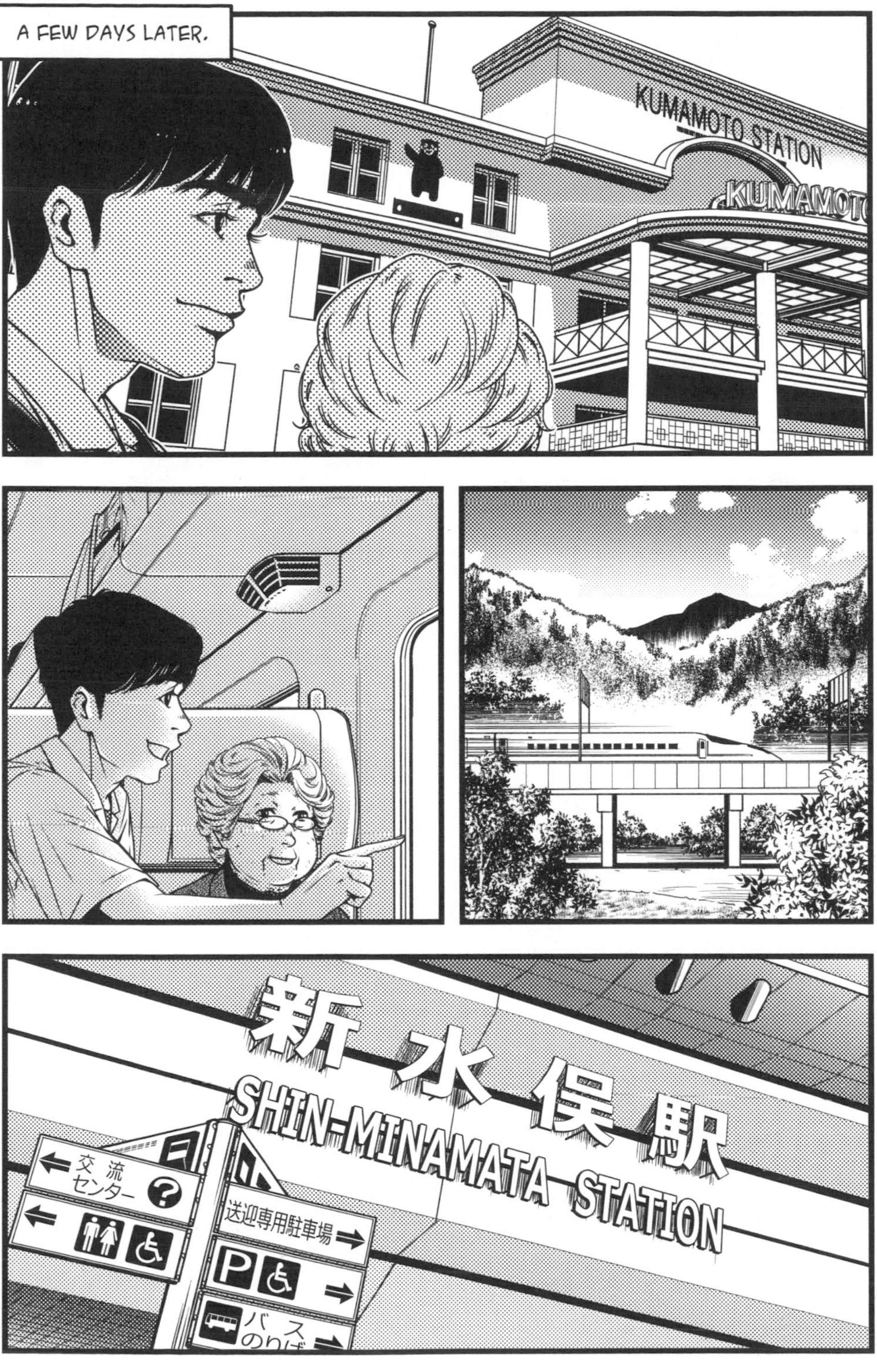
A FEW DAYS LATER.
KUMAMOTO STATION
新水俣駅
SHIN-MINAMATA STATION
交流センター
送迎専用駐車場
バス
のりば

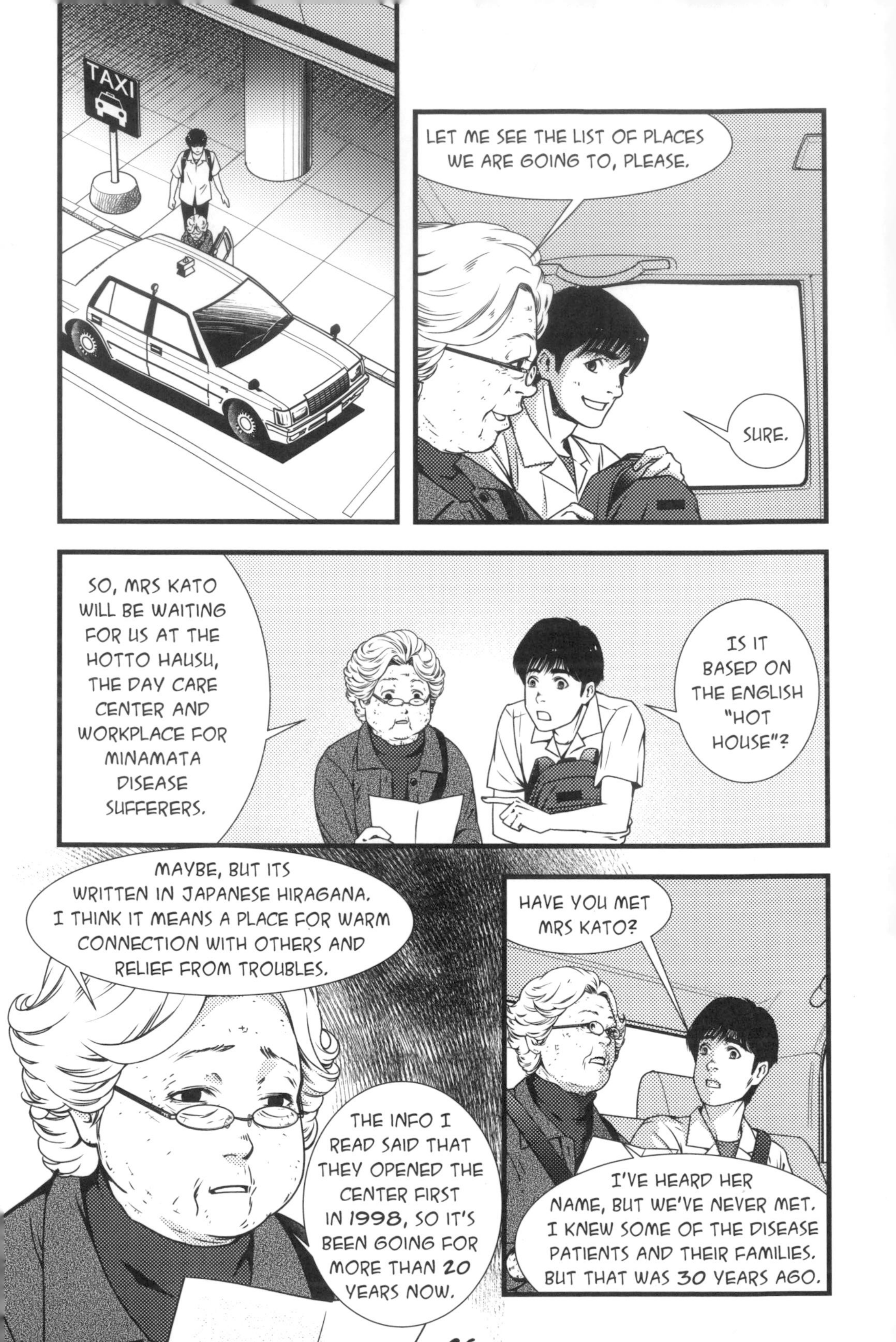
TAXI
LET ME SEE THE LIST OF PLACES WE ARE GOING TO, PLEASE.
SURE.
SO, MRS KATO WILL BE WAITING FOR US AT THE HOTTO HAUSU, THE DAY CARE CENTER AND WORKPLACE FOR MINAMATA DISEASE SUFFERERS.
IS IT BASED ON THE ENGLISH "HOT HOUSE"?
MAYBE, BUT ITS WRITTEN IN JAPANESE HIRAGANA. I THINK IT MEANS A PLACE FOR WARM CONNECTION WITH OTHERS AND RELIEF FROM TROUBLES.
THE INFO I READ SAID THAT THEY OPENED THE CENTER FIRST IN 1998, SO IT'S BEEN GOING FOR MORE THAN 20 YEARS NOW.
HAVE YOU MET MRS KATO?
I'VE HEARD HER NAME, BUT WE'VE NEVER MET. I KNEW SOME OF THE DISEASE PATIENTS AND THEIR FAMILIES. BUT THAT WAS 30 YEARS AGO.

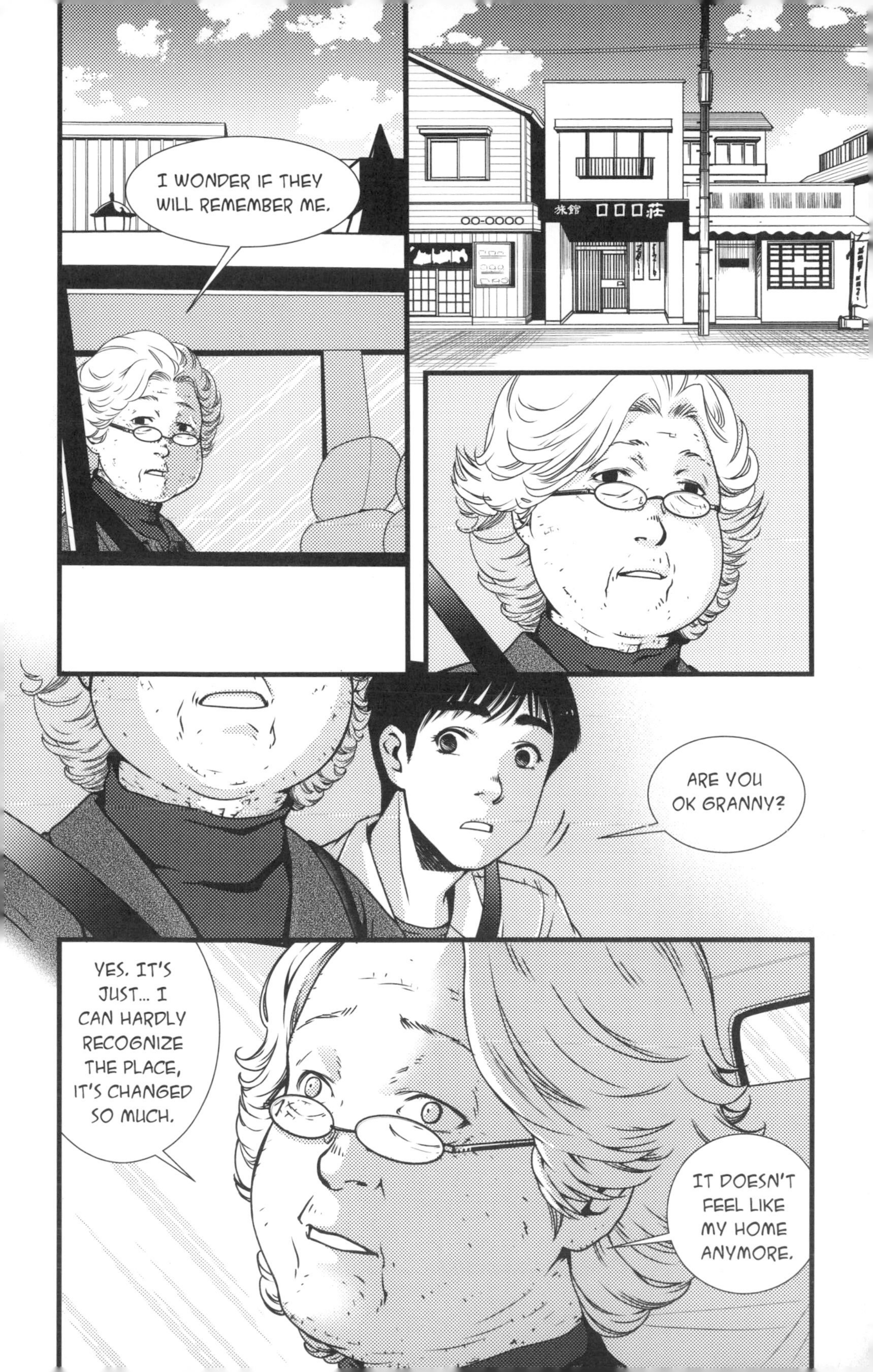
I WONDER IF THEY WILL REMEMBER ME.
ARE YOU OK GRANNY?
YES. IT'S JUST... I CAN HARDLY RECOGNIZE THE PLACE, IT'S CHANGED SO MUCH.
IT DOESN'T FEEL LIKE MY HOME ANYMORE.

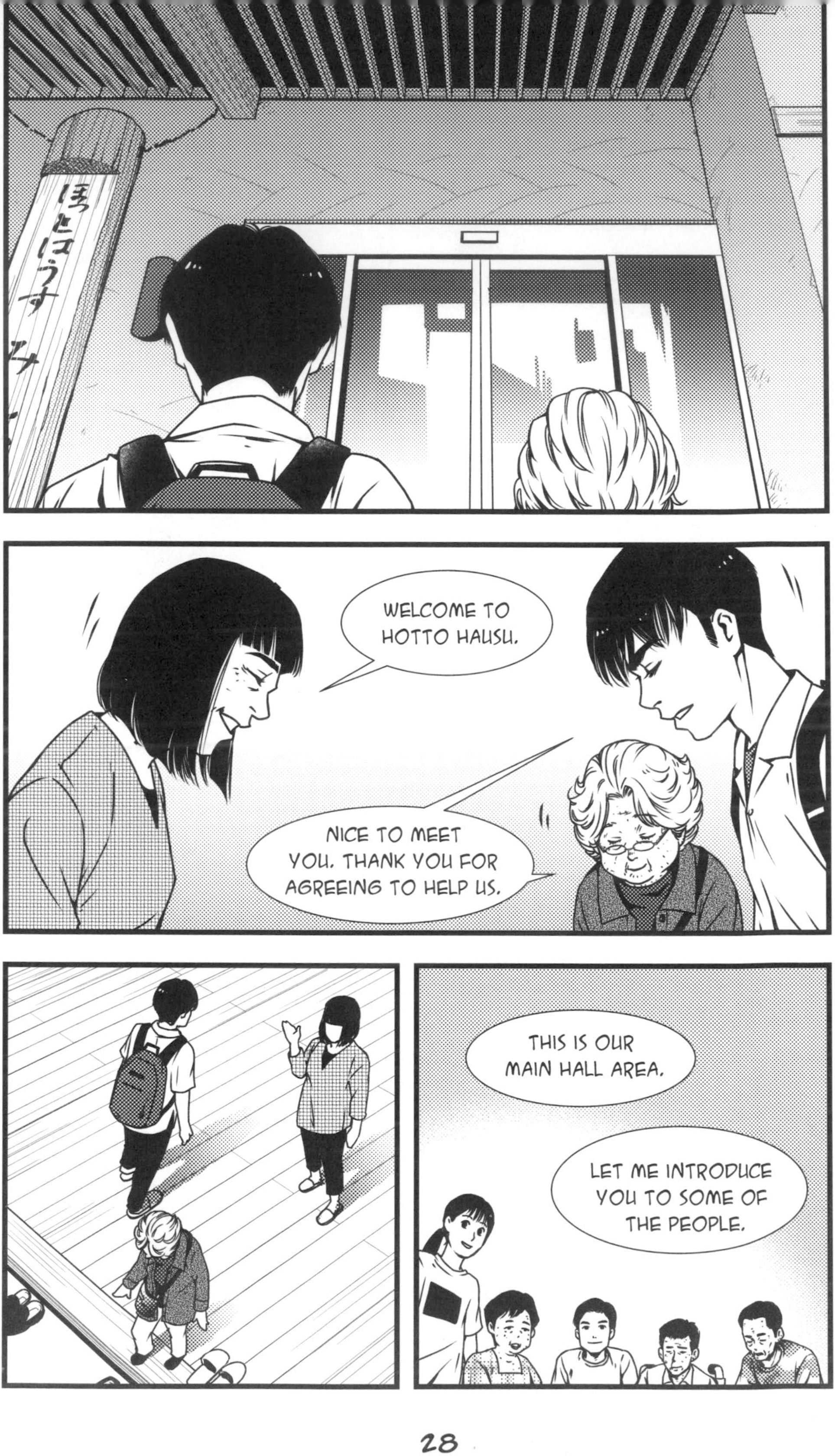
ほっとはうす
WELCOME TO HOTTO HAUSU.
NICE TO MEET YOU. THANK YOU FOR AGREEING TO HELP US.
THIS IS OUR MAIN HALL AREA.
LET ME INTRODUCE YOU TO SOME OF THE PEOPLE.

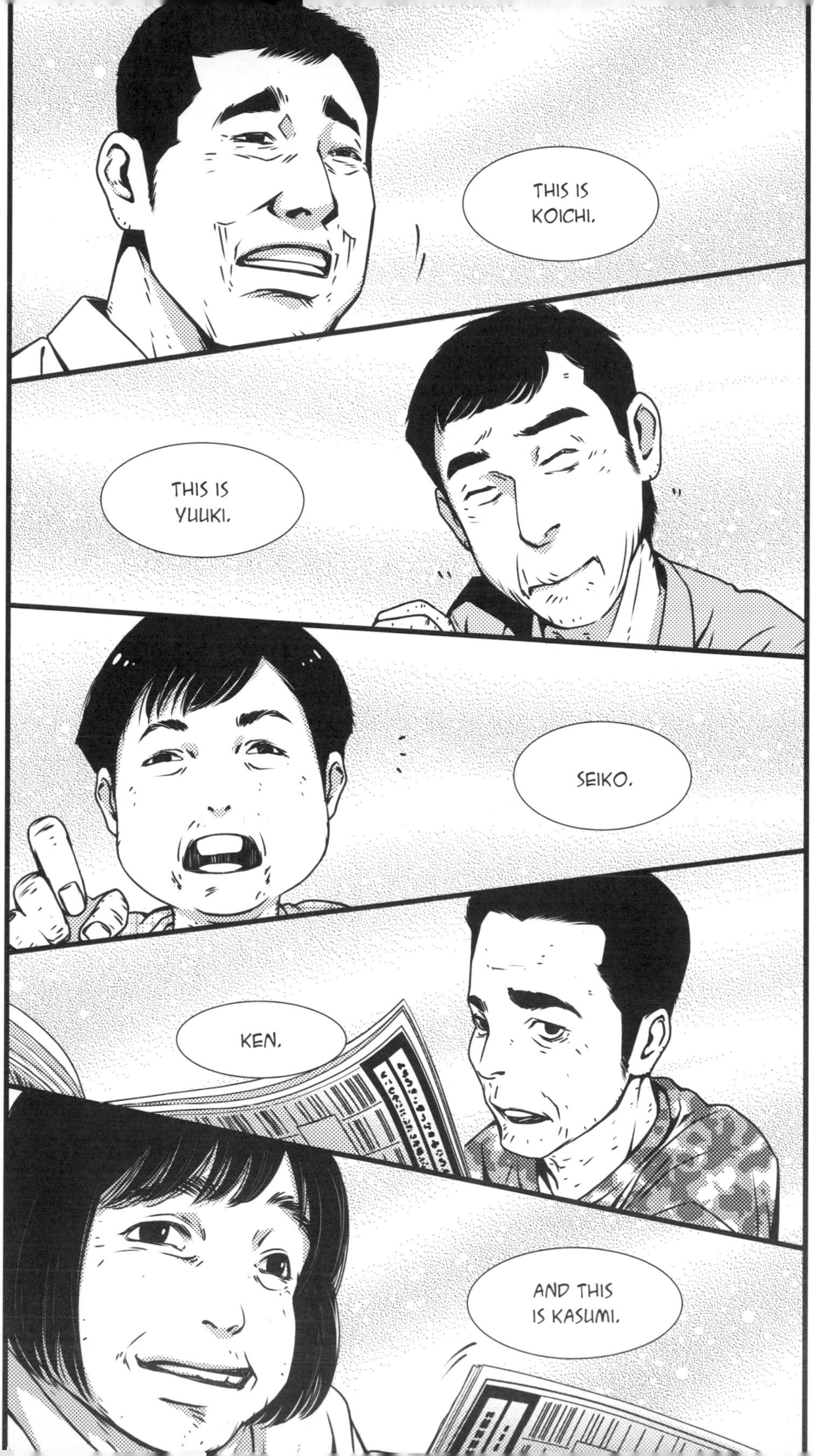
THIS IS KOICHI.
THIS IS YUUKI.
SEIKO.
KEN.
AND THIS IS KASUMI.

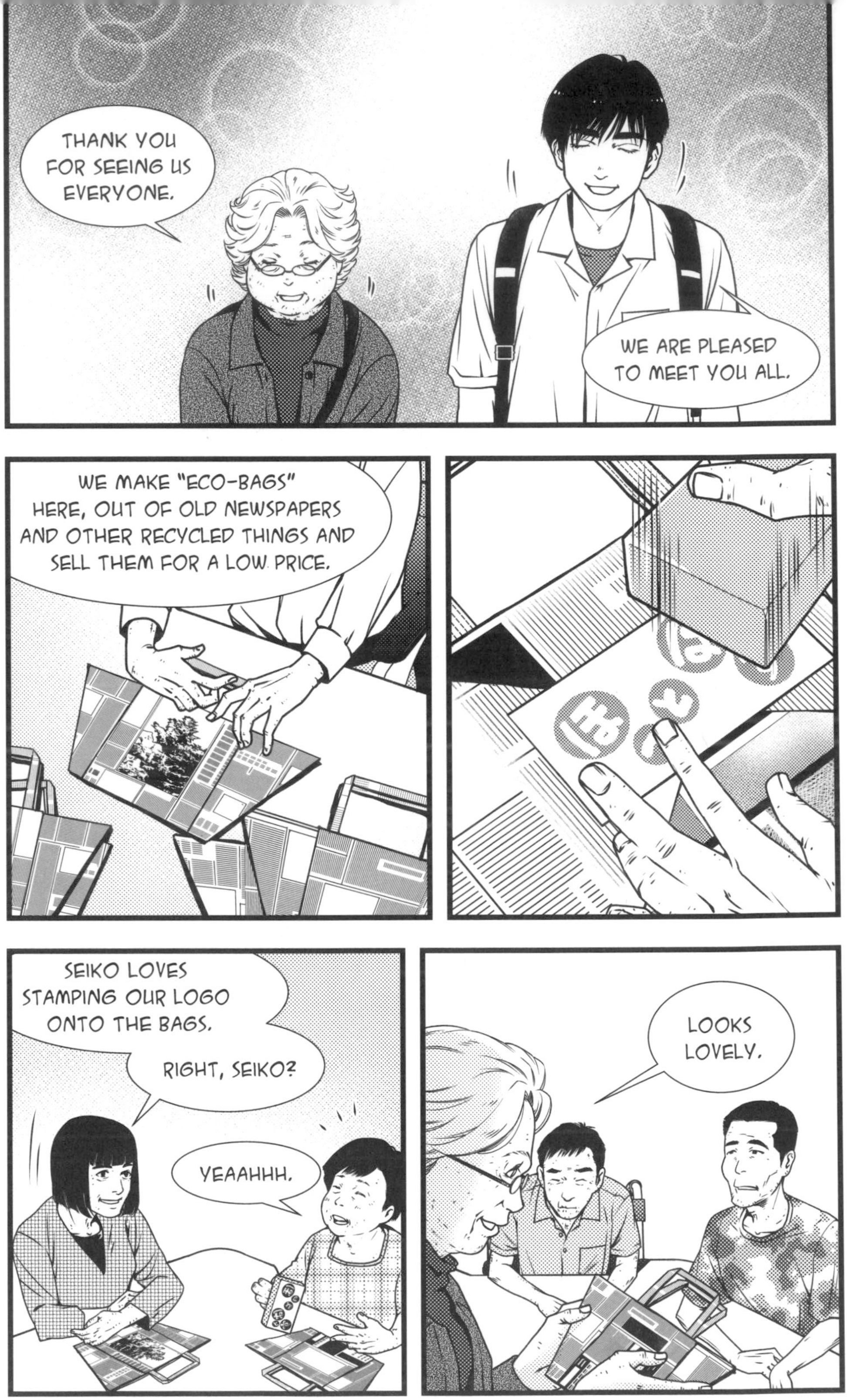
THANK YOU FOR SEEING US EVERYONE.
WE ARE PLEASED TO MEET YOU ALL.
WE MAKE "ECO-BAGS" HERE, OUT OF OLD NEWSPAPERS AND OTHER RECYCLED THINGS AND SELL THEM FOR A LOW PRICE.
SEIKO LOVES STAMPING OUR LOGO ONTO THE BAGS.
RIGHT, SEIKO?
YEAAHHH.
LOOKS LOVELY.

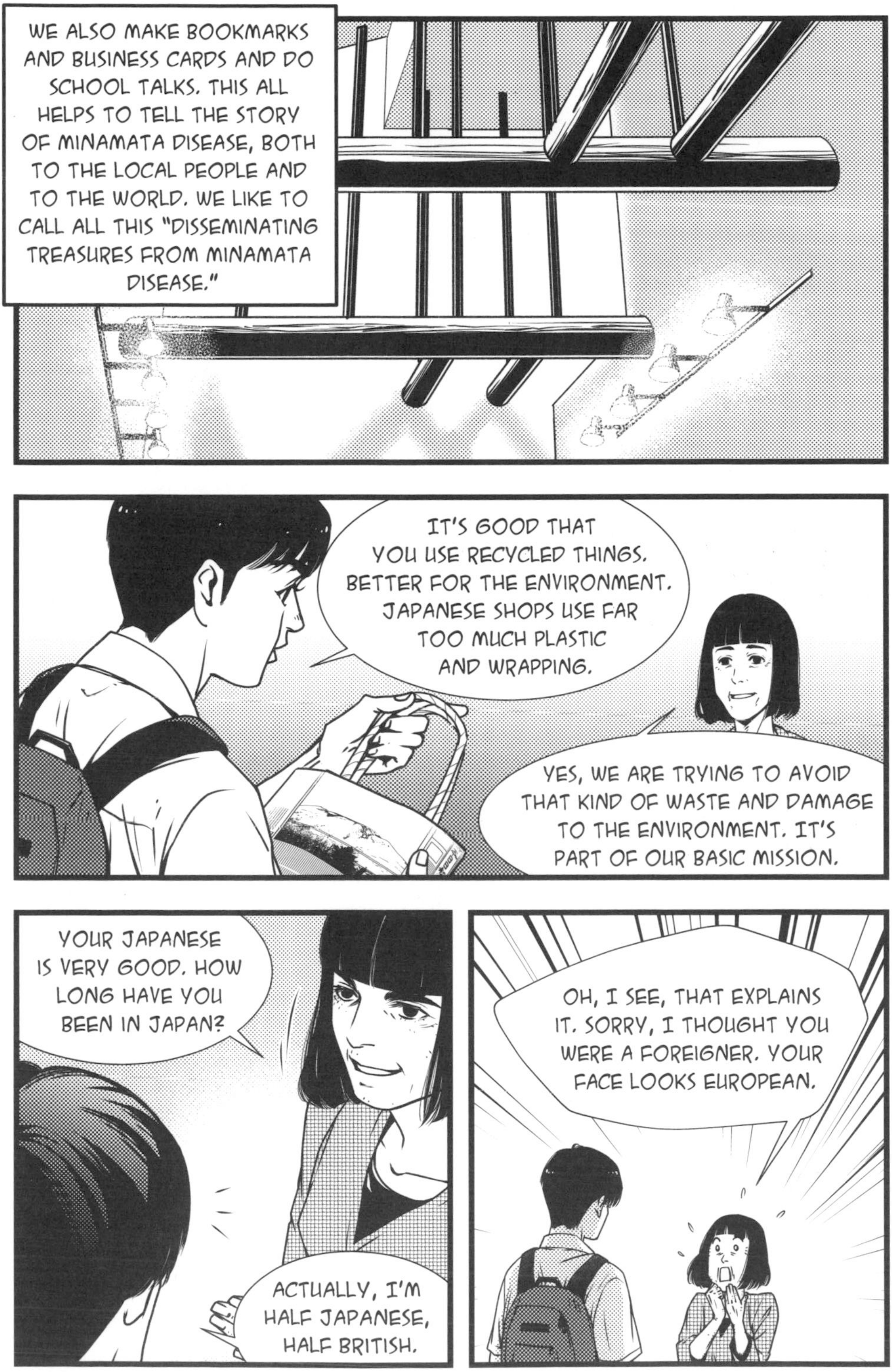
WE ALSO MAKE BOOKMARKS AND BUSINESS CARDS AND DO SCHOOL TALKS. THIS ALL HELPS TO TELL THE STORY OF MINAMATA DISEASE, BOTH TO THE LOCAL PEOPLE AND TO THE WORLD. WE LIKE TO CALL ALL THIS "DISSEMINATING TREASURES FROM MINAMATA DISEASE."
IT'S GOOD THAT YOU USE RECYCLED THINGS. BETTER FOR THE ENVIRONMENT. JAPANESE SHOPS USE FAR TOO MUCH PLASTIC AND WRAPPING.
YES, WE ARE TRYING TO AVOID THAT KIND OF WASTE AND DAMAGE TO THE ENVIRONMENT. IT'S PART OF OUR BASIC MISSION.
YOUR JAPANESE IS VERY GOOD. HOW LONG HAVE YOU BEEN IN JAPAN?
ACTUALLY, I'M HALF JAPANESE, HALF BRITISH.
OH, I SEE, THAT EXPLAINS IT. SORRY, I THOUGHT YOU WERE A FOREIGNER. YOUR FACE LOOKS EUROPEAN.

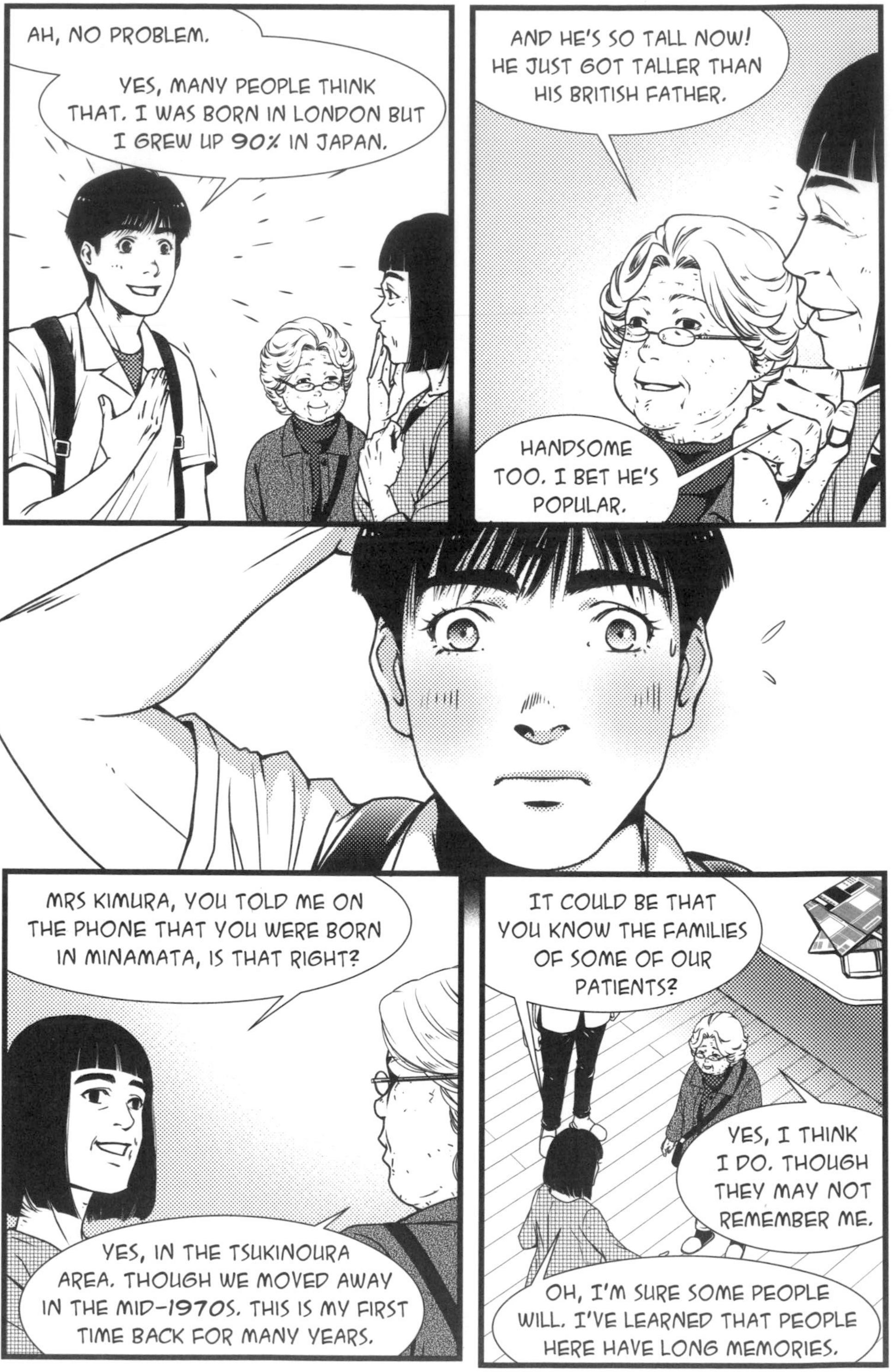
AH, NO PROBLEM.
YES, MANY PEOPLE THINK THAT. I WAS BORN IN LONDON BUT I GREW UP 90% IN JAPAN.
AND HE'S SO TALL NOW! HE JUST GOT TALLER THAN HIS BRITISH FATHER.
HANDSOME TOO. I BET HE'S POPULAR.
MRS KIMURA, YOU TOLD ME ON THE PHONE THAT YOU WERE BORN IN MINAMATA, IS THAT RIGHT?
YES, IN THE TSUKINOURA AREA. THOUGH WE MOVED AWAY IN THE MID-1970S. THIS IS MY FIRST TIME BACK FOR MANY YEARS.
IT COULD BE THAT YOU KNOW THE FAMILIES OF SOME OF OUR PATIENTS?
YES, I THINK I DO. THOUGH THEY MAY NOT REMEMBER ME.
OH, I'M SURE SOME PEOPLE WILL. I'VE LEARNED THAT PEOPLE HERE HAVE LONG MEMORIES.

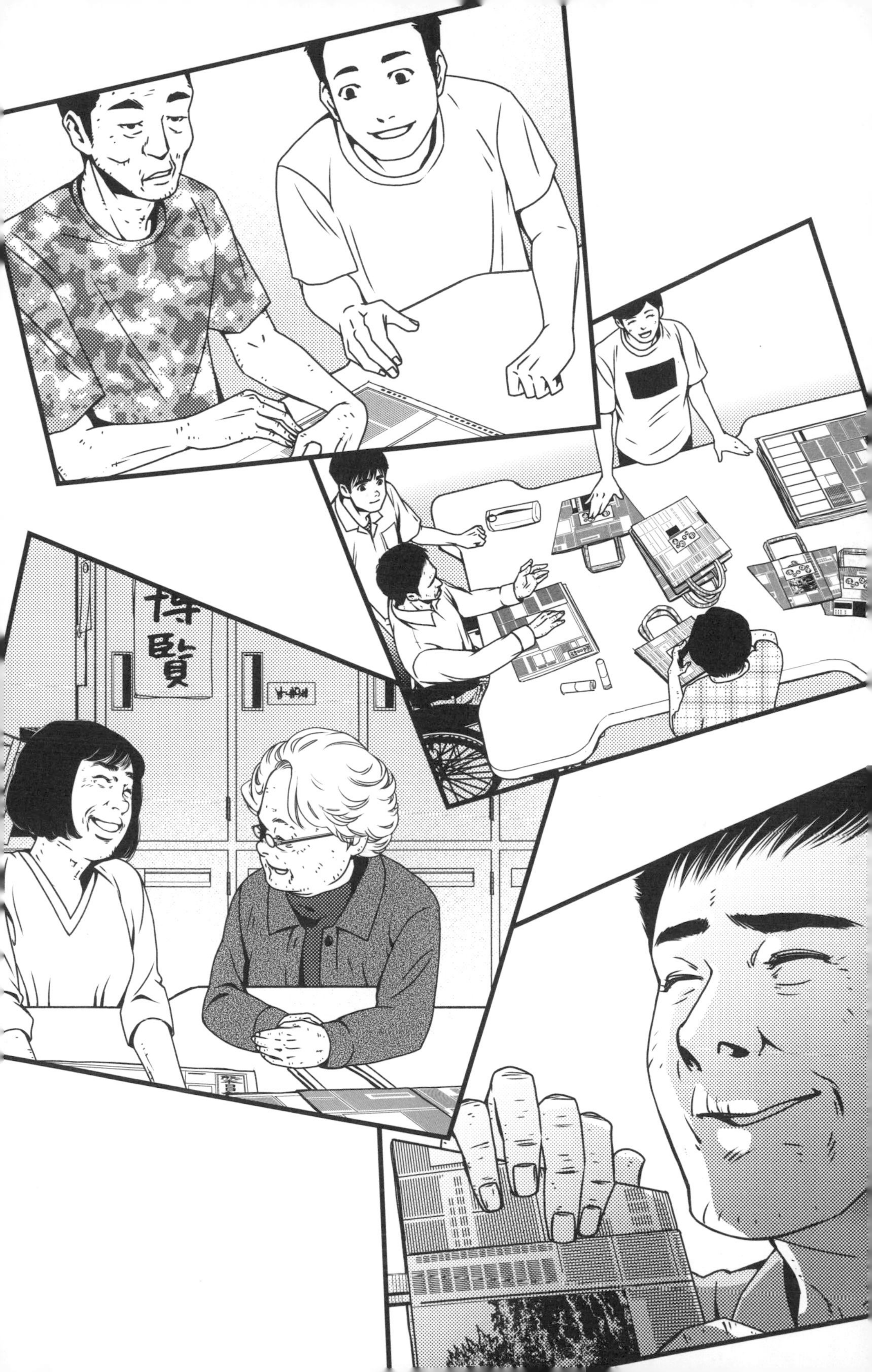

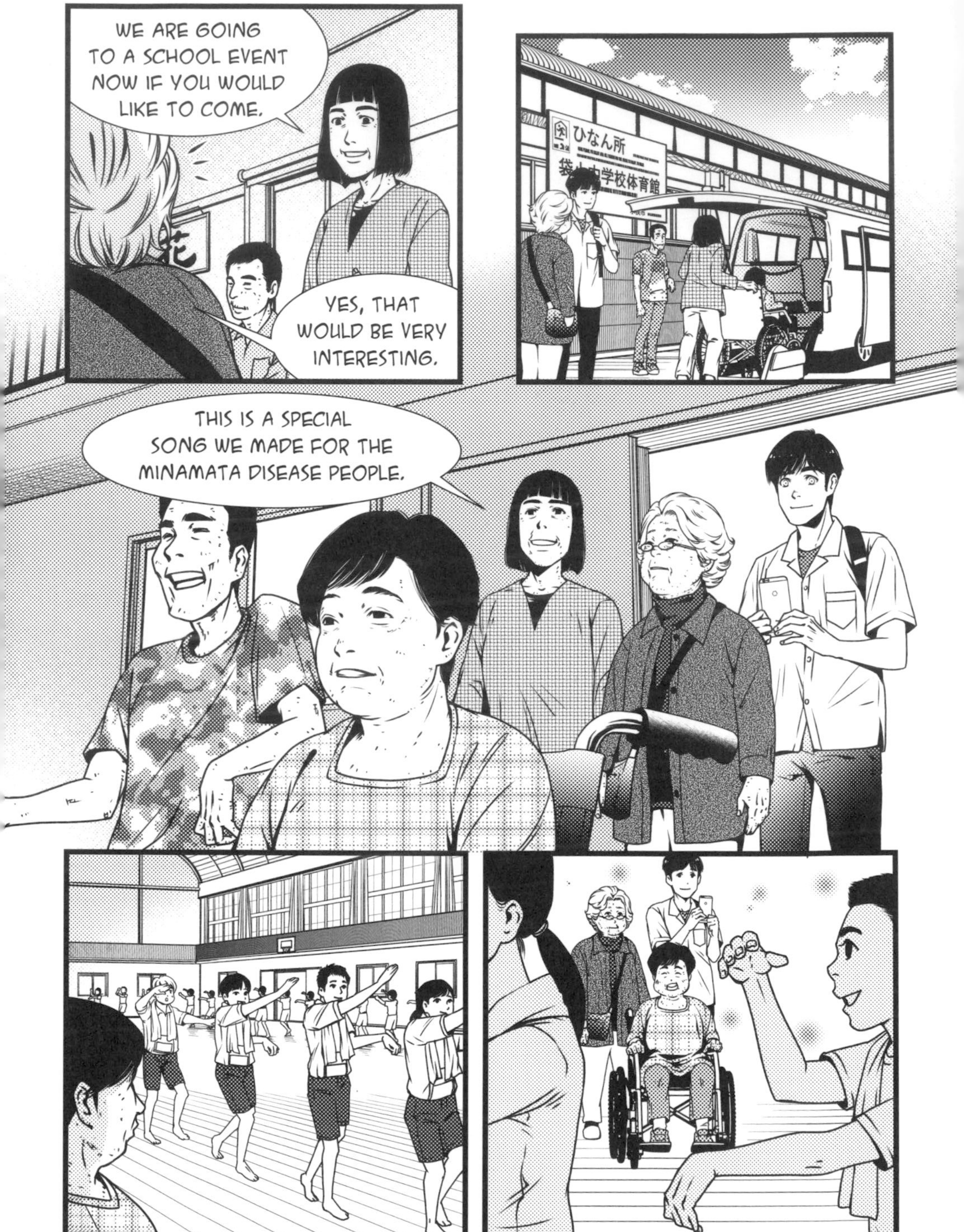
WE ARE GOING TO A SCHOOL EVENT NOW IF YOU WOULD LIKE TO COME.
YES, THAT WOULD BE VERY INTERESTING.
ひなん所
THIS IS A SPECIAL SONG WE MADE FOR THE MINAMATA DISEASE PEOPLE.

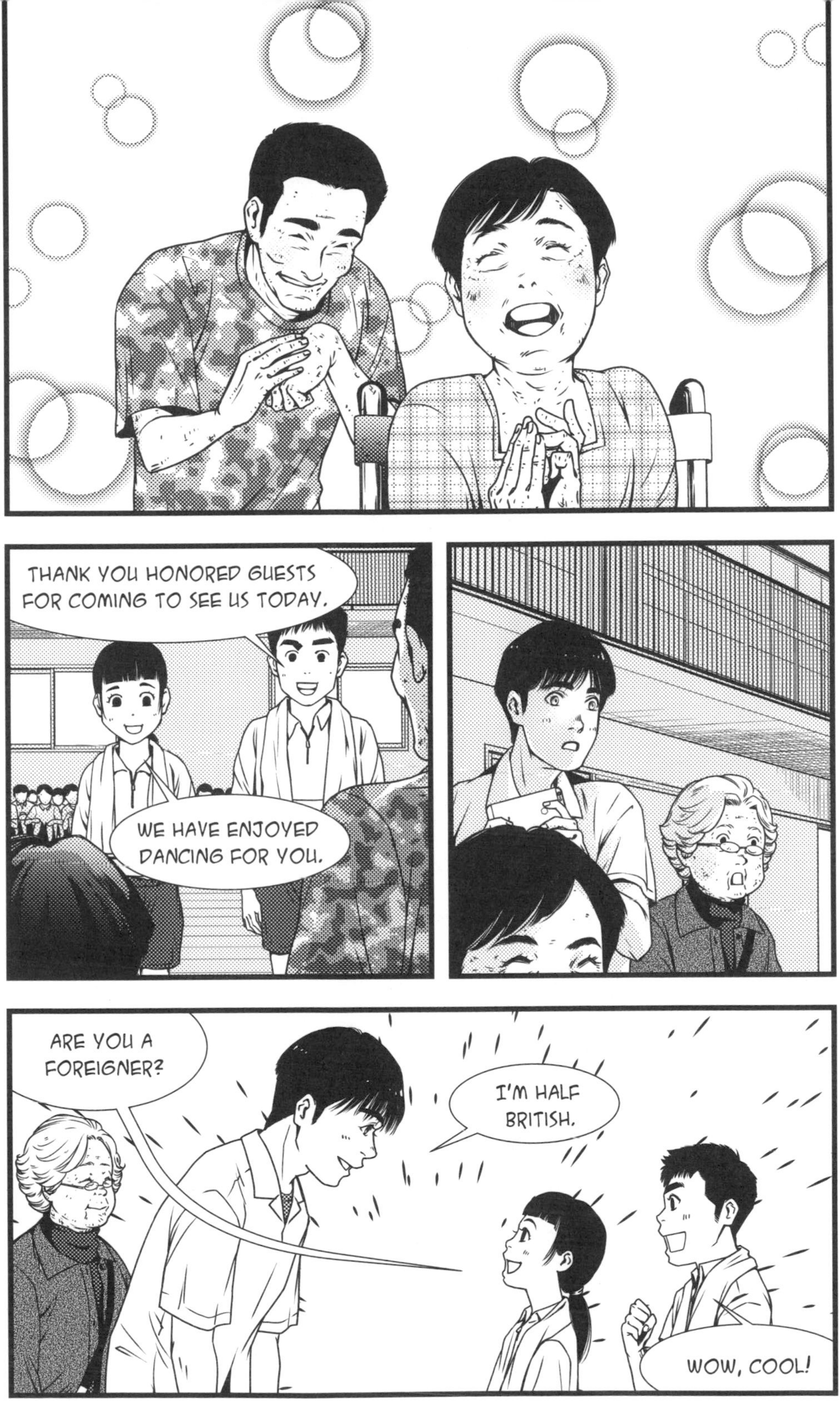
THANK YOU HONORED GUESTS FOR COMING TO SEE US TODAY.
WE HAVE ENJOYED DANCING FOR YOU.
ARE YOU A FOREIGNER?
I'M HALF BRITISH.
WOW, COOL!

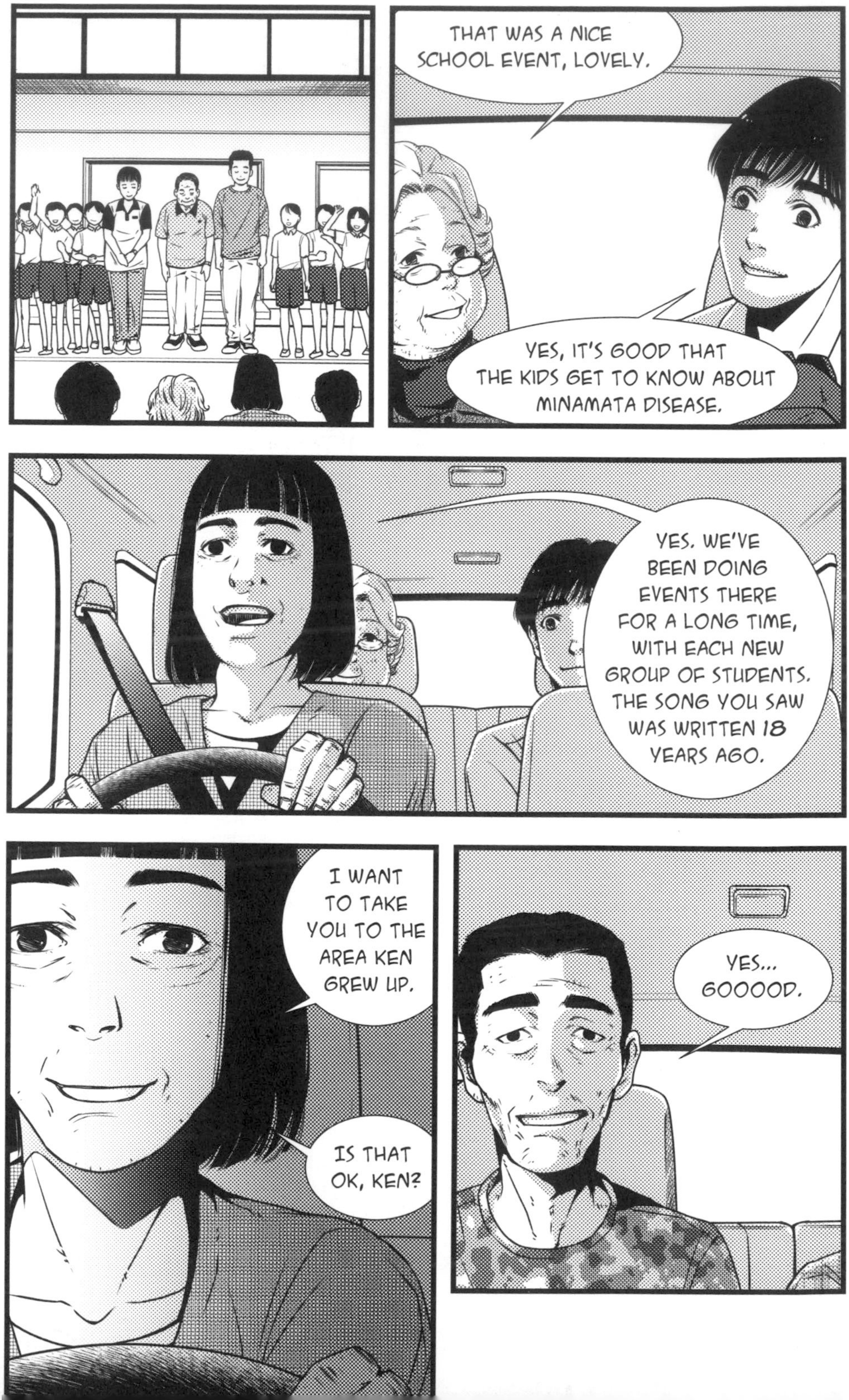
THAT WAS A NICE SCHOOL EVENT, LOVELY.
YES, IT'S GOOD THAT THE KIDS GET TO KNOW ABOUT MINAMATA DISEASE.
YES. WE'VE BEEN DOING EVENTS THERE FOR A LONG TIME, WITH EACH NEW GROUP OF STUDENTS. THE SONG YOU SAW WAS WRITTEN 18 YEARS AGO.
I WANT TO TAKE YOU TO THE AREA KEN GREW UP.
IS THAT OK, KEN?
YES... GOOOOD.

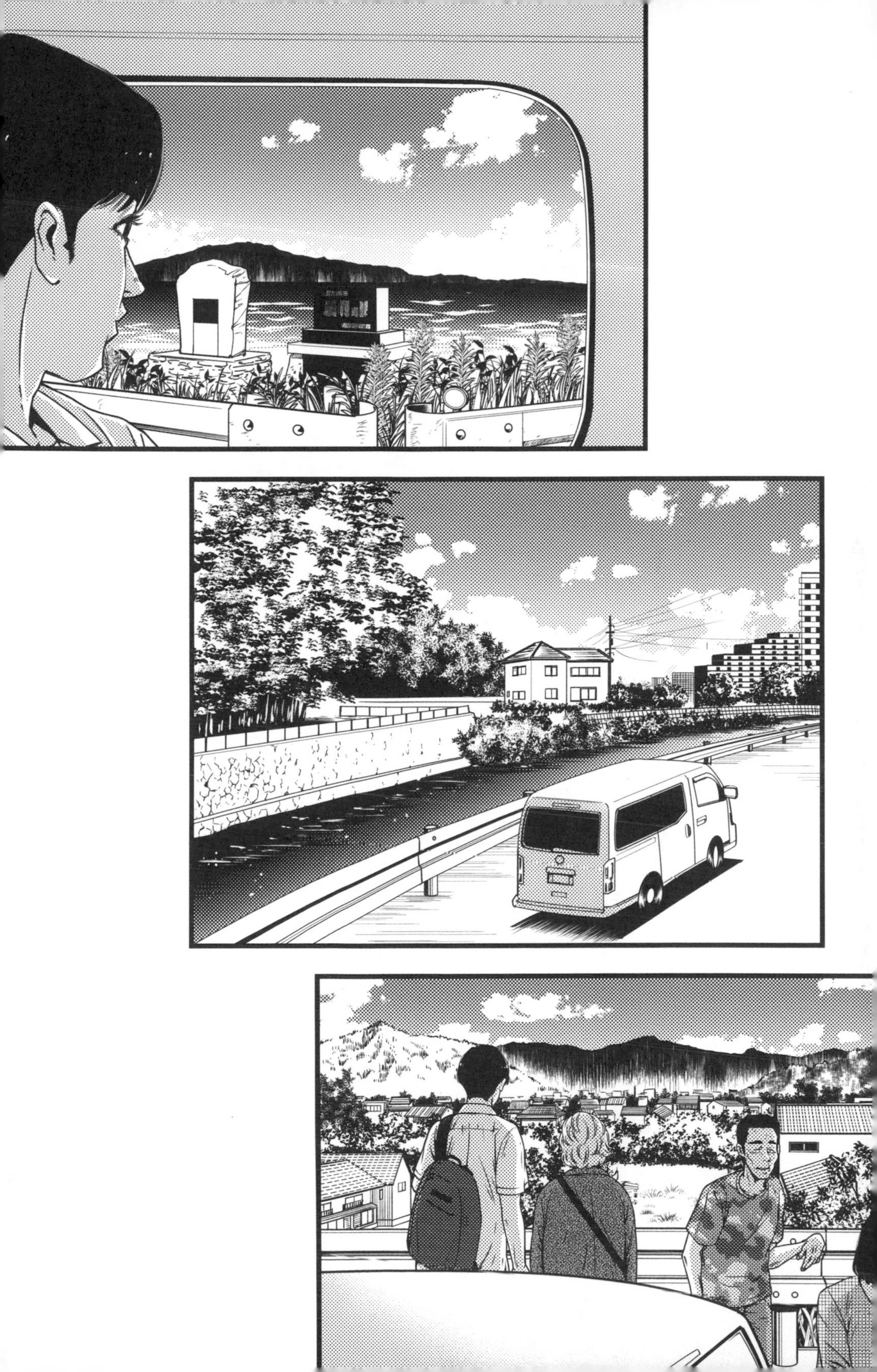

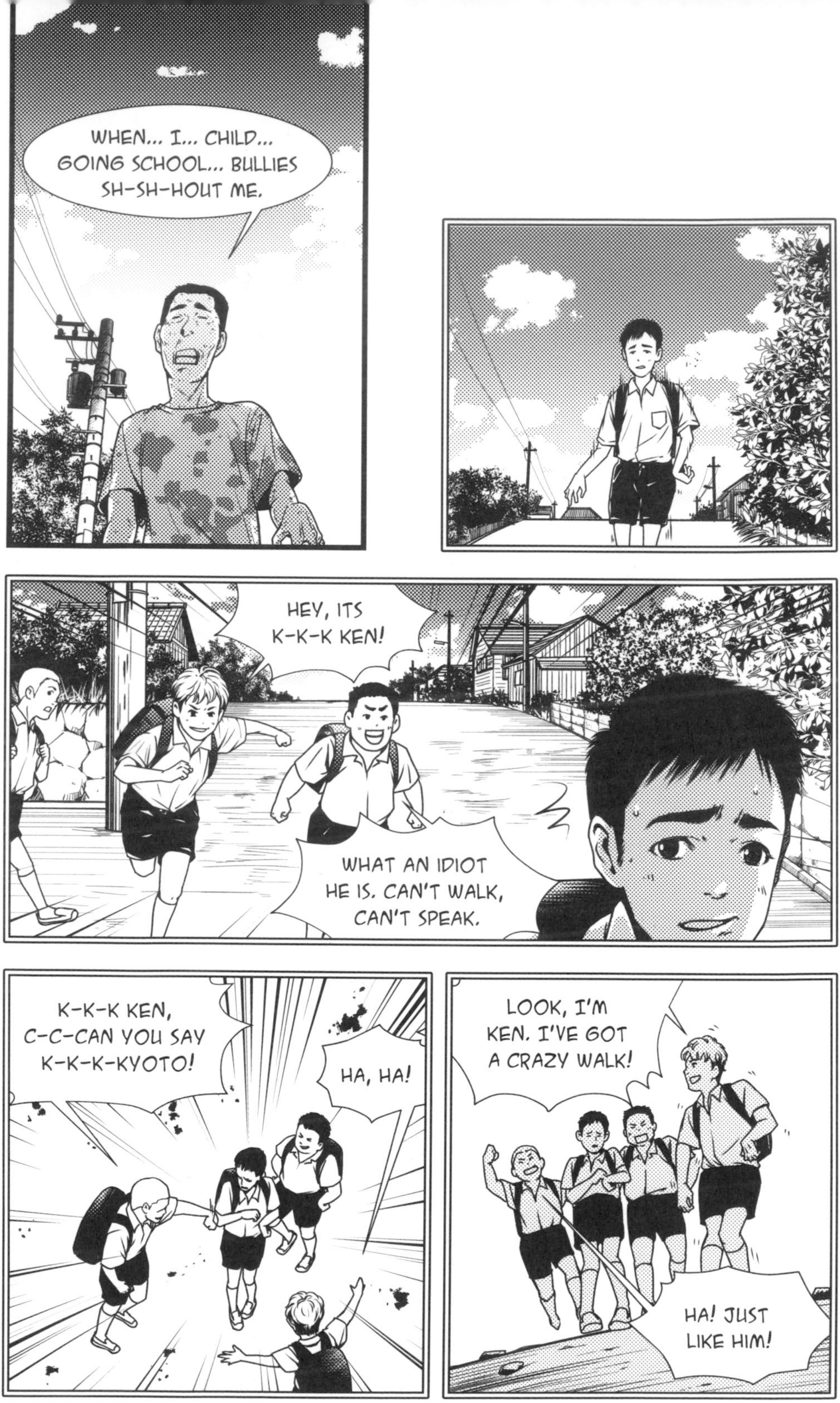
WHEN... I... CHILD... GOING SCHOOL... BULLIES SH-SH-HOUT ME.
HEY, ITS K-K-K KEN!
WHAT AN IDIOT HE IS. CAN'T WALK, CAN'T SPEAK.
K-K-K KEN, C-C-CAN YOU SAY K-K-K-KYOTO!
HA, HA!
LOOK, I'M KEN. I'VE GOT A CRAZY WALK!
HA! JUST LIKE HIM!

MY FATHER LOST HIS JOB IN CHISSO BECAUSE OF SICK FOOLS LIKE YOU!

HE HAD TO MOVE TO FUKUOKA! WE HARDLY EVER SEE HIM ANYMORE!

BAM!

AAHH.

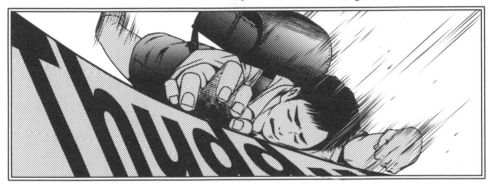

WHY DON'T YOU JUST DIE!

COME ON, TOSHI. SOMEONE'S COMING.

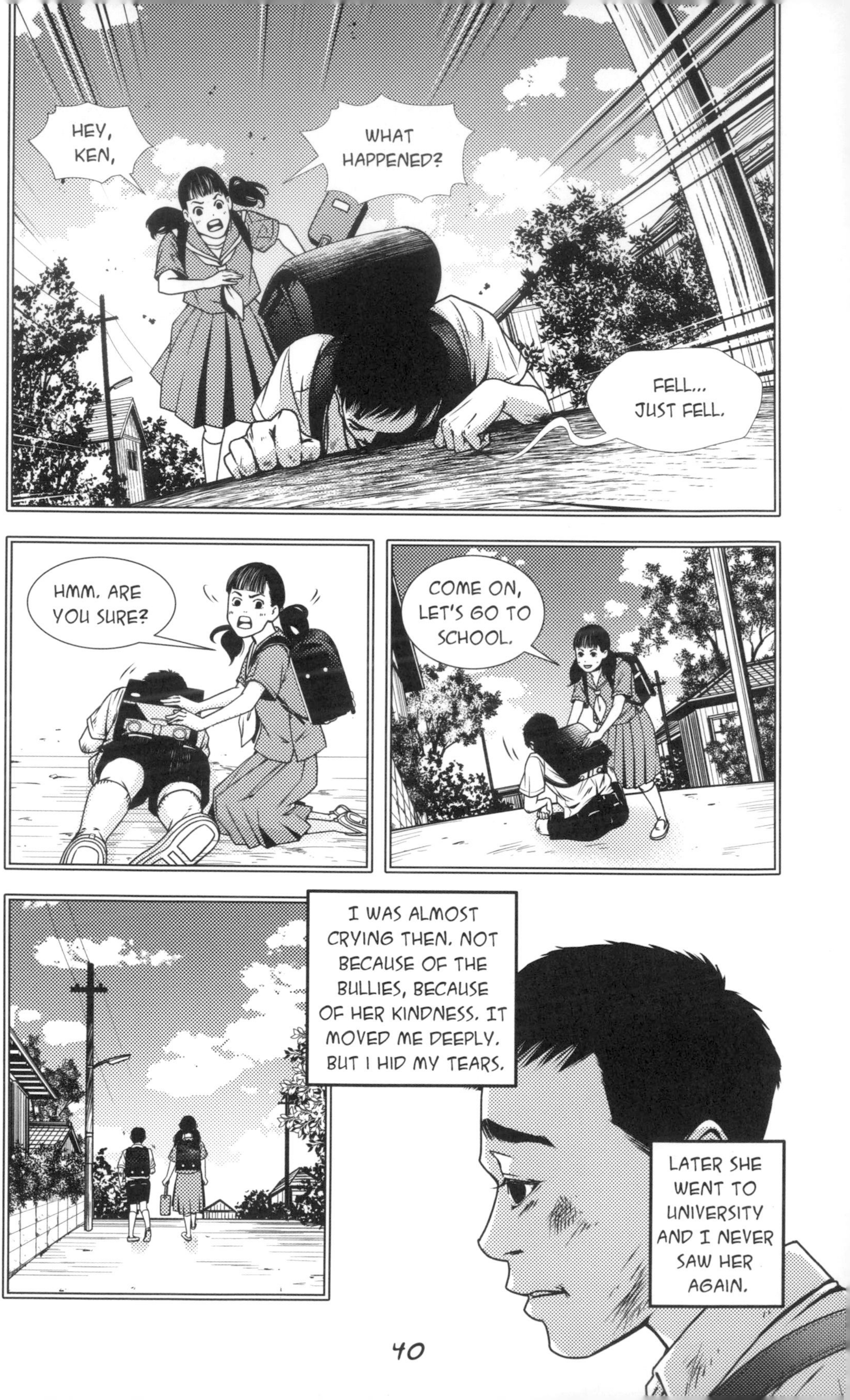
HEY, KEN,
WHAT HAPPENED?
FELL... JUST FELL.
HMM. ARE YOU SURE?
COME ON, LET'S GO TO SCHOOL.
I WAS ALMOST CRYING THEN. NOT BECAUSE OF THE BULLIES, BECAUSE OF HER KINDNESS. IT MOVED ME DEEPLY. BUT I HID MY TEARS.
LATER SHE WENT TO UNIVERSITY AND I NEVER SAW HER AGAIN.

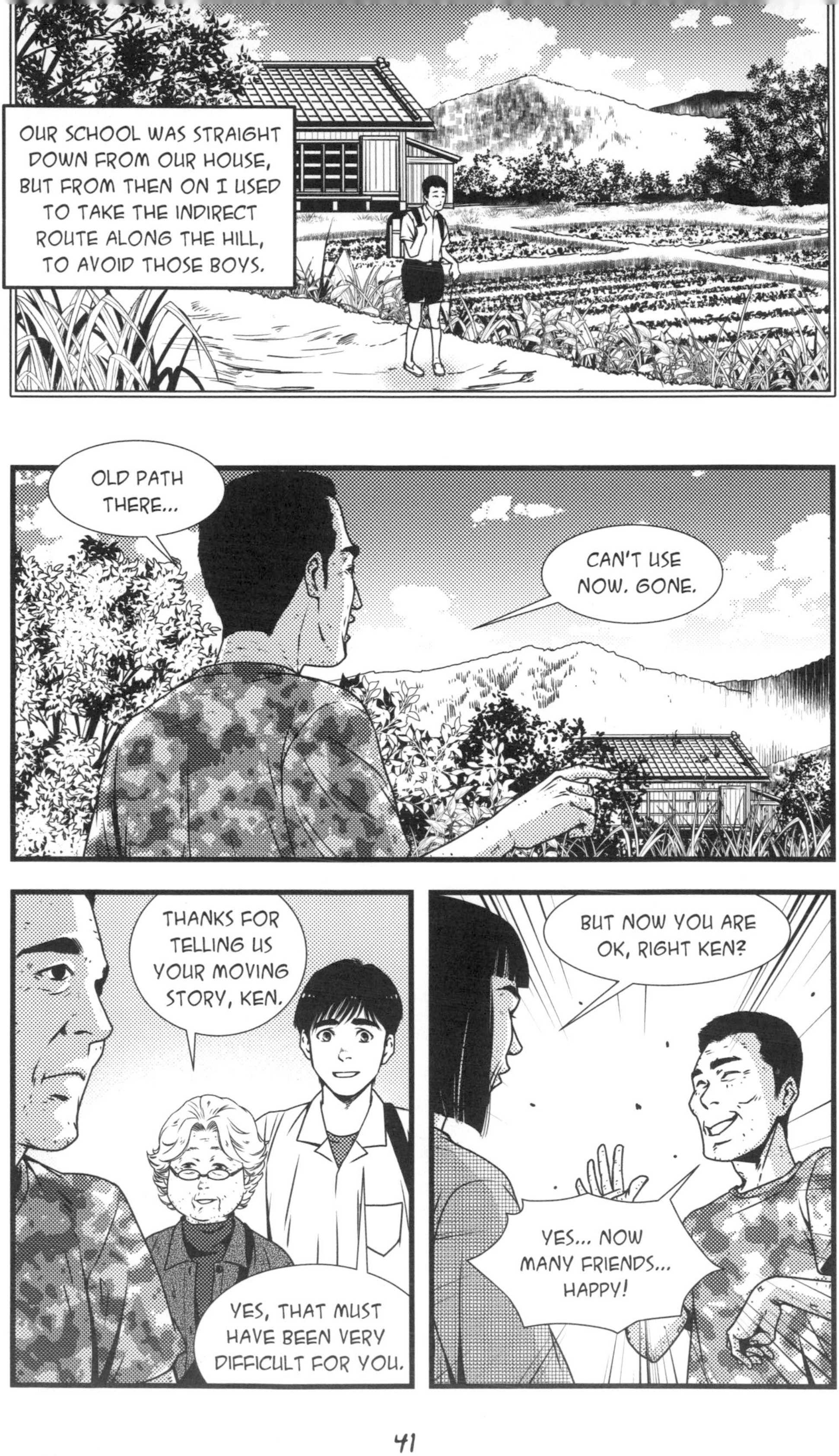
OUR SCHOOL WAS STRAIGHT DOWN FROM OUR HOUSE, BUT FROM THEN ON I USED TO TAKE THE INDIRECT ROUTE ALONG THE HILL, TO AVOID THOSE BOYS.
OLD PATH THERE...
CAN'T USE NOW. GONE.
THANKS FOR TELLING US YOUR MOVING STORY, KEN.
YES, THAT MUST HAVE BEEN VERY DIFFICULT FOR YOU.
BUT NOW YOU ARE OK, RIGHT KEN?
YES... NOW MANY FRIENDS... HAPPY!

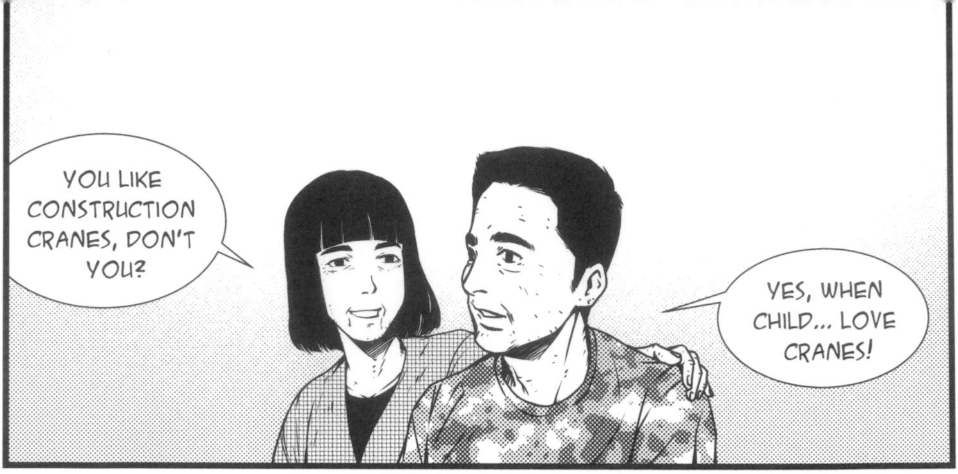
YOU LIKE CONSTRUCTION CRANES, DON'T YOU?
YES, WHEN CHILD... LOVE CRANES!

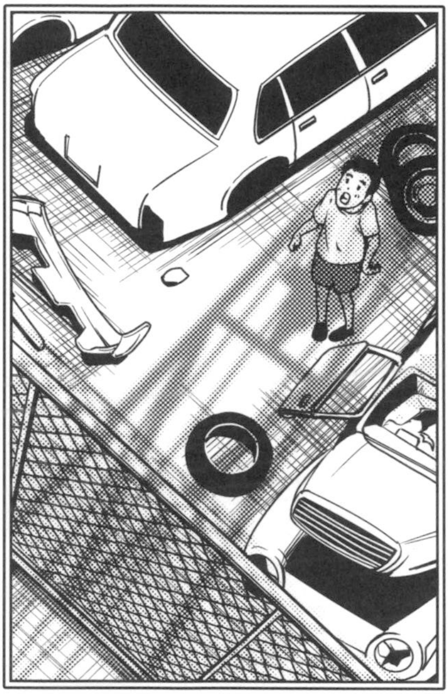

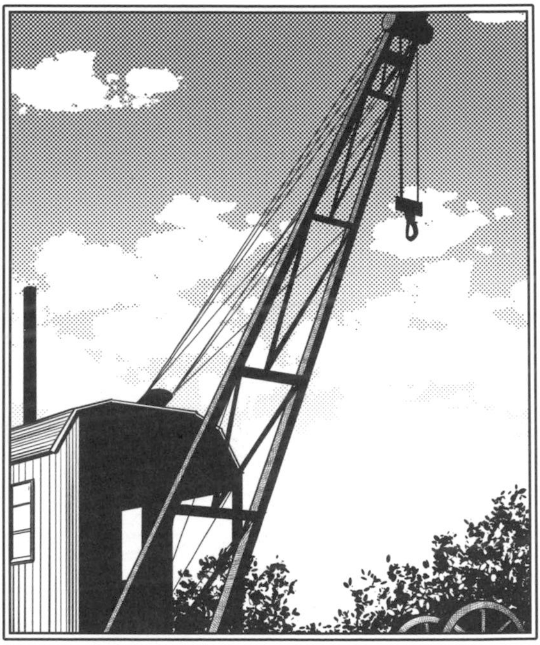

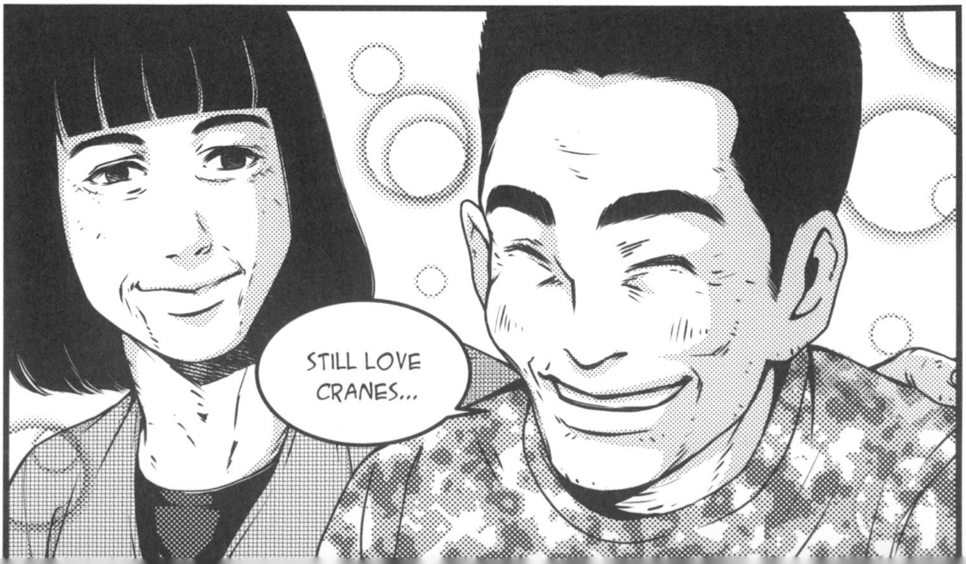
STILL LOVE CRANES...

HE FIRST SAW CRANES WHEN THEY WERE EXTENDING THE CHISSO FACTORY. SO, IT'S A LOVE-HATE FEELING FOR HIM.

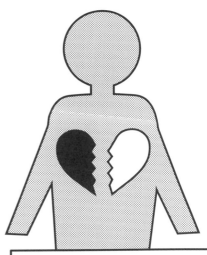

LIKE MANY PEOPLE AROUND HERE IT WAS A VERY DIFFICULT MIX OF FEELINGS. THEY WERE ANGRY ABOUT WHAT HAD HAPPENED TO THEM BUT REMEMBERED THE TIME THAT THE FACTORY BROUGHT NEW LIFE TO THE AREA.

KEN IS JUST ONE EXAMPLE OF THAT SPLIT IN MANY PEOPLE HERE – HE HATED AND FEARED THOSE KIDS FOR BULLYING HIM...

BUT HE ALSO PITIED THEM, UNDERSTOOD THAT THE PROBLEMS THE DISEASE CREATED FOR THE COMPANY ALSO DEEPLY AFFECTED THEIR LIVES.

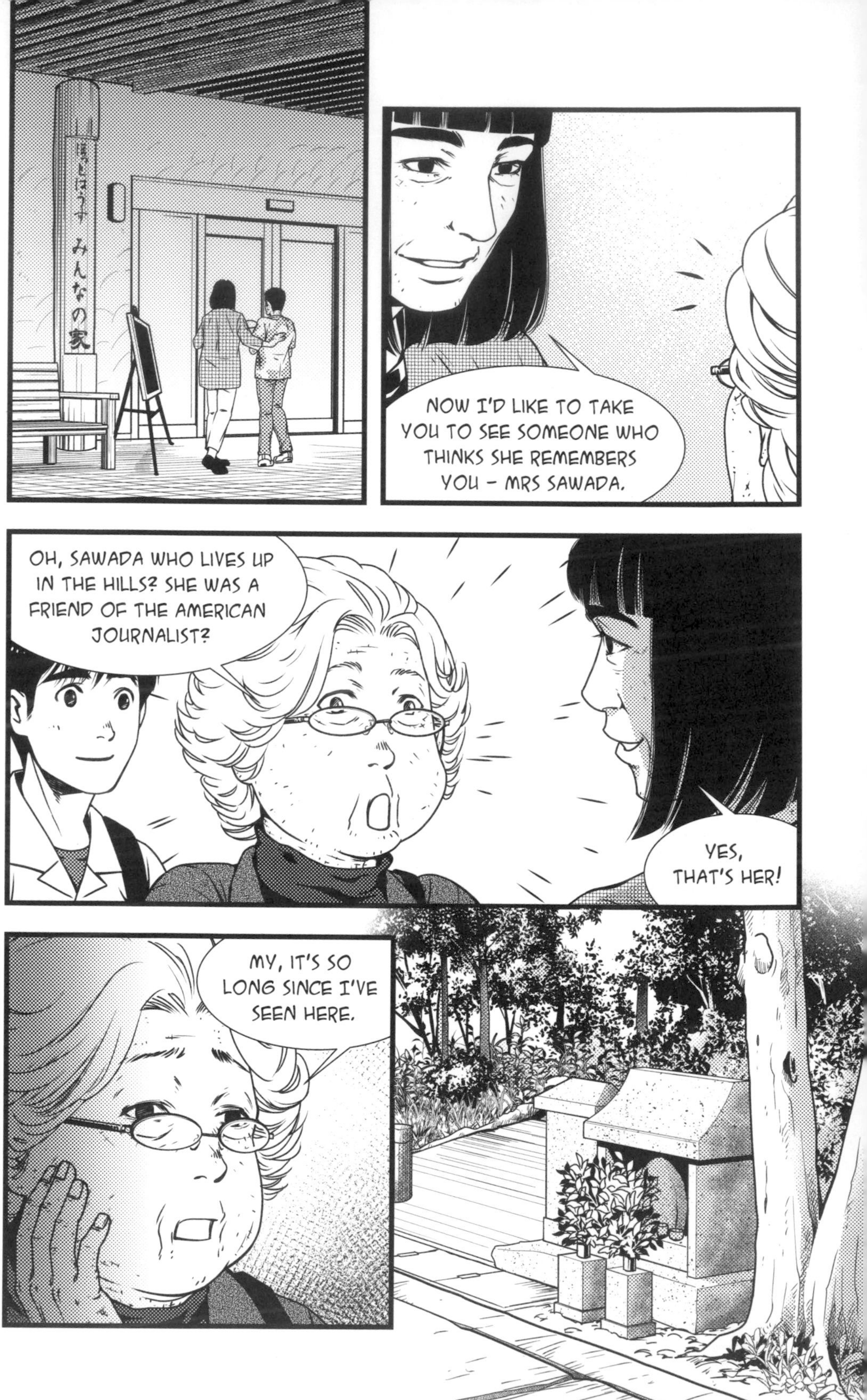
ほっとはうす みんなの家
NOW I'D LIKE TO TAKE YOU TO SEE SOMEONE WHO THINKS SHE REMEMBERS YOU - MRS SAWADA.
OH, SAWADA WHO LIVES UP IN THE HILLS? SHE WAS A FRIEND OF THE AMERICAN JOURNALIST?
YES, THAT'S HER!
MY, IT'S SO LONG SINCE I'VE SEEN HERE.

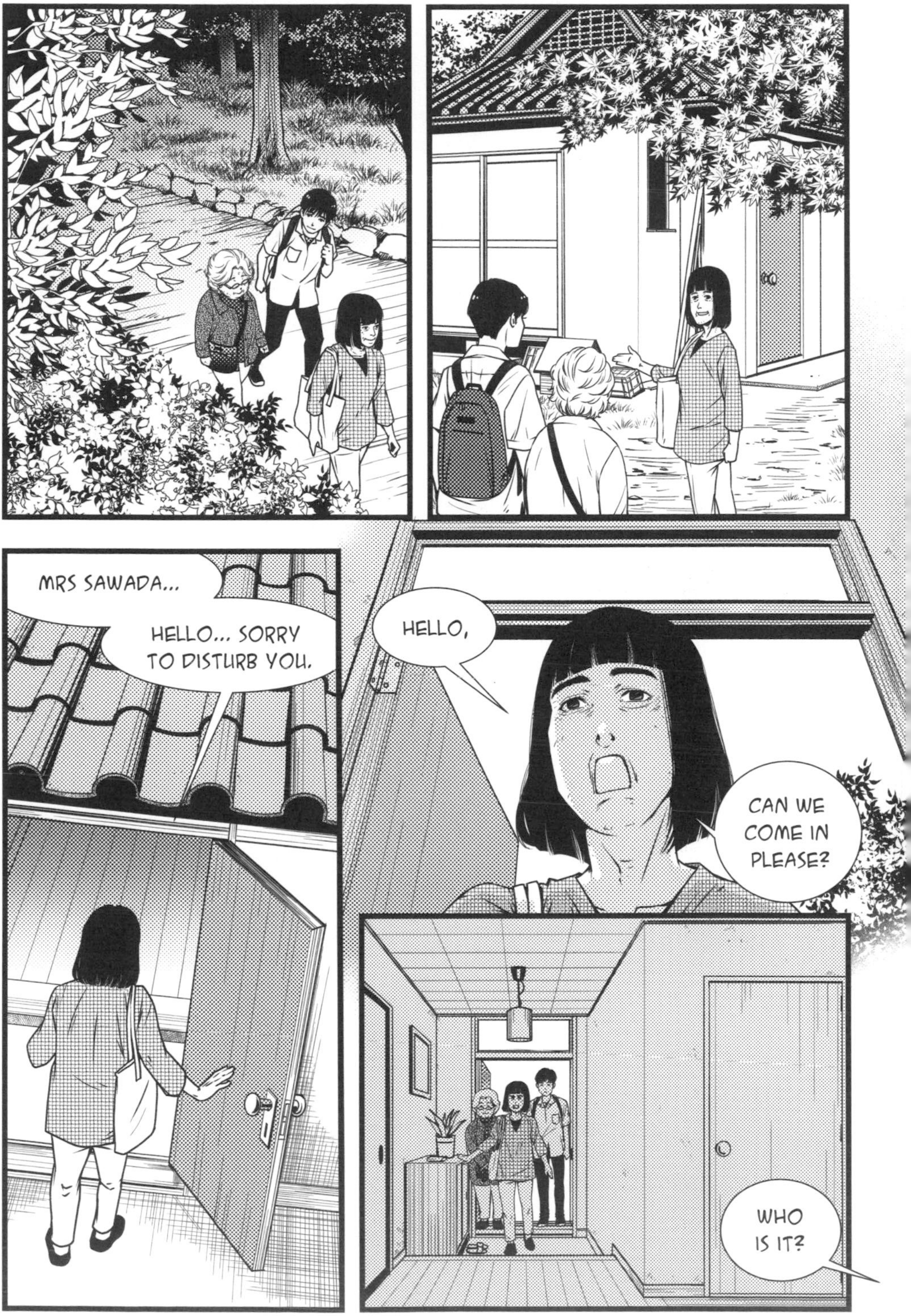
MRS SAWADA...
HELLO... SORRY TO DISTURB YOU.
HELLO,
CAN WE COME IN PLEASE?
WHO IS IT?

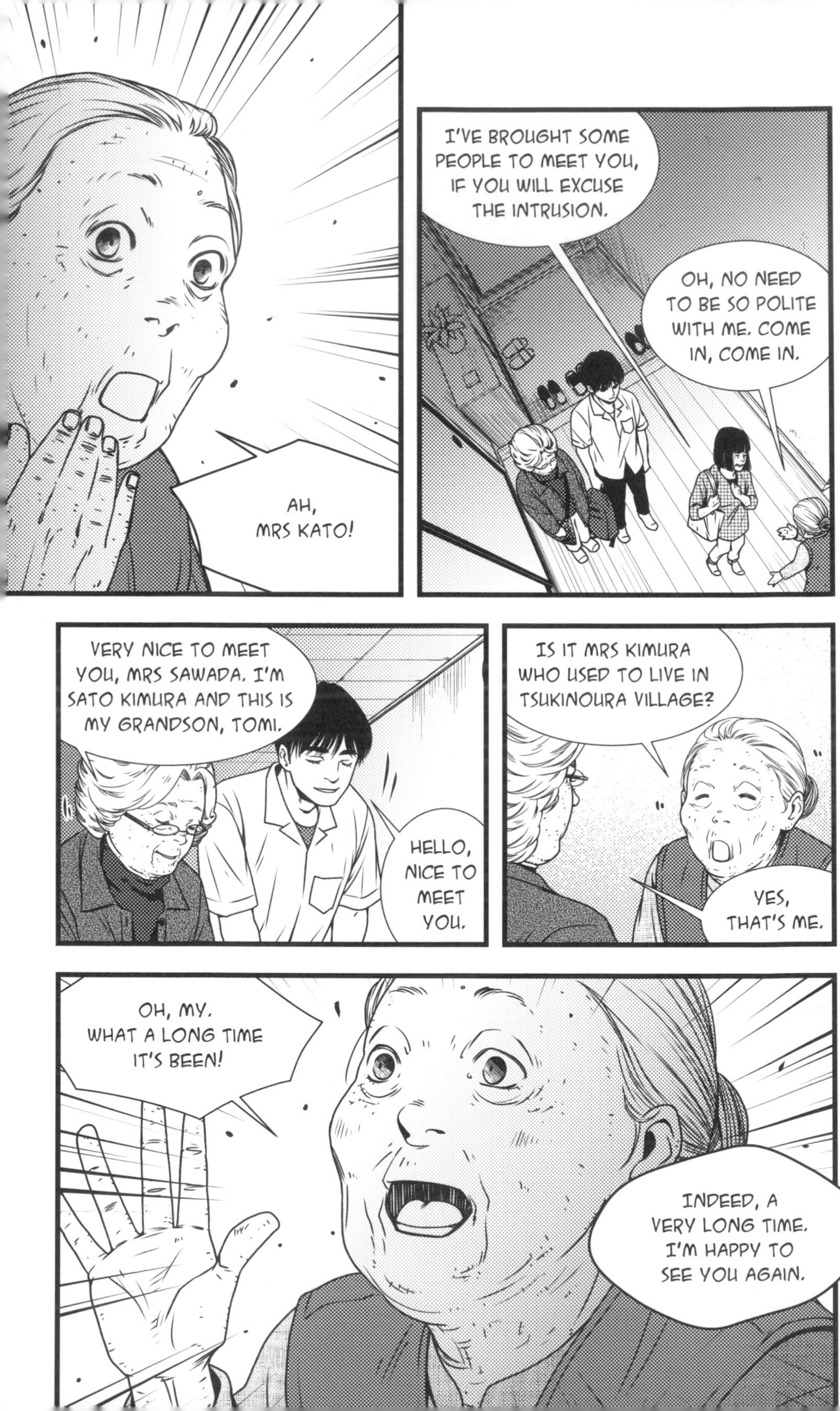
AH,
MRS KATO!
I'VE BROUGHT SOME PEOPLE TO MEET YOU, IF YOU WILL EXCUSE THE INTRUSION.
OH, NO NEED TO BE SO POLITE WITH ME. COME IN, COME IN.
VERY NICE TO MEET YOU, MRS SAWADA. I'M SATO KIMURA AND THIS IS MY GRANDSON, TOMI.
HELLO, NICE TO MEET YOU.
IS IT MRS KIMURA WHO USED TO LIVE IN TSUKINOURA VILLAGE?
YES, THAT'S ME.
OH, MY. WHAT A LONG TIME IT'S BEEN!
INDEED, A VERY LONG TIME. I'M HAPPY TO SEE YOU AGAIN.

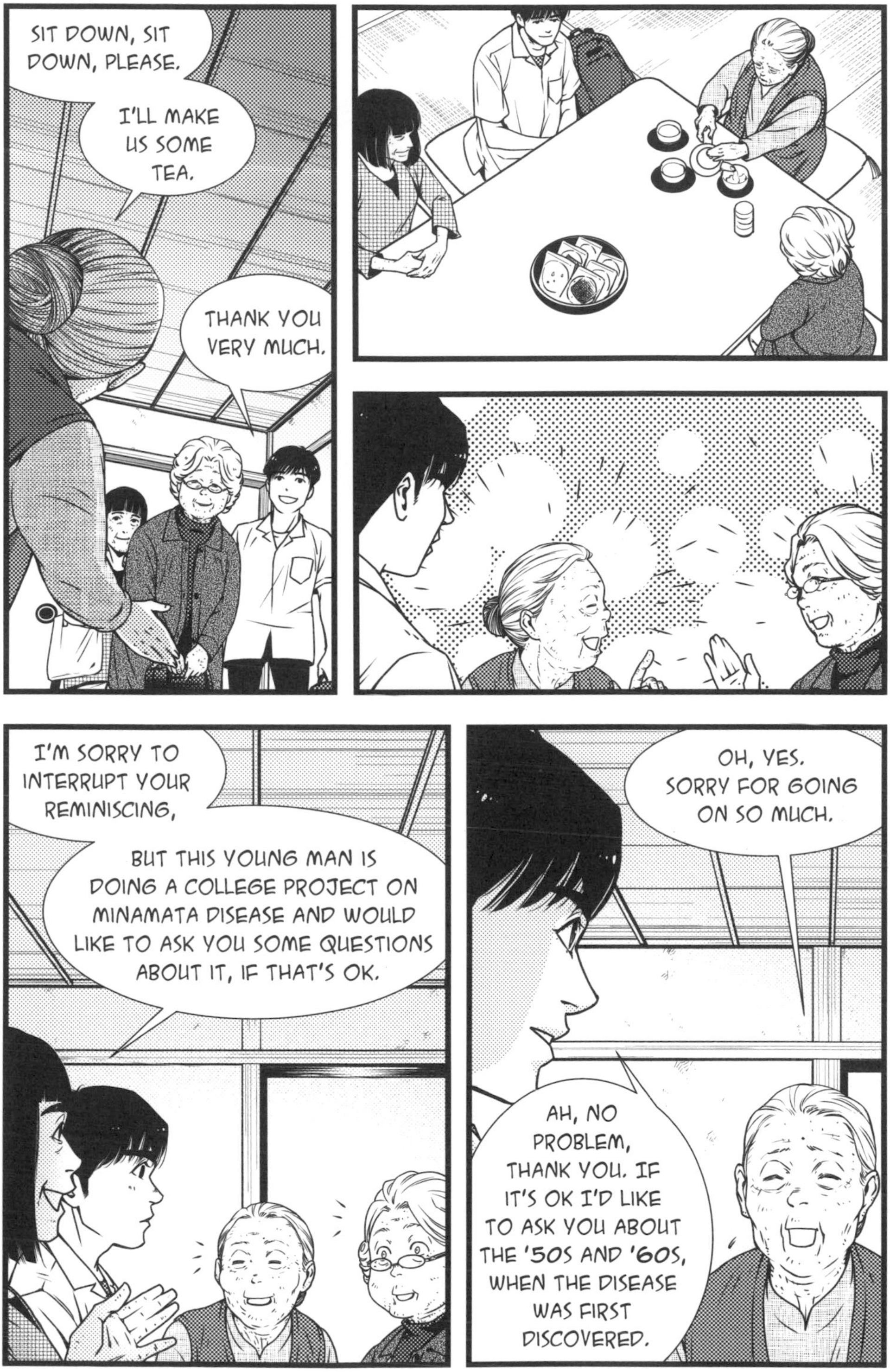
SIT DOWN, SIT DOWN, PLEASE.
I'LL MAKE US SOME TEA.
THANK YOU VERY MUCH.
I'M SORRY TO INTERRUPT YOUR REMINISCING,
BUT THIS YOUNG MAN IS DOING A COLLEGE PROJECT ON MINAMATA DISEASE AND WOULD LIKE TO ASK YOU SOME QUESTIONS ABOUT IT, IF THAT'S OK.
OH, YES. SORRY FOR GOING ON SO MUCH.
AH, NO PROBLEM, THANK YOU. IF IT'S OK I'D LIKE TO ASK YOU ABOUT THE '50S AND '60S, WHEN THE DISEASE WAS FIRST DISCOVERED.

I SEEM TO BE TALKING ABOUT IT A LOT RECENTLY. THERE WAS AN AMERICAN FILM CREW HERE A FEW MONTHS AGO, DRESSED UP LIKE IT WAS THE 1970S.

OH, REALLY? WHO WAS THE MAIN ACTOR?

OH, I FORGET HIS NAME. A HANDSOME GUY, JOHNNY SOMETHING. THEY MADE HIM UP TO LOOK LIKE OUR MR SMITH.

YOU MEAN EUGENE SMITH, THE PHOTOGRAPHER WHO TOOK ALL THOSE FAMOUS PHOTOS OF MINAMATA IN THE '70S?

YES, THAT'S HIM IN THE PHOTO THERE,

WITH US IN... AH, 1973 I THINK.

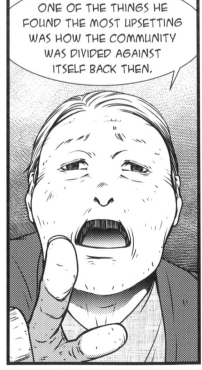

ONE OF THE THINGS HE FOUND THE MOST UPSETTING WAS HOW THE COMMUNITY WAS DIVIDED AGAINST ITSELF BACK THEN.

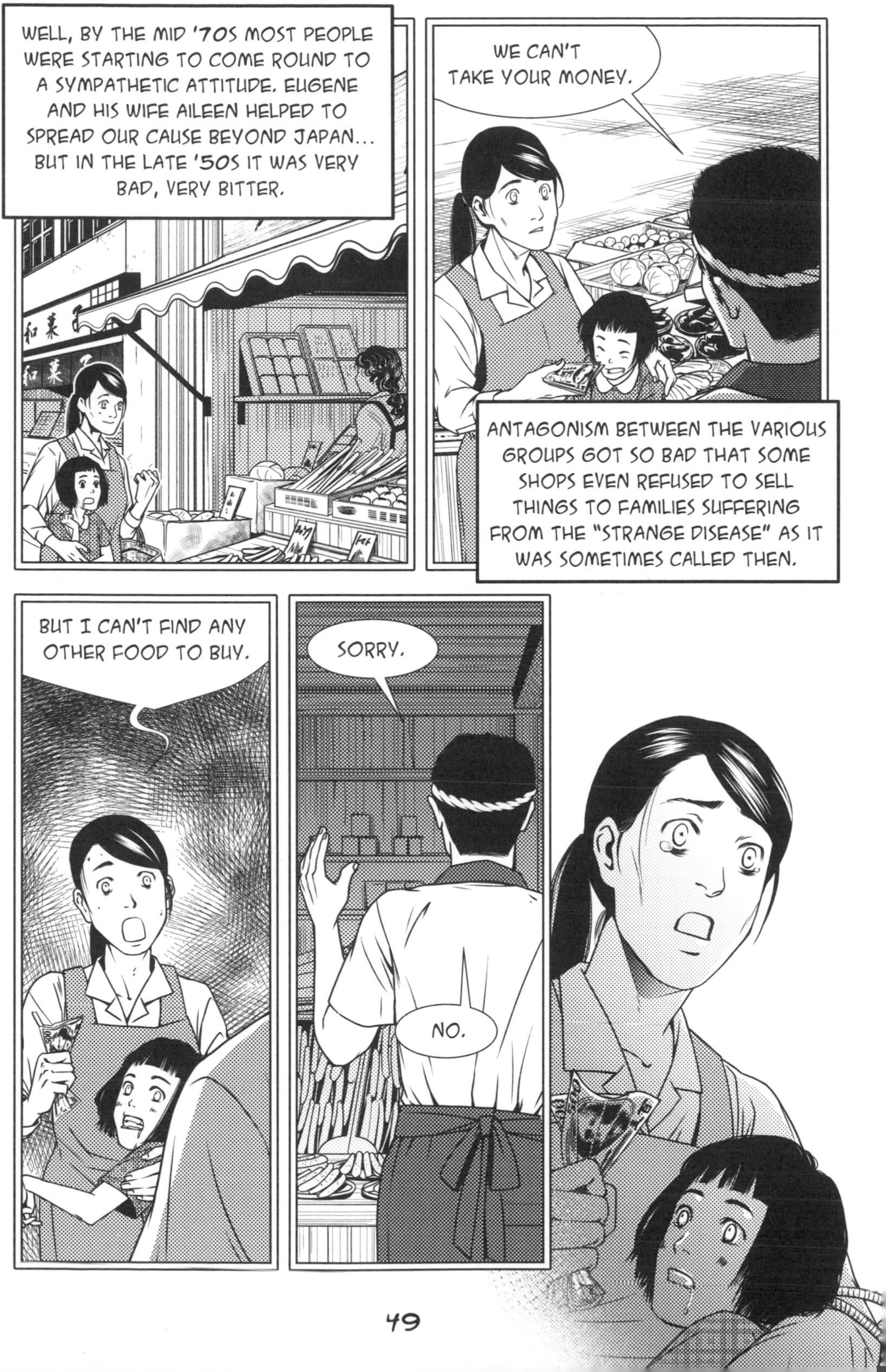
WELL, BY THE MID '70S MOST PEOPLE WERE STARTING TO COME ROUND TO A SYMPATHETIC ATTITUDE. EUGENE AND HIS WIFE AILEEN HELPED TO SPREAD OUR CAUSE BEYOND JAPAN... BUT IN THE LATE '50S IT WAS VERY BAD, VERY BITTER.
WE CAN'T TAKE YOUR MONEY.
ANTAGONISM BETWEEN THE VARIOUS GROUPS GOT SO BAD THAT SOME SHOPS EVEN REFUSED TO SELL THINGS TO FAMILIES SUFFERING FROM THE "STRANGE DISEASE" AS IT WAS SOMETIMES CALLED THEN.
BUT I CAN'T FIND ANY OTHER FOOD TO BUY.
SORRY.
NO.

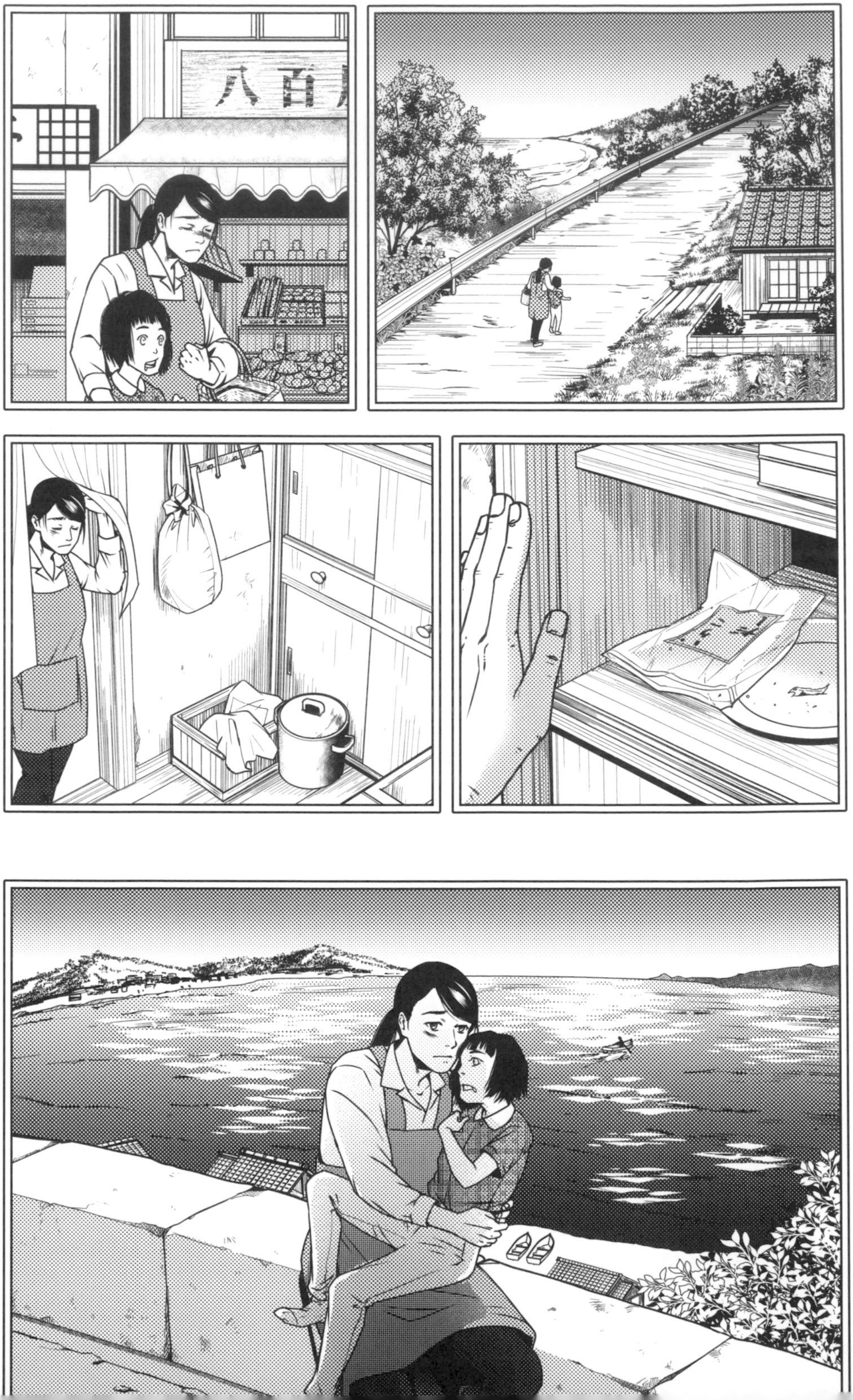
八百

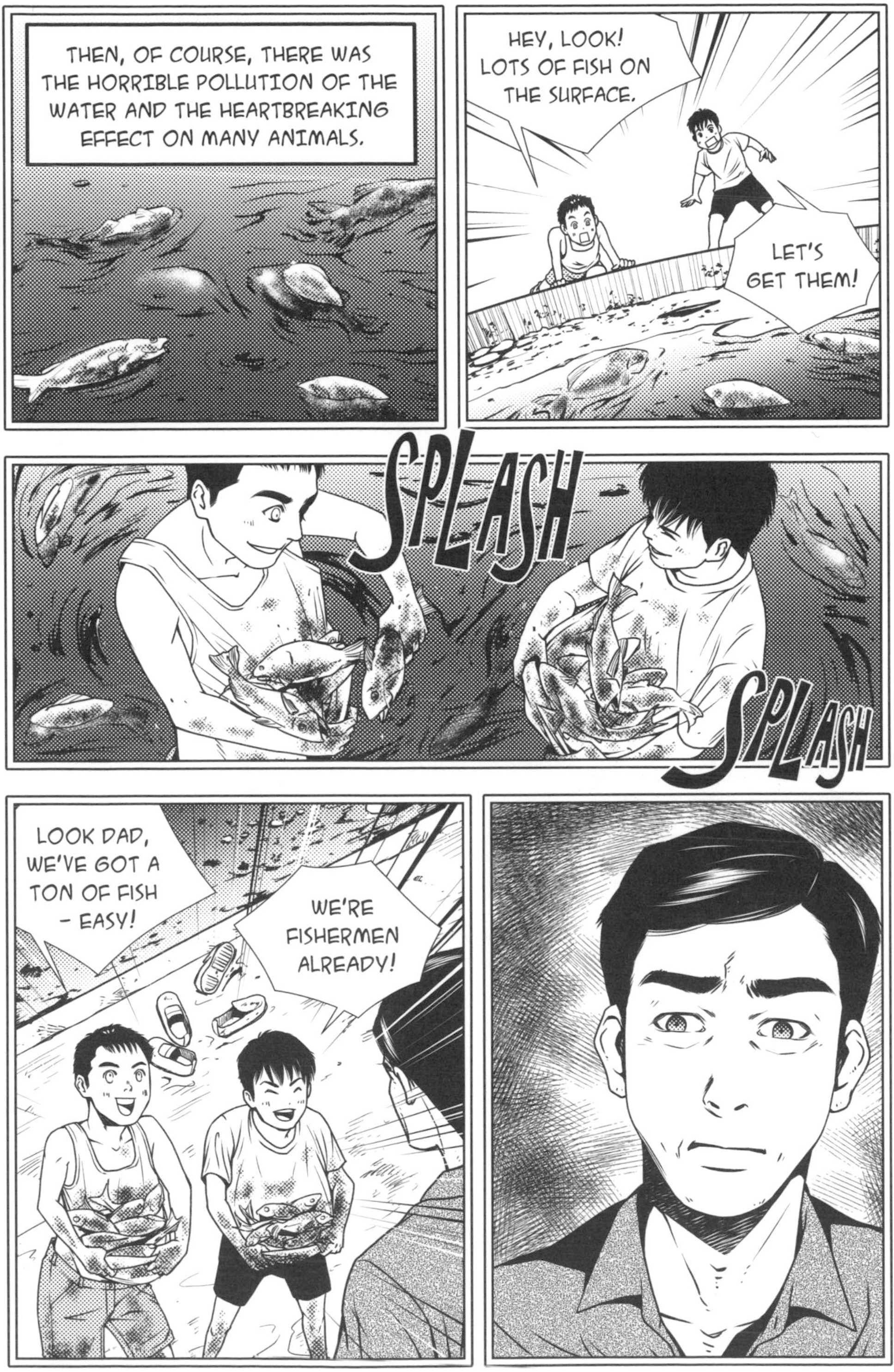

THEN, OF COURSE, THERE WAS THE HORRIBLE POLLUTION OF THE WATER AND THE HEARTBREAKING EFFECT ON MANY ANIMALS.
HEY, LOOK! LOTS OF FISH ON THE SURFACE.
LET'S GET THEM!
SPLASH
SPLASH
LOOK DAD, WE'VE GOT A TON OF FISH - EASY!
WE'RE FISHERMEN ALREADY!

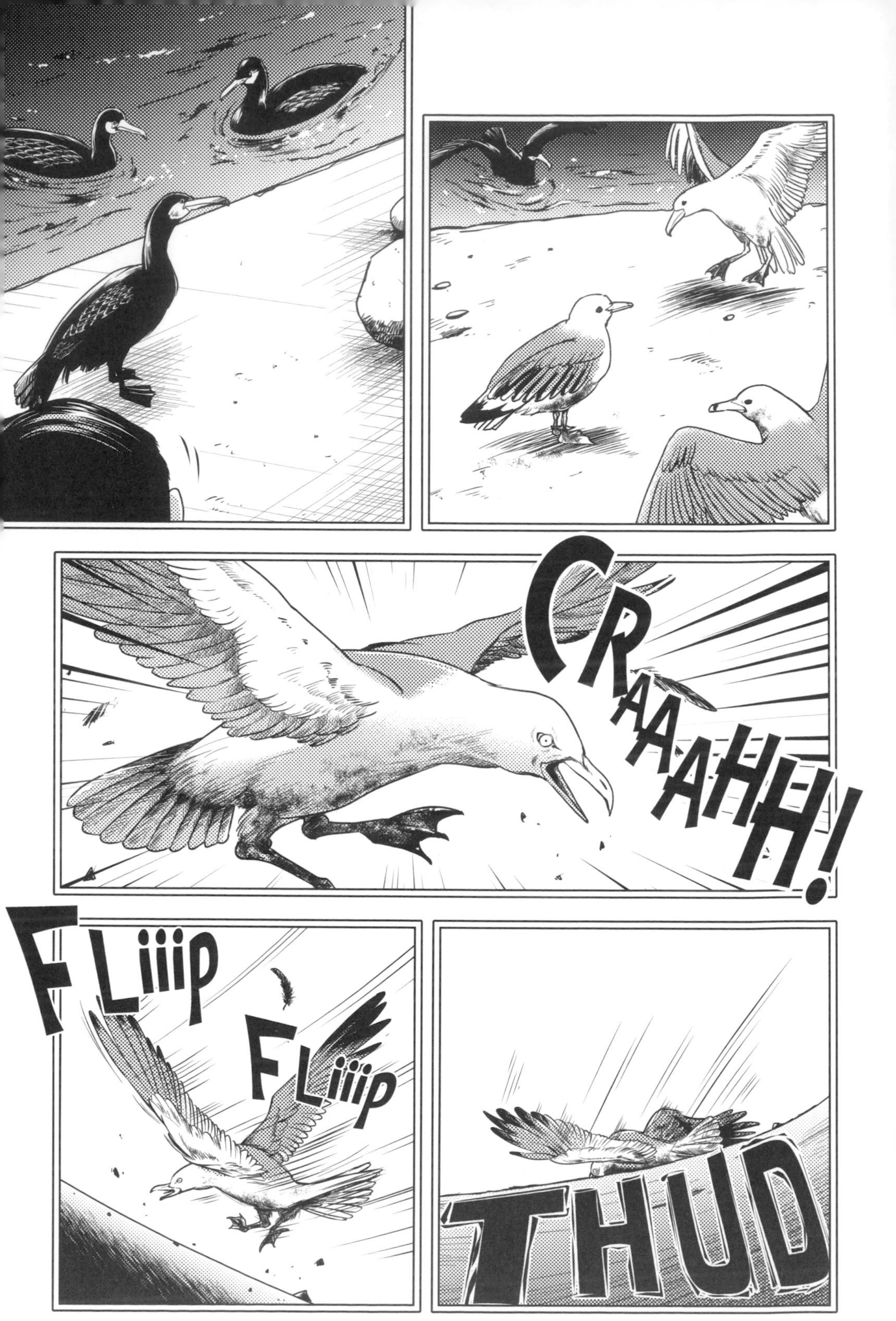
CRAAAHH!
FLiiip
FLiiip
THUD

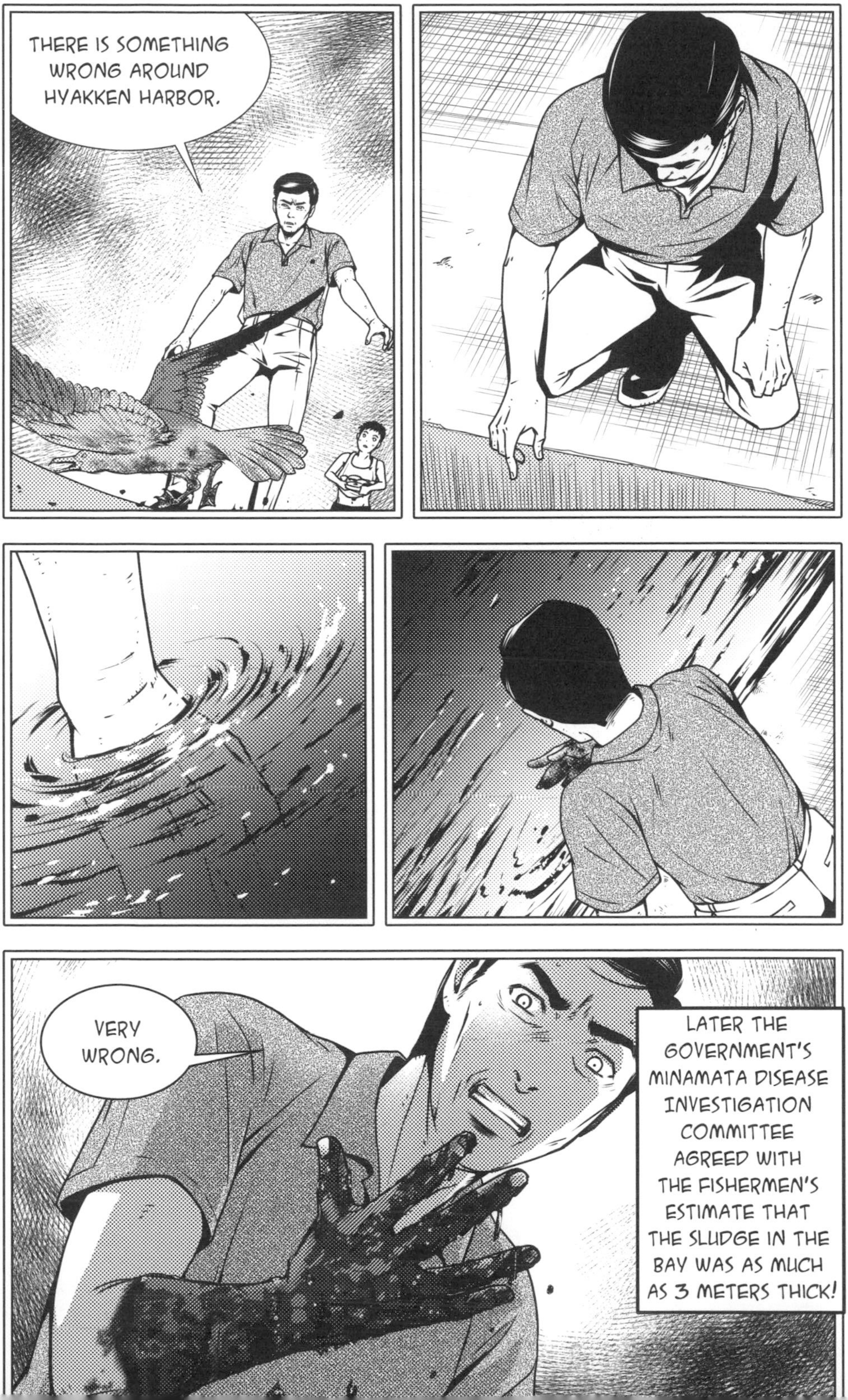
THERE IS SOMETHING WRONG AROUND HYAKKEN HARBOR.
VERY WRONG.
LATER THE GOVERNMENT'S MINAMATA DISEASE INVESTIGATION COMMITTEE AGREED WITH THE FISHERMEN'S ESTIMATE THAT THE SLUDGE IN THE BAY WAS AS MUCH AS 3 METERS THICK!

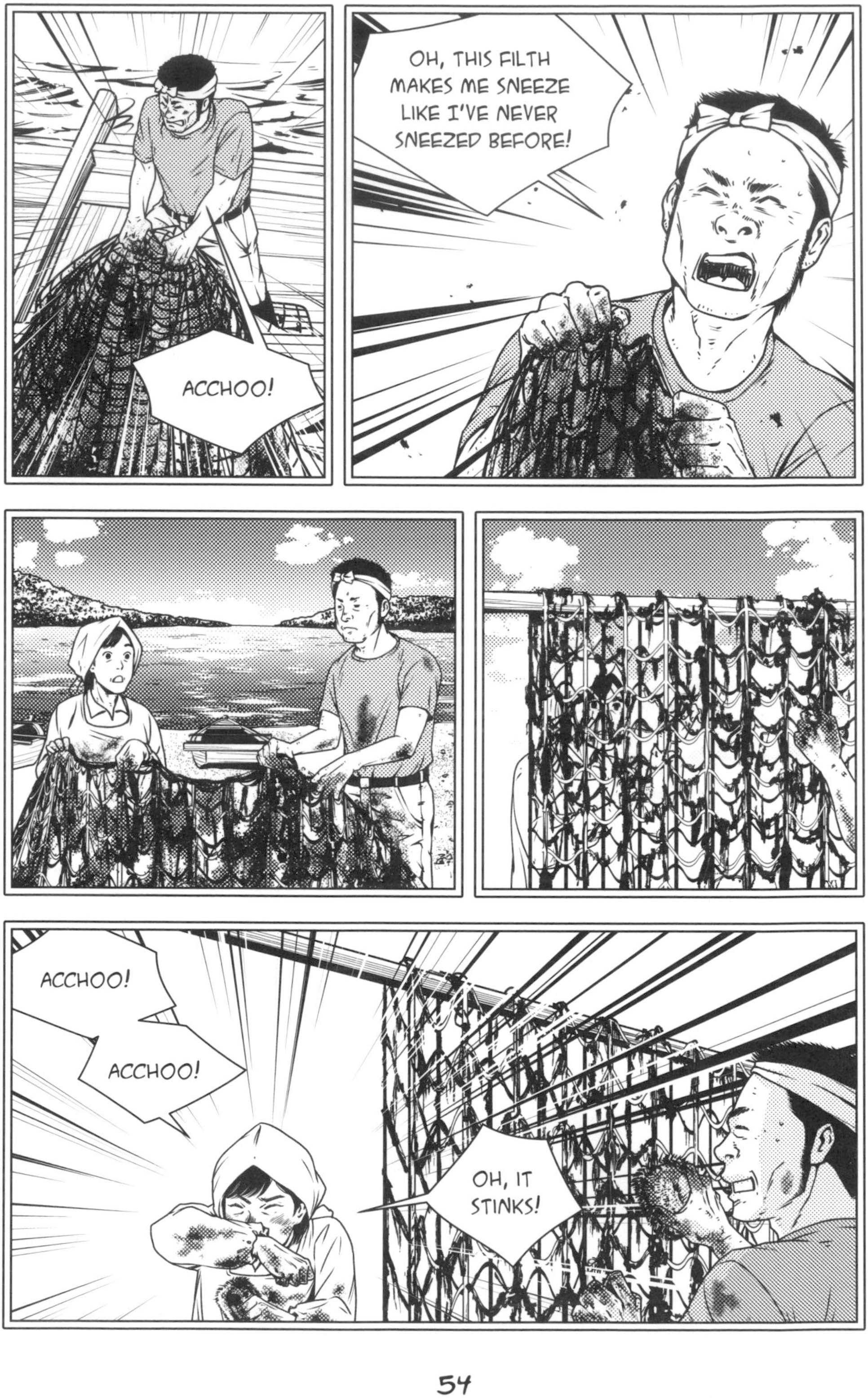
ACCHOO!
OH, THIS FILTH MAKES ME SNEEZE LIKE I'VE NEVER SNEEZED BEFORE!
ACCHOO!
ACCHOO!
OH, IT STINKS!

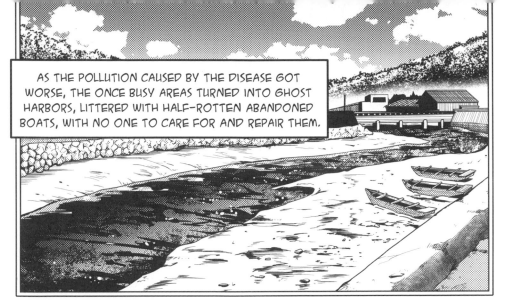

AS THE POLLUTION CAUSED BY THE DISEASE GOT WORSE, THE ONCE BUSY AREAS TURNED INTO GHOST HARBORS, LITTERED WITH HALF-ROTTEN ABANDONED BOATS, WITH NO ONE TO CARE FOR AND REPAIR THEM.

BEFORE THE DISEASE WORMED AND SCUTTLED ITS WAY INTO THE PEOPLE AND THE AREA THERE WERE 318 HOUSEHOLDS ENGAGED IN FISHERY, OFTEN FOR MANY GENERATIONS IN THE SAME FAMILY. A PROUD TRADITION. BY 1961 THIS HAD SHRUNK TO ONLY 168 HOUSEHOLDS, WHILE THE FISHING CATCH HAD REDUCED TO LESS THAN 10% OF WHAT IT USED TO BE, "IN THE GOOD OLD DAYS."

IT WAS ESPECIALLY HARD WHEN WE THOUGHT BACK TO HOW SIMPLE, CLEAN, AND BEAUTIFUL THE SEA WAS BEFORE.

HELLO AGAIN LOVELY FISH. IT'S US – SEIKO AND SHUICHI.

HOW WONDERFULLY YOUR SKIN REFLECTS THE SUN!

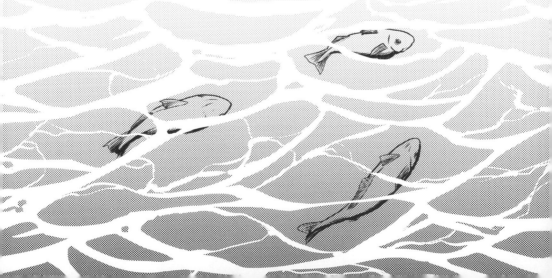

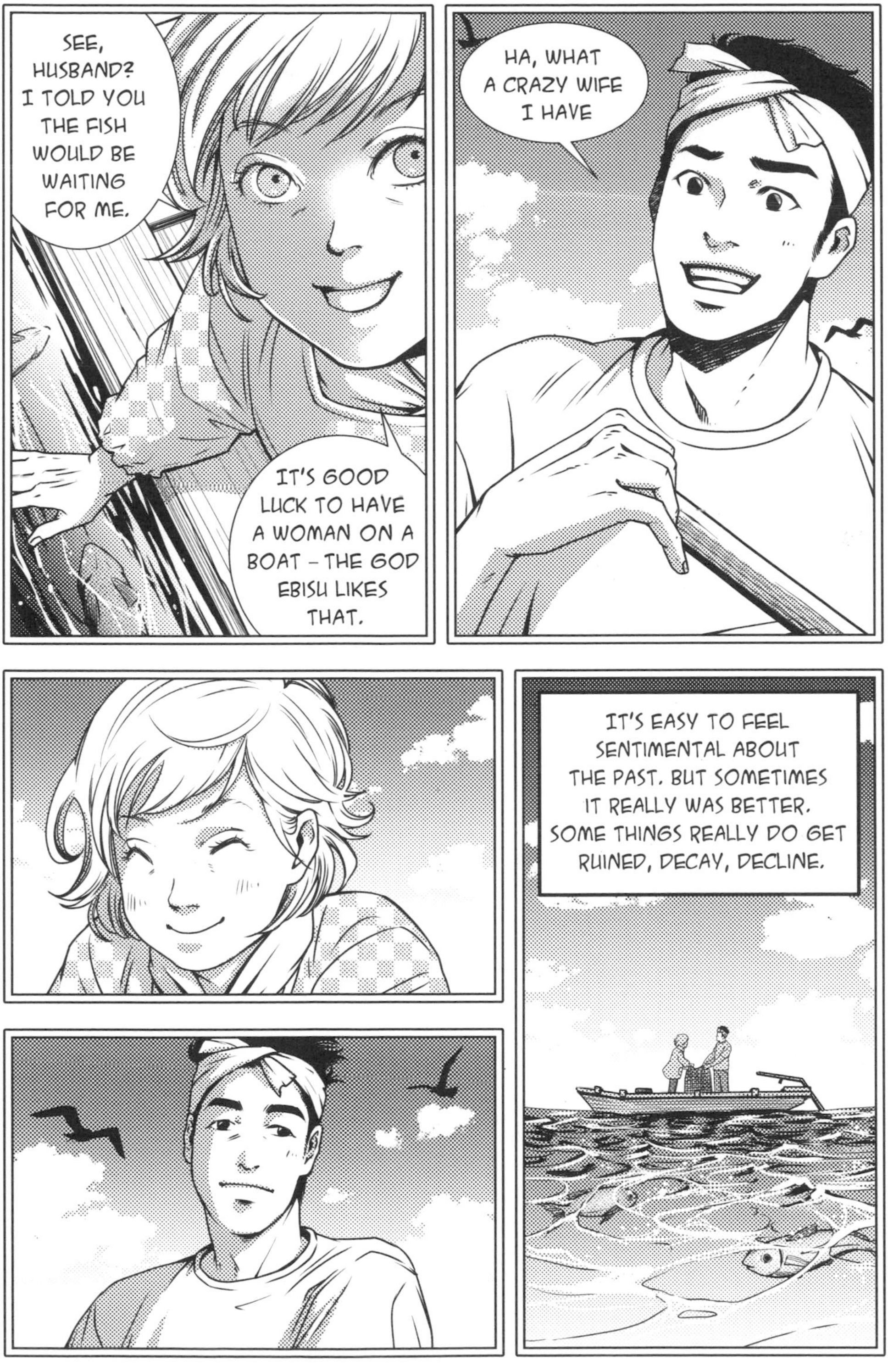
SEE, HUSBAND? I TOLD YOU THE FISH WOULD BE WAITING FOR ME.
IT'S GOOD LUCK TO HAVE A WOMAN ON A BOAT – THE GOD EBISU LIKES THAT.
HA, WHAT A CRAZY WIFE I HAVE
IT'S EASY TO FEEL SENTIMENTAL ABOUT THE PAST. BUT SOMETIMES IT REALLY WAS BETTER. SOME THINGS REALLY DO GET RUINED, DECAY, DECLINE.

I CLEARLY REMEMBER THE TIME THAT I SAW A FISHERMAN, WHO WAS VERY STRONG, WITH A WIDE CHEST AND BEAUTIFULLY TONED MUSCLES...

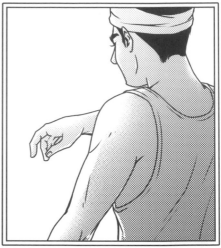

NOW SOBBING LIKE A BABY.

HE WAS CRYING UNCONTROLLABLY TO THINK OF HOW THE NATURAL BEAUTY OF THE SEA THAT HE LOVED HAD BEEN DESTROYED BY THIS DISGUSTING HUMAN-MADE POLLUTION. IT BROKE HIS HEART.

AND IT BROKE MINE TO SEE SUCH PROUD FISHERMEN REDUCED TO HELPLESS TEARS.

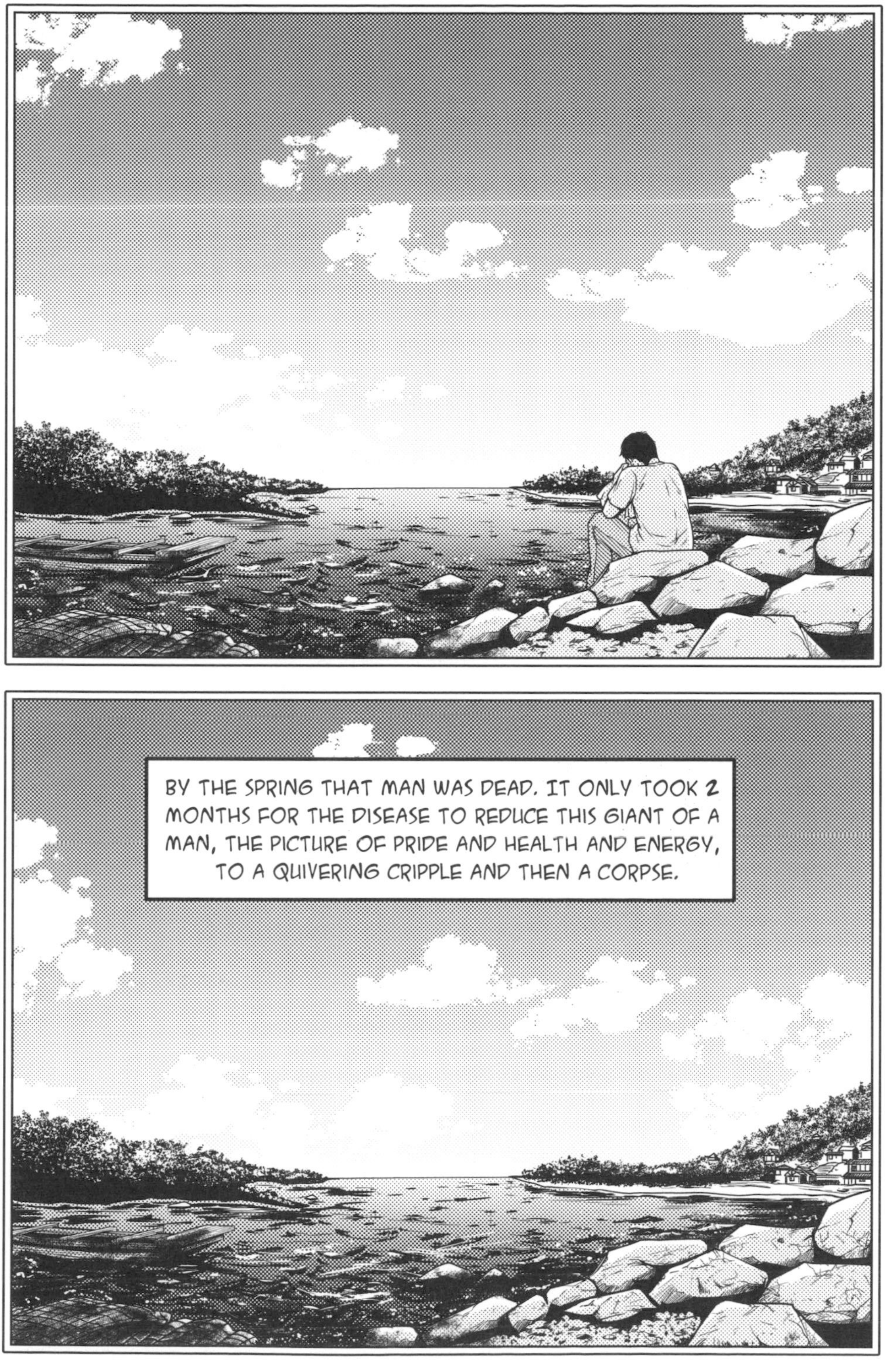
BY THE SPRING THAT MAN WAS DEAD. IT ONLY TOOK 2 MONTHS FOR THE DISEASE TO REDUCE THIS GIANT OF A MAN, THE PICTURE OF PRIDE AND HEALTH AND ENERGY, TO A QUIVERING CRIPPLE AND THEN A CORPSE.

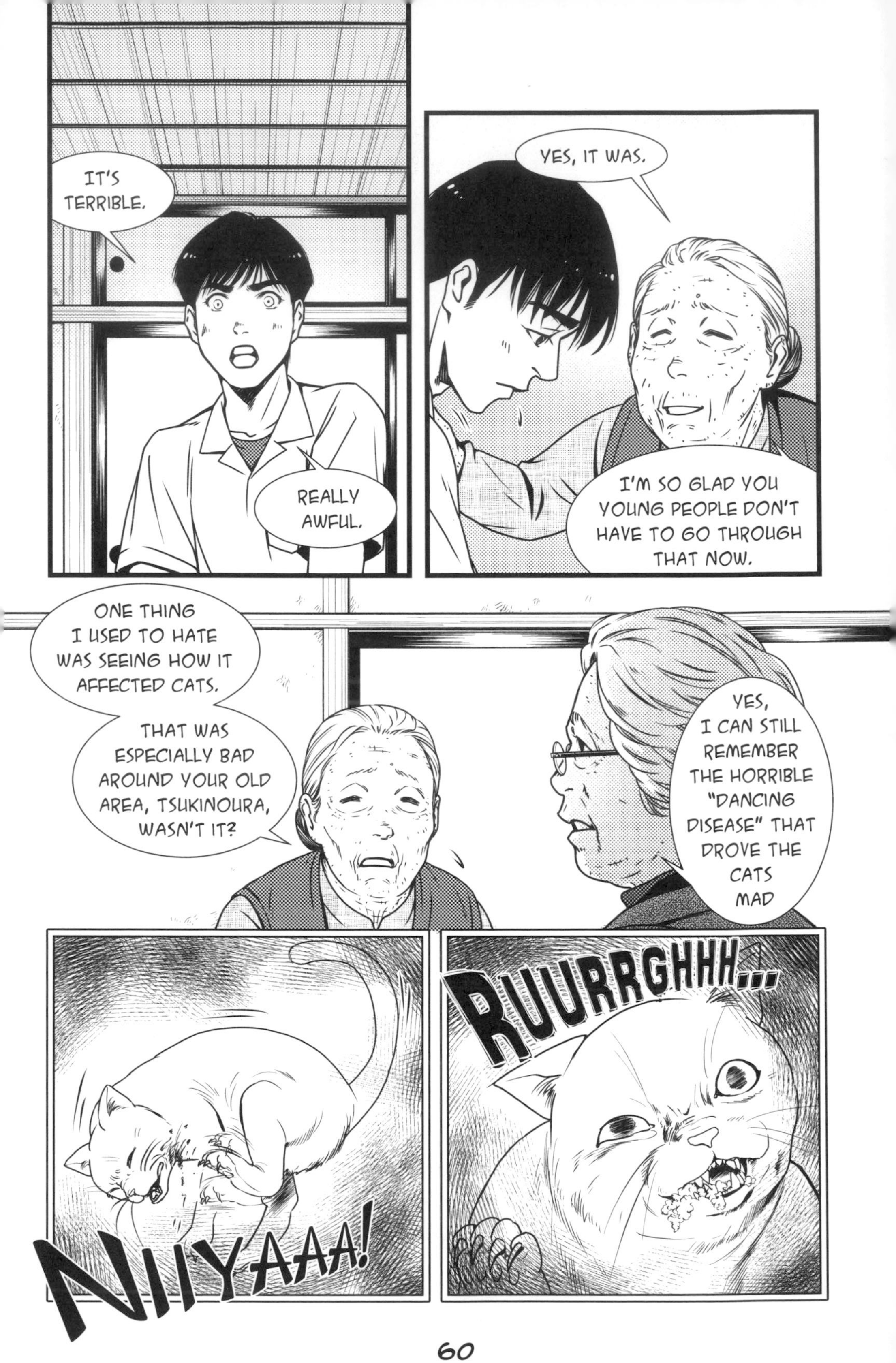
IT'S TERRIBLE.
REALLY AWFUL.
YES, IT WAS.
I'M SO GLAD YOU YOUNG PEOPLE DON'T HAVE TO GO THROUGH THAT NOW.
ONE THING I USED TO HATE WAS SEEING HOW IT AFFECTED CATS.
THAT WAS ESPECIALLY BAD AROUND YOUR OLD AREA, TSUKINOURA, WASN'T IT?
YES, I CAN STILL REMEMBER THE HORRIBLE "DANCING DISEASE" THAT DROVE THE CATS MAD
NIIYAAA!
RUURRGHHH...

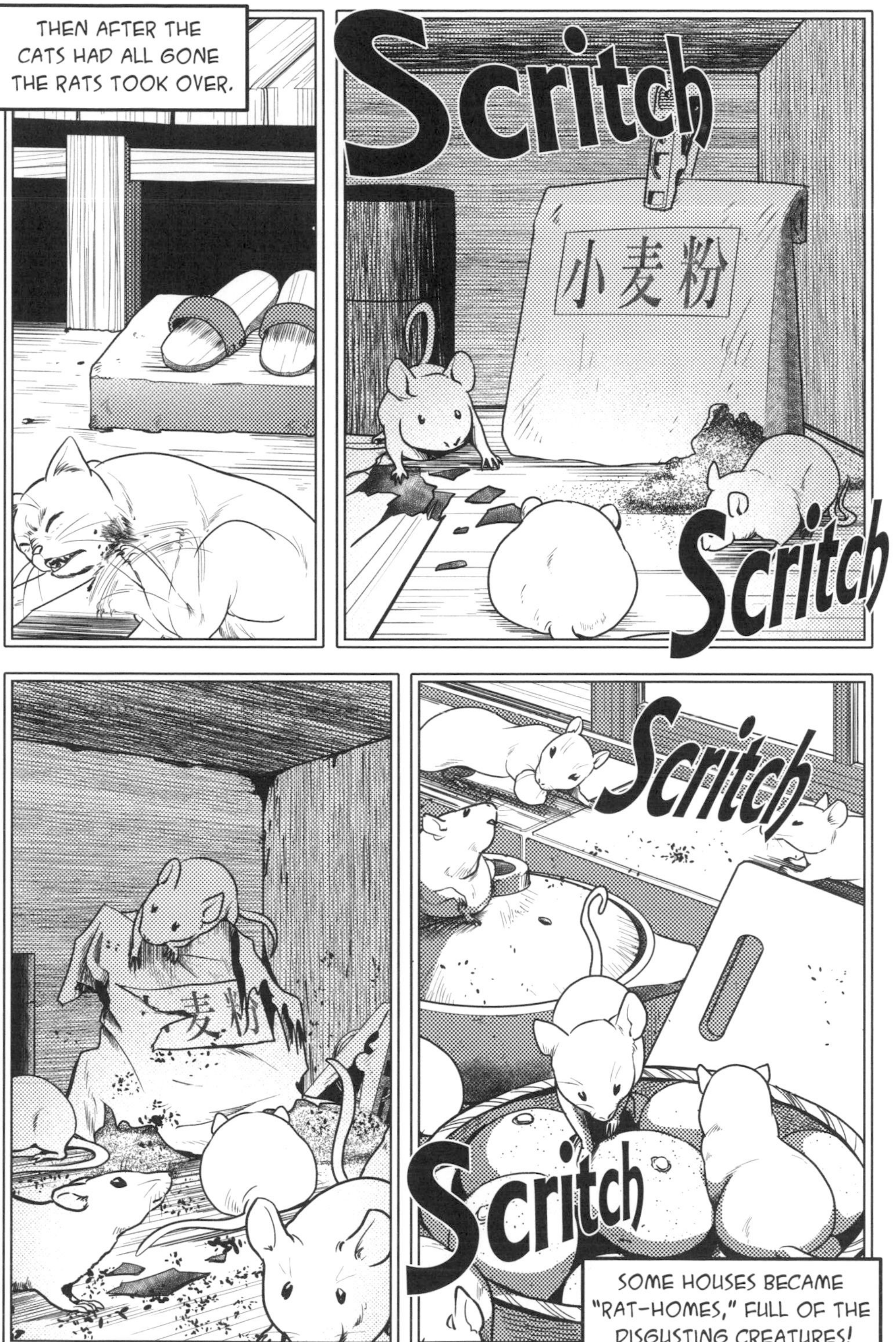
THEN AFTER THE CATS HAD ALL GONE THE RATS TOOK OVER.
Scritch
小麦粉
Scritch
麦粉
Scritch
Scritch
SOME HOUSES BECAME "RAT-HOMES," FULL OF THE DISGUSTING CREATURES!

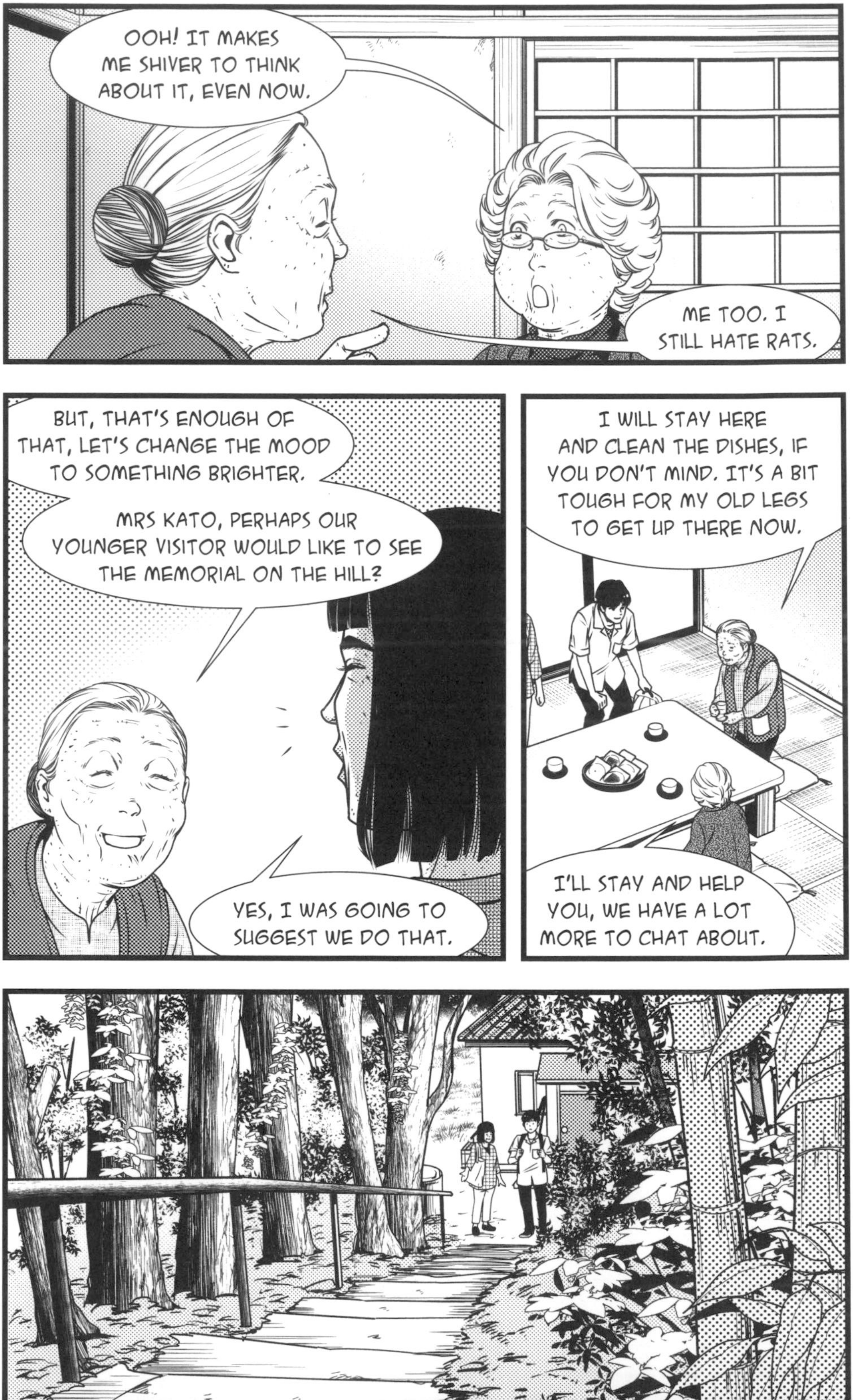
OOH! IT MAKES ME SHIVER TO THINK ABOUT IT, EVEN NOW.
ME TOO. I STILL HATE RATS.
BUT, THAT'S ENOUGH OF THAT, LET'S CHANGE THE MOOD TO SOMETHING BRIGHTER.
MRS KATO, PERHAPS OUR YOUNGER VISITOR WOULD LIKE TO SEE THE MEMORIAL ON THE HILL?
YES, I WAS GOING TO SUGGEST WE DO THAT.
I WILL STAY HERE AND CLEAN THE DISHES, IF YOU DON'T MIND. IT'S A BIT TOUGH FOR MY OLD LEGS TO GET UP THERE NOW.
I'LL STAY AND HELP YOU, WE HAVE A LOT MORE TO CHAT ABOUT.

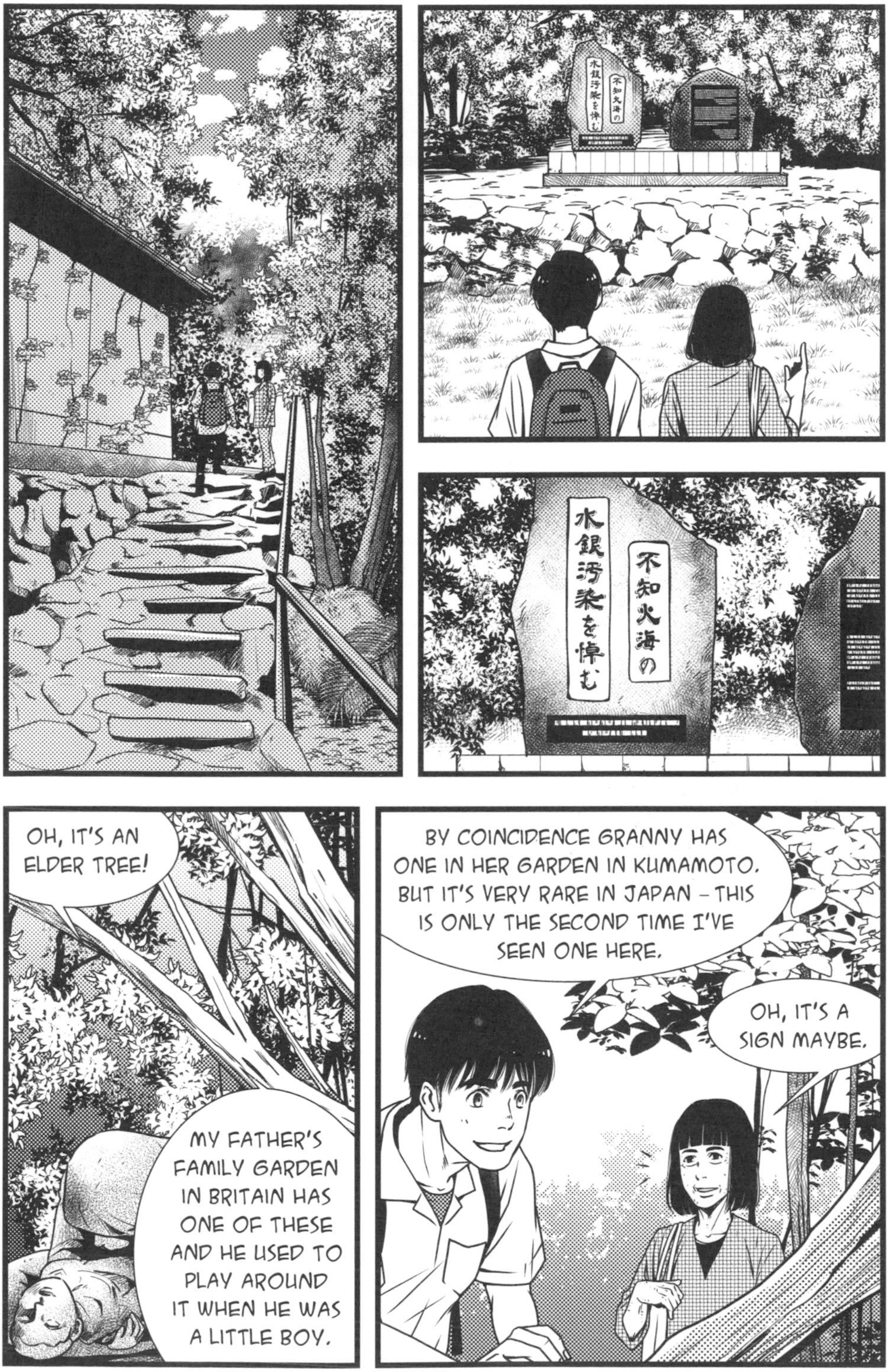
不知火海の
水銀汚染を悼む
OH, IT'S AN ELDER TREE!
MY FATHER'S FAMILY GARDEN IN BRITAIN HAS ONE OF THESE AND HE USED TO PLAY AROUND IT WHEN HE WAS A LITTLE BOY.
BY COINCIDENCE GRANNY HAS ONE IN HER GARDEN IN KUMAMOTO. BUT IT'S VERY RARE IN JAPAN – THIS IS ONLY THE SECOND TIME I'VE SEEN ONE HERE.
OH, IT'S A SIGN MAYBE.

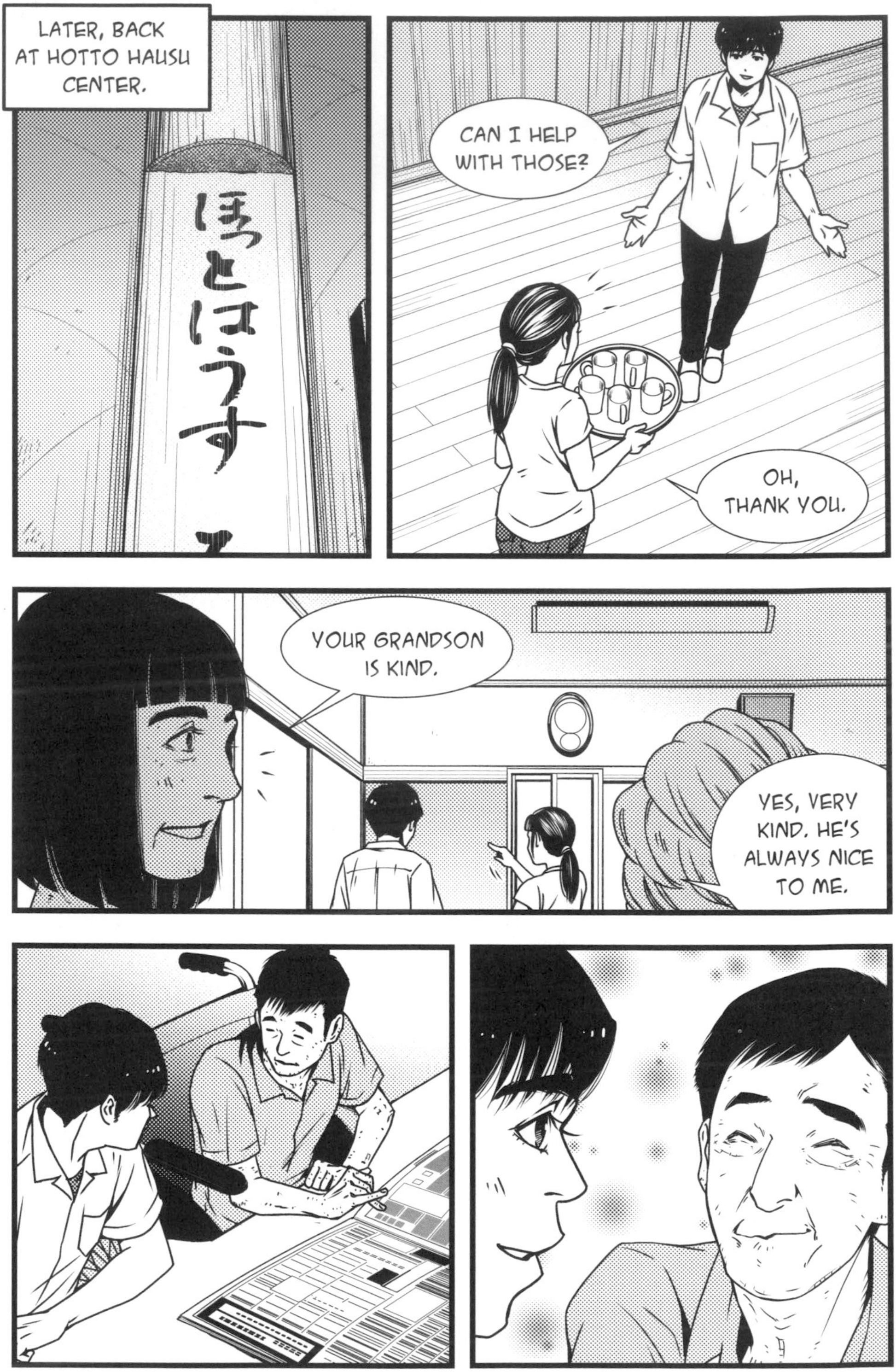
LATER, BACK AT HOTTO HAUSU CENTER.
ほっとはうす
CAN I HELP WITH THOSE?
OH, THANK YOU.
YOUR GRANDSON IS KIND.
YES, VERY KIND. HE'S ALWAYS NICE TO ME.

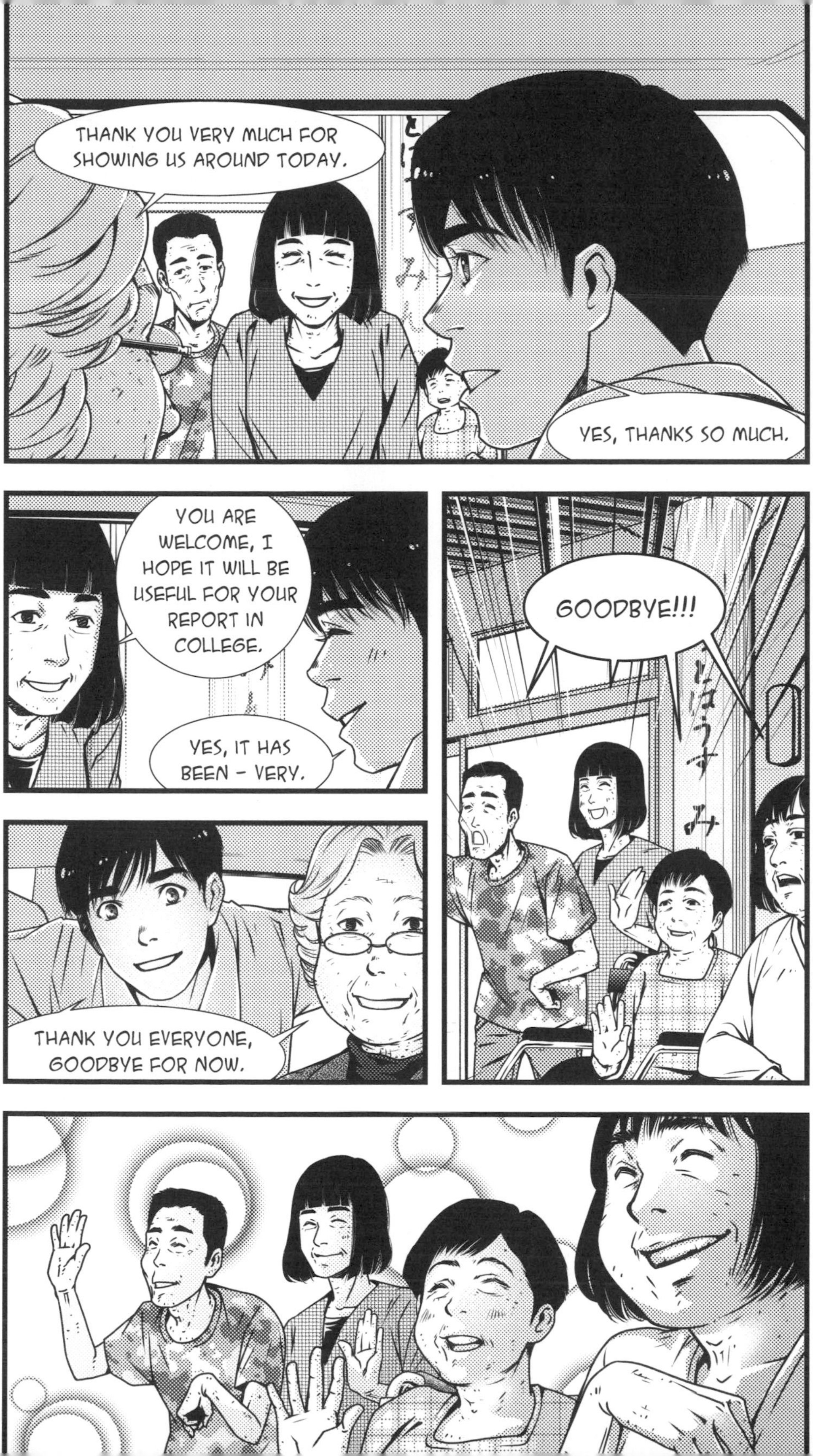
THANK YOU VERY MUCH FOR SHOWING US AROUND TODAY.
YES, THANKS SO MUCH.
YOU ARE WELCOME, I HOPE IT WILL BE USEFUL FOR YOUR REPORT IN COLLEGE.
YES, IT HAS BEEN - VERY.
THANK YOU EVERYONE, GOODBYE FOR NOW.
GOODBYE!!!

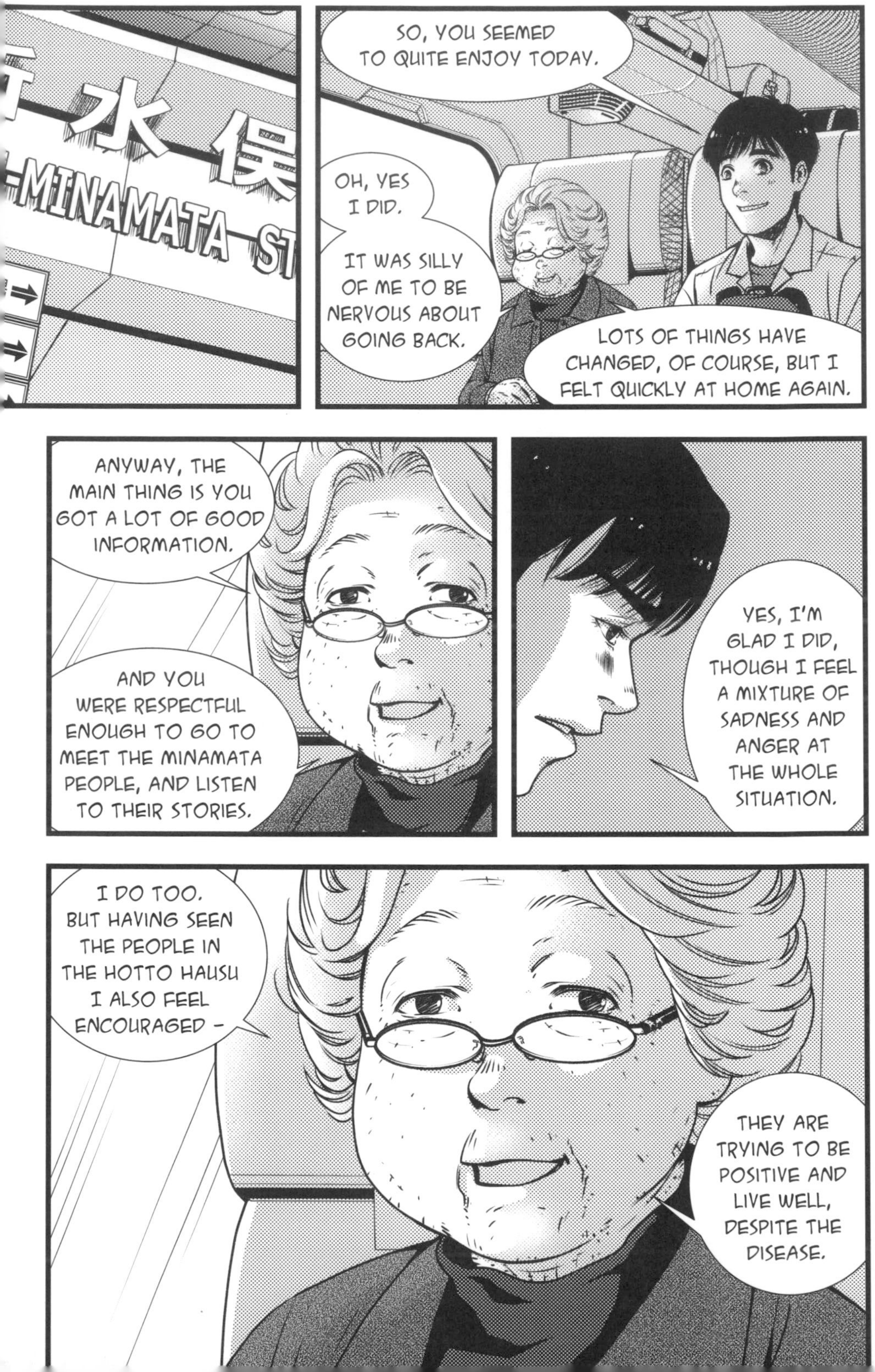

水俣
MINAMATA ST
SO, YOU SEEMED TO QUITE ENJOY TODAY.
OH, YES I DID.
IT WAS SILLY OF ME TO BE NERVOUS ABOUT GOING BACK.
LOTS OF THINGS HAVE CHANGED, OF COURSE, BUT I FELT QUICKLY AT HOME AGAIN.
ANYWAY, THE MAIN THING IS YOU GOT A LOT OF GOOD INFORMATION.
AND YOU WERE RESPECTFUL ENOUGH TO GO TO MEET THE MINAMATA PEOPLE, AND LISTEN TO THEIR STORIES.
YES, I'M GLAD I DID, THOUGH I FEEL A MIXTURE OF SADNESS AND ANGER AT THE WHOLE SITUATION.
I DO TOO. BUT HAVING SEEN THE PEOPLE IN THE HOTTO HAUSU I ALSO FEEL ENCOURAGED –
THEY ARE TRYING TO BE POSITIVE AND LIVE WELL, DESPITE THE DISEASE.

DEFIANCE

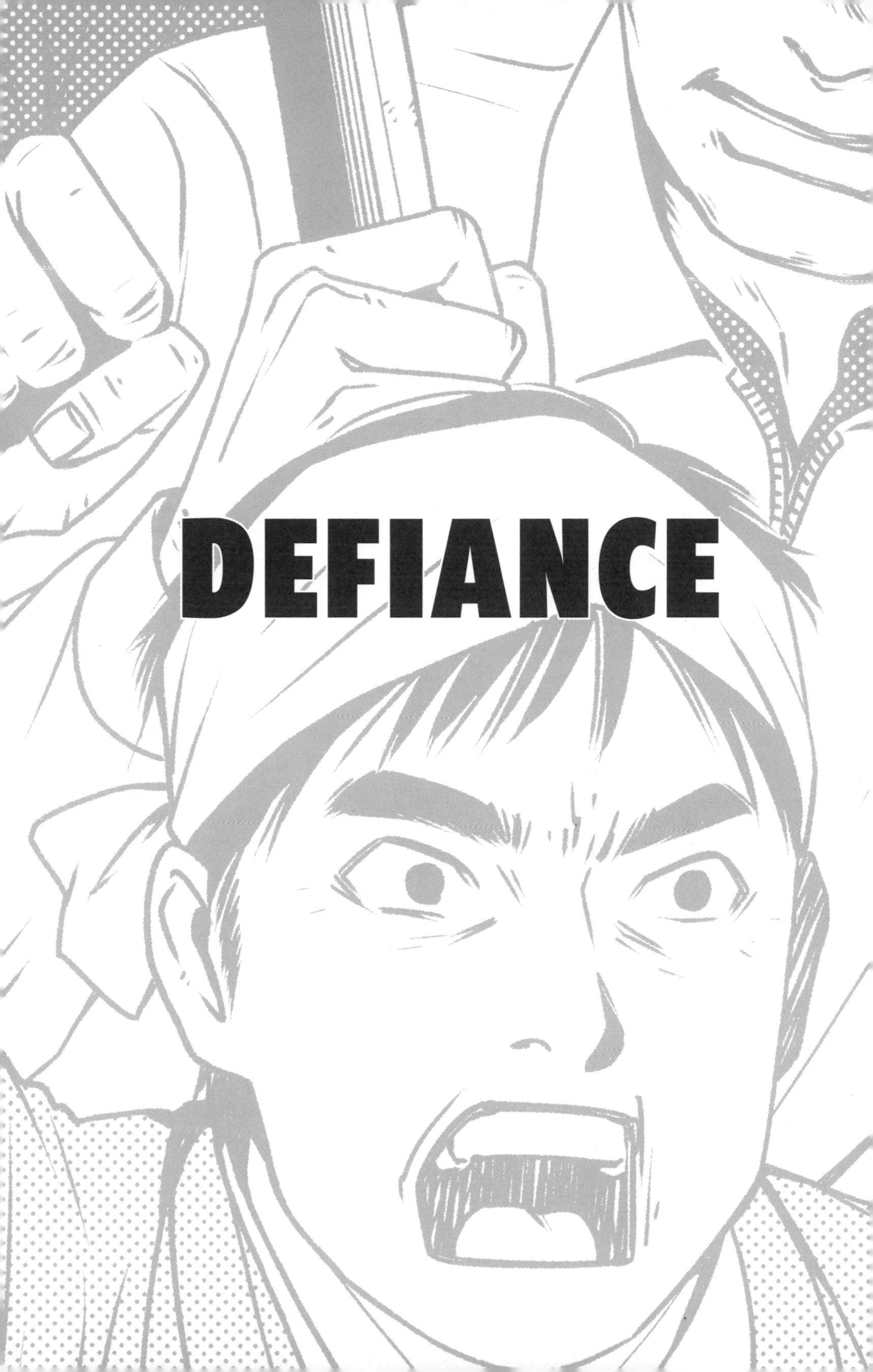

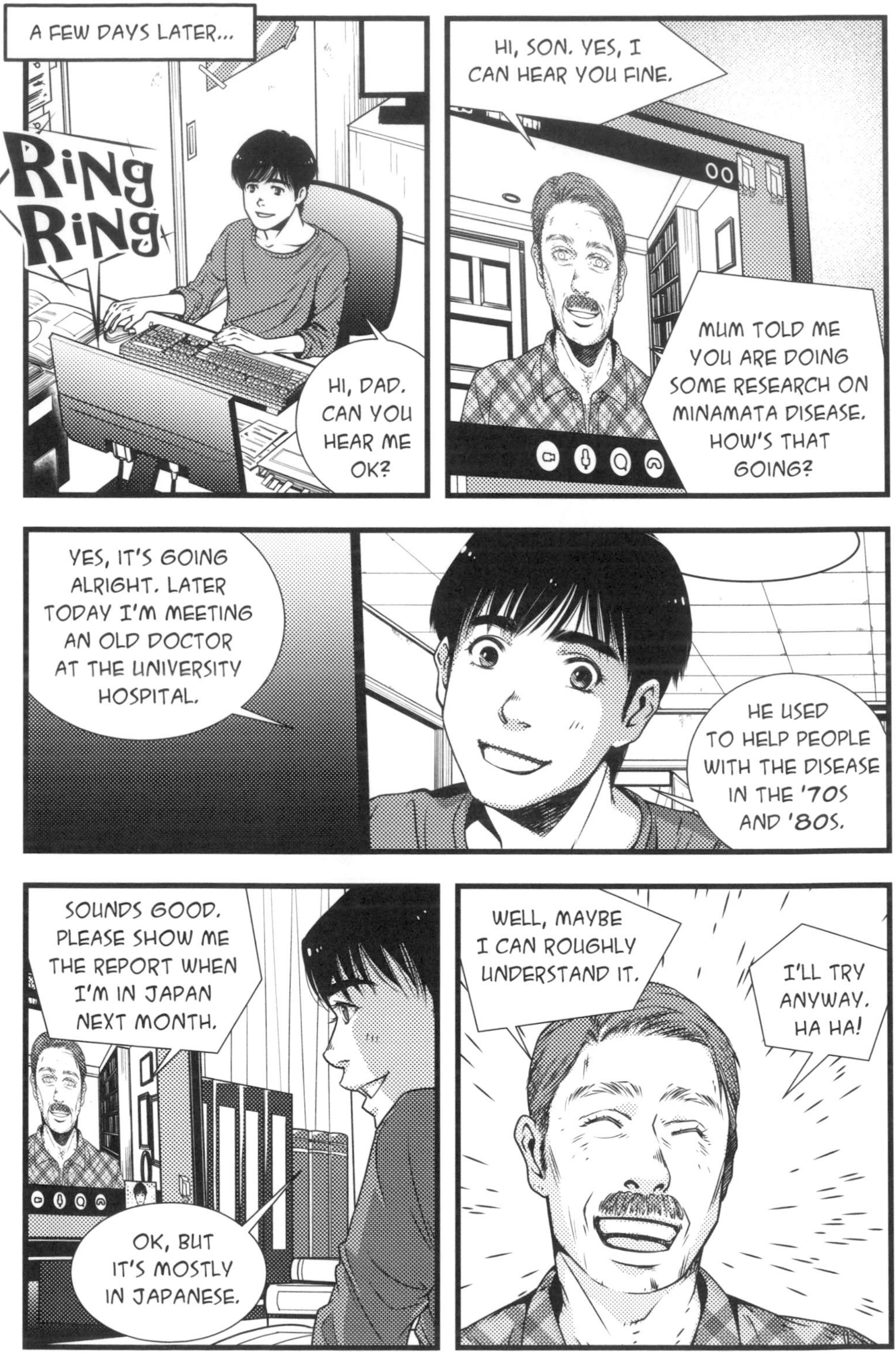
A FEW DAYS LATER...
RING RING
HI, DAD. CAN YOU HEAR ME OK?
HI, SON. YES, I CAN HEAR YOU FINE.
MUM TOLD ME YOU ARE DOING SOME RESEARCH ON MINAMATA DISEASE. HOW'S THAT GOING?
YES, IT'S GOING ALRIGHT. LATER TODAY I'M MEETING AN OLD DOCTOR AT THE UNIVERSITY HOSPITAL.
HE USED TO HELP PEOPLE WITH THE DISEASE IN THE '70S AND '80S.
SOUNDS GOOD. PLEASE SHOW ME THE REPORT WHEN I'M IN JAPAN NEXT MONTH.
OK, BUT IT'S MOSTLY IN JAPANESE.
WELL, MAYBE I CAN ROUGHLY UNDERSTAND IT.
I'LL TRY ANYWAY. HA HA!

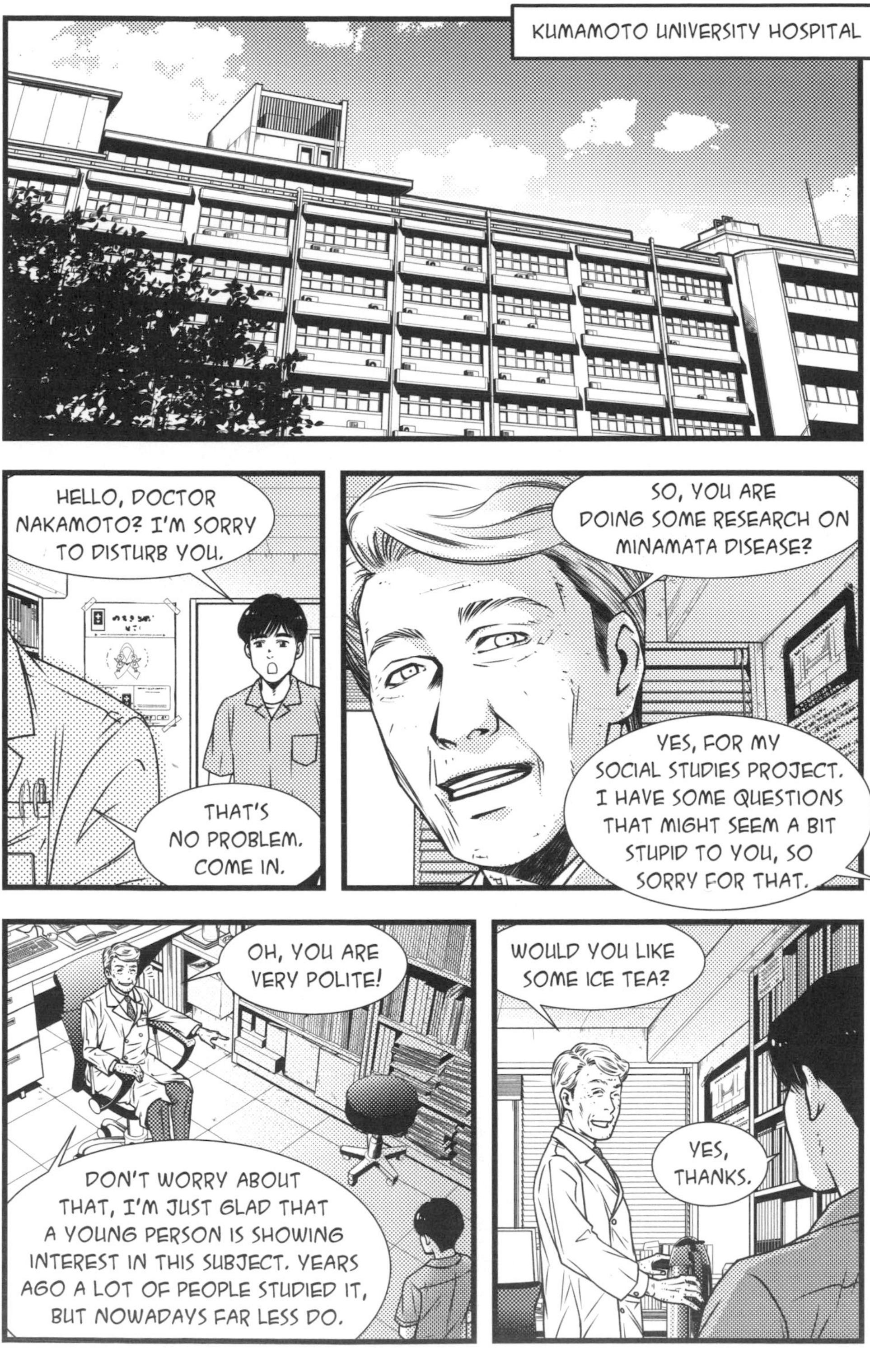
KUMAMOTO UNIVERSITY HOSPITAL
HELLO, DOCTOR NAKAMOTO? I'M SORRY TO DISTURB YOU.
THAT'S NO PROBLEM. COME IN.
SO, YOU ARE DOING SOME RESEARCH ON MINAMATA DISEASE?
YES, FOR MY SOCIAL STUDIES PROJECT. I HAVE SOME QUESTIONS THAT MIGHT SEEM A BIT STUPID TO YOU, SO SORRY FOR THAT.
OH, YOU ARE VERY POLITE!
DON'T WORRY ABOUT THAT, I'M JUST GLAD THAT A YOUNG PERSON IS SHOWING INTEREST IN THIS SUBJECT. YEARS AGO A LOT OF PEOPLE STUDIED IT, BUT NOWADAYS FAR LESS DO.
WOULD YOU LIKE SOME ICE TEA?
YES, THANKS.

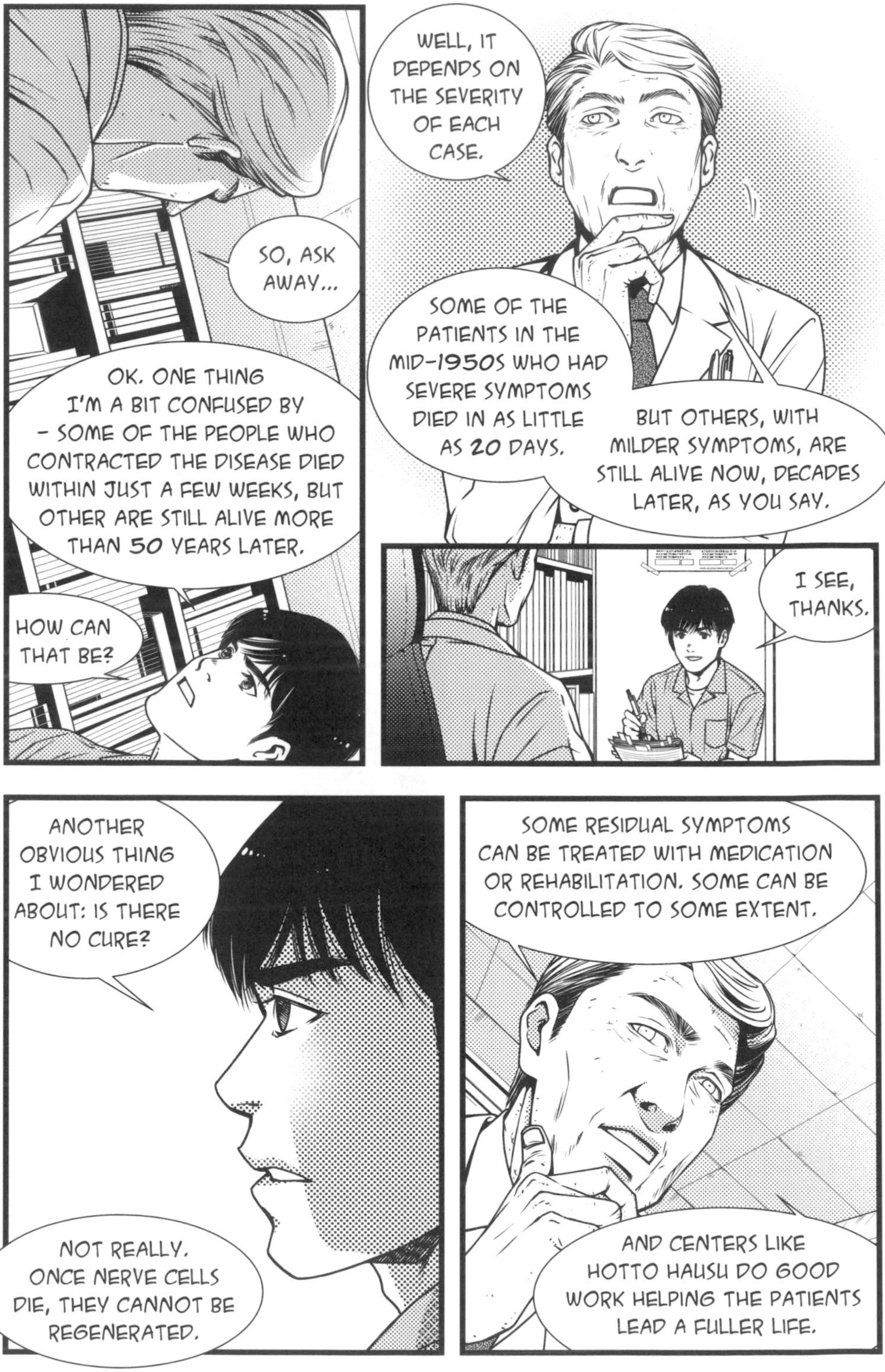
SO, ASK AWAY...
OK. ONE THING I'M A BIT CONFUSED BY - SOME OF THE PEOPLE WHO CONTRACTED THE DISEASE DIED WITHIN JUST A FEW WEEKS, BUT OTHER ARE STILL ALIVE MORE THAN 50 YEARS LATER.
HOW CAN THAT BE?
WELL, IT DEPENDS ON THE SEVERITY OF EACH CASE.
SOME OF THE PATIENTS IN THE MID-1950S WHO HAD SEVERE SYMPTOMS DIED IN AS LITTLE AS 20 DAYS.
BUT OTHERS, WITH MILDER SYMPTOMS, ARE STILL ALIVE NOW, DECADES LATER, AS YOU SAY.
I SEE, THANKS.
ANOTHER OBVIOUS THING I WONDERED ABOUT: IS THERE NO CURE?
NOT REALLY. ONCE NERVE CELLS DIE, THEY CANNOT BE REGENERATED.
SOME RESIDUAL SYMPTOMS CAN BE TREATED WITH MEDICATION OR REHABILITATION. SOME CAN BE CONTROLLED TO SOME EXTENT.
AND CENTERS LIKE HOTTO HAUSU DO GOOD WORK HELPING THE PATIENTS LEAD A FULLER LIFE.

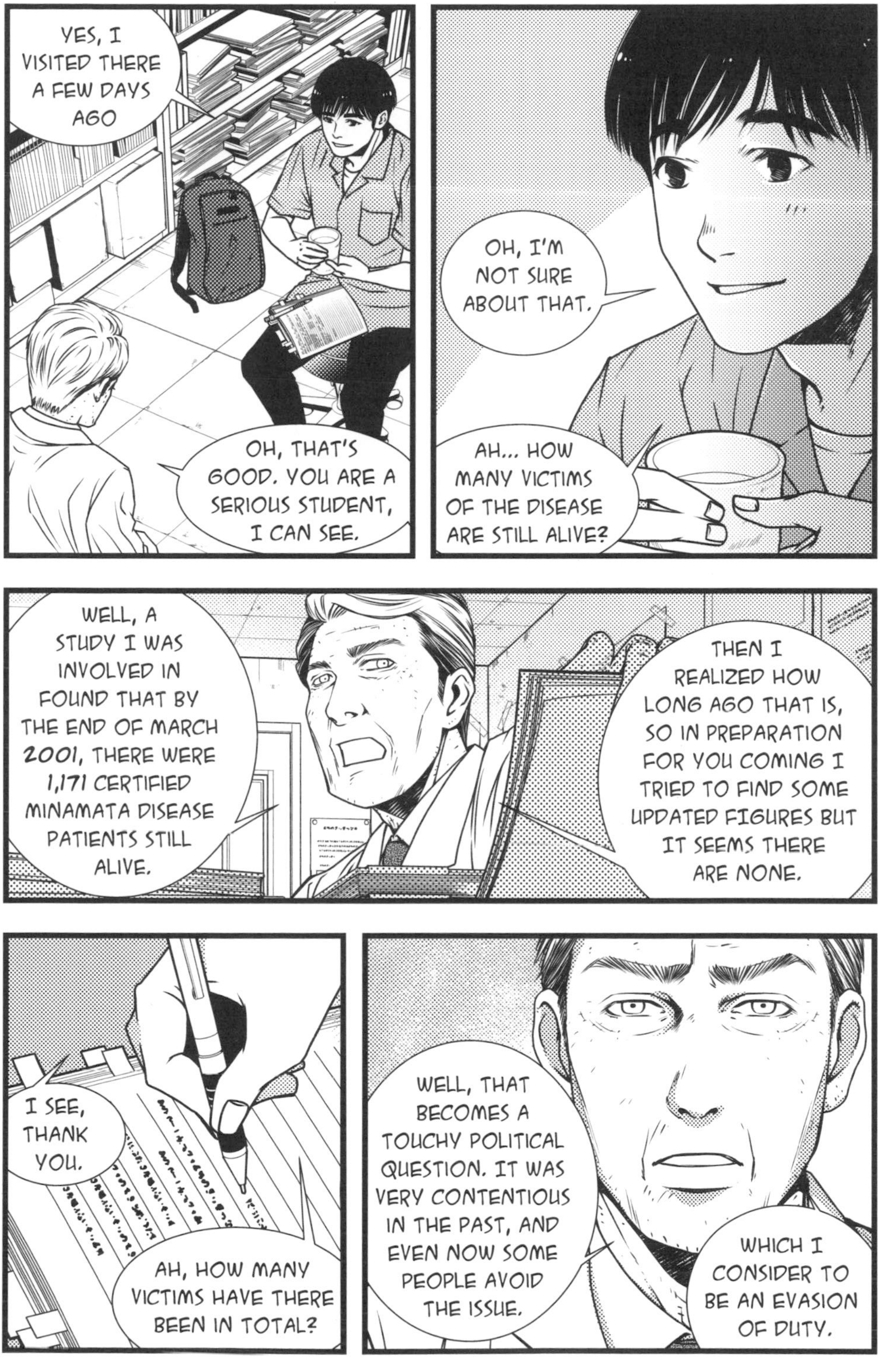
YES, I VISITED THERE A FEW DAYS AGO
OH, THAT'S GOOD. YOU ARE A SERIOUS STUDENT, I CAN SEE.
OH, I'M NOT SURE ABOUT THAT.
AH... HOW MANY VICTIMS OF THE DISEASE ARE STILL ALIVE?
WELL, A STUDY I WAS INVOLVED IN FOUND THAT BY THE END OF MARCH 2001, THERE WERE 1,171 CERTIFIED MINAMATA DISEASE PATIENTS STILL ALIVE.
THEN I REALIZED HOW LONG AGO THAT IS, SO IN PREPARATION FOR YOU COMING I TRIED TO FIND SOME UPDATED FIGURES BUT IT SEEMS THERE ARE NONE.
I SEE, THANK YOU.
AH, HOW MANY VICTIMS HAVE THERE BEEN IN TOTAL?
WELL, THAT BECOMES A TOUCHY POLITICAL QUESTION. IT WAS VERY CONTENTIOUS IN THE PAST, AND EVEN NOW SOME PEOPLE AVOID THE ISSUE.
WHICH I CONSIDER TO BE AN EVASION OF DUTY.

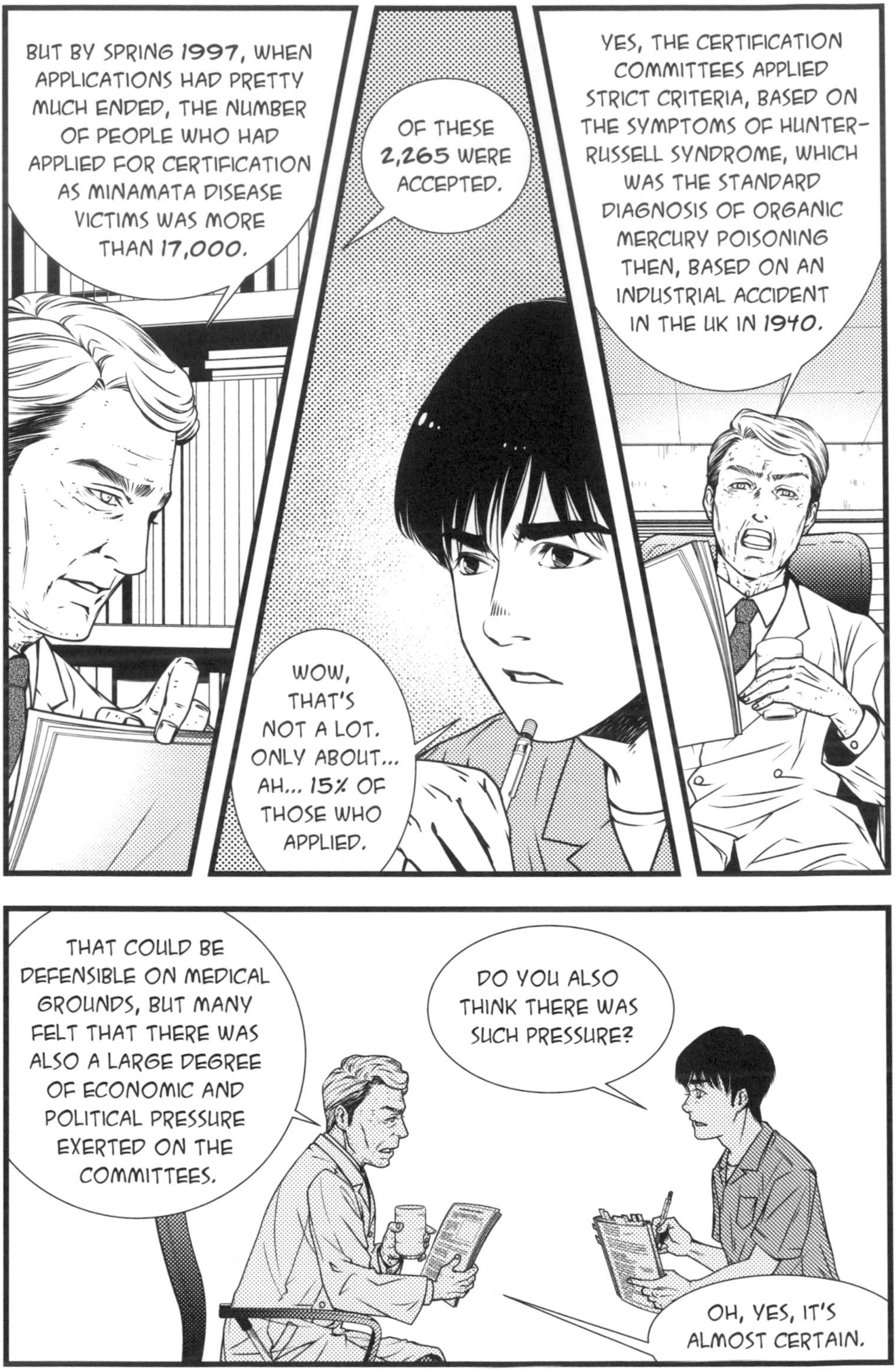
BUT BY SPRING 1997, WHEN APPLICATIONS HAD PRETTY MUCH ENDED, THE NUMBER OF PEOPLE WHO HAD APPLIED FOR CERTIFICATION AS MINAMATA DISEASE VICTIMS WAS MORE THAN 17,000.
OF THESE 2,265 WERE ACCEPTED.
WOW, THAT'S NOT A LOT. ONLY ABOUT... AH... 15% OF THOSE WHO APPLIED.
YES, THE CERTIFICATION COMMITTEES APPLIED STRICT CRITERIA, BASED ON THE SYMPTOMS OF HUNTER-RUSSELL SYNDROME, WHICH WAS THE STANDARD DIAGNOSIS OF ORGANIC MERCURY POISONING THEN, BASED ON AN INDUSTRIAL ACCIDENT IN THE UK IN 1940.
THAT COULD BE DEFENSIBLE ON MEDICAL GROUNDS, BUT MANY FELT THAT THERE WAS ALSO A LARGE DEGREE OF ECONOMIC AND POLITICAL PRESSURE EXERTED ON THE COMMITTEES.
DO YOU ALSO THINK THERE WAS SUCH PRESSURE?
OH, YES, IT'S ALMOST CERTAIN.

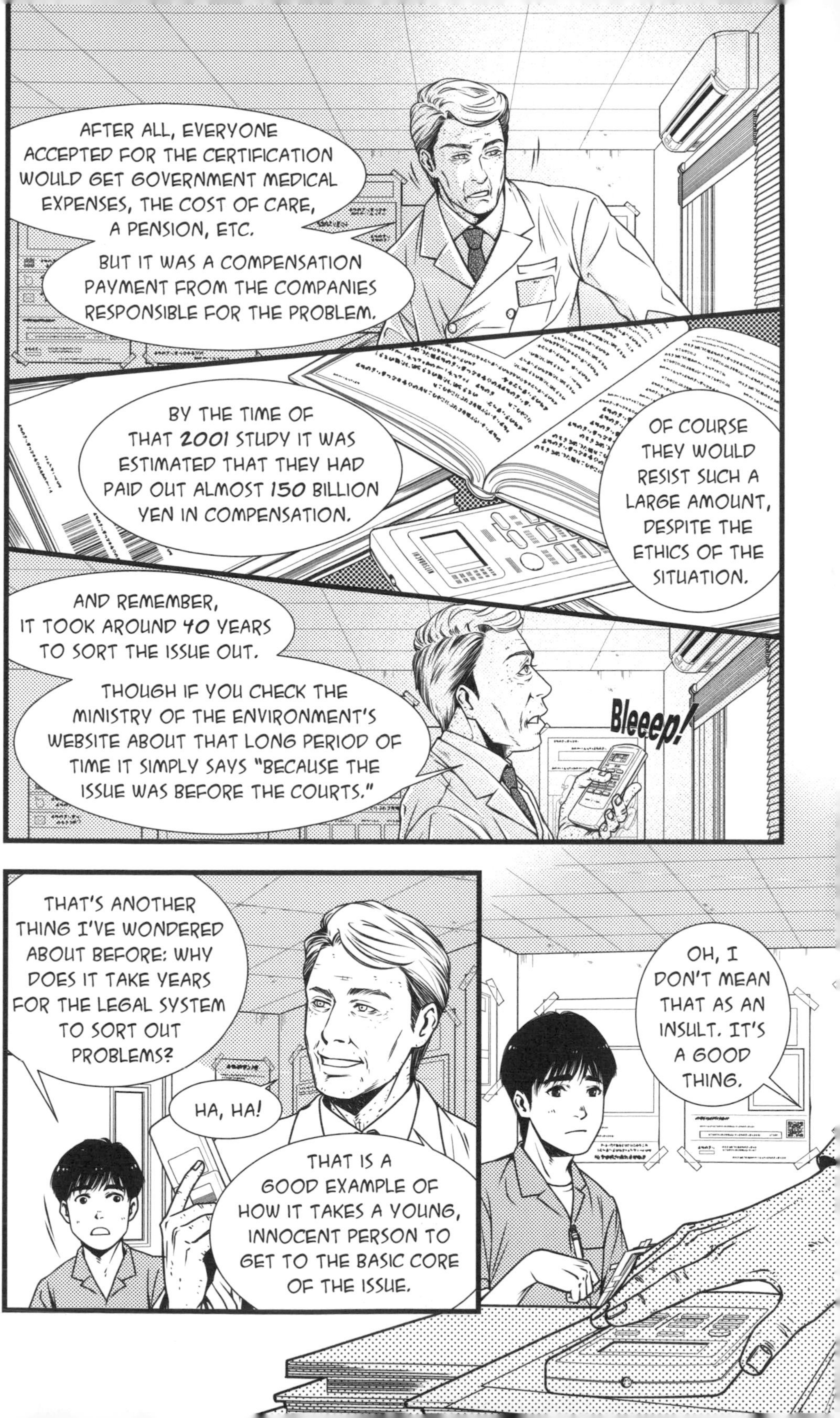
AFTER ALL, EVERYONE ACCEPTED FOR THE CERTIFICATION WOULD GET GOVERNMENT MEDICAL EXPENSES, THE COST OF CARE, A PENSION, ETC.
BUT IT WAS A COMPENSATION PAYMENT FROM THE COMPANIES RESPONSIBLE FOR THE PROBLEM.
BY THE TIME OF THAT 2001 STUDY IT WAS ESTIMATED THAT THEY HAD PAID OUT ALMOST 150 BILLION YEN IN COMPENSATION.
OF COURSE THEY WOULD RESIST SUCH A LARGE AMOUNT, DESPITE THE ETHICS OF THE SITUATION.
AND REMEMBER, IT TOOK AROUND 40 YEARS TO SORT THE ISSUE OUT.
THOUGH IF YOU CHECK THE MINISTRY OF THE ENVIRONMENT'S WEBSITE ABOUT THAT LONG PERIOD OF TIME IT SIMPLY SAYS "BECAUSE THE ISSUE WAS BEFORE THE COURTS."
Bleeep!
THAT'S ANOTHER THING I'VE WONDERED ABOUT BEFORE: WHY DOES IT TAKE YEARS FOR THE LEGAL SYSTEM TO SORT OUT PROBLEMS?
HA, HA!
THAT IS A GOOD EXAMPLE OF HOW IT TAKES A YOUNG, INNOCENT PERSON TO GET TO THE BASIC CORE OF THE ISSUE.
OH, I DON'T MEAN THAT AS AN INSULT. IT'S A GOOD THING.

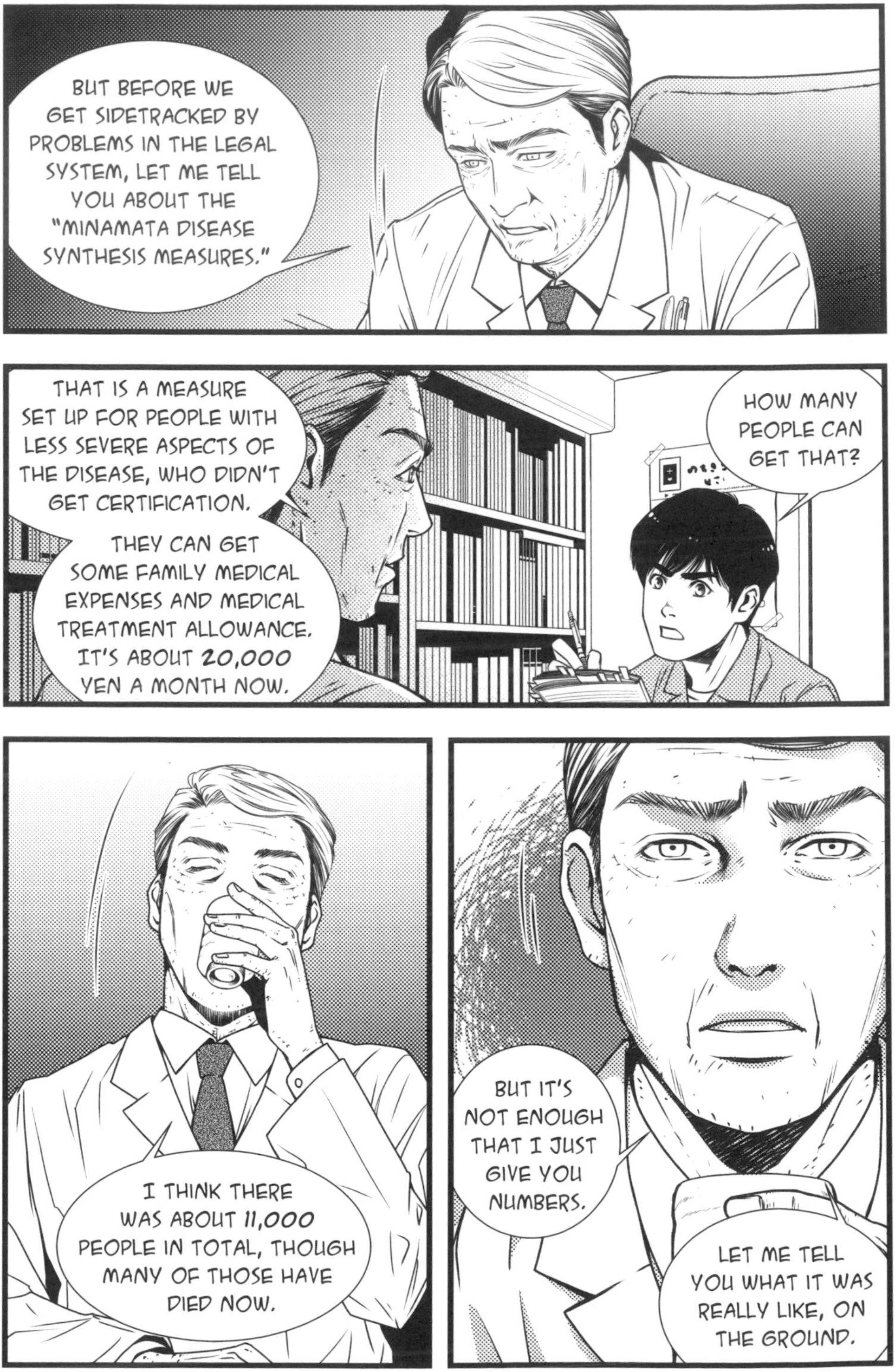
BUT BEFORE WE GET SIDETRACKED BY PROBLEMS IN THE LEGAL SYSTEM, LET ME TELL YOU ABOUT THE "MINAMATA DISEASE SYNTHESIS MEASURES."
THAT IS A MEASURE SET UP FOR PEOPLE WITH LESS SEVERE ASPECTS OF THE DISEASE, WHO DIDN'T GET CERTIFICATION.
THEY CAN GET SOME FAMILY MEDICAL EXPENSES AND MEDICAL TREATMENT ALLOWANCE. IT'S ABOUT 20,000 YEN A MONTH NOW.
HOW MANY PEOPLE CAN GET THAT?
I THINK THERE WAS ABOUT 11,000 PEOPLE IN TOTAL, THOUGH MANY OF THOSE HAVE DIED NOW.
BUT IT'S NOT ENOUGH THAT I JUST GIVE YOU NUMBERS.
LET ME TELL YOU WHAT IT WAS REALLY LIKE, ON THE GROUND.

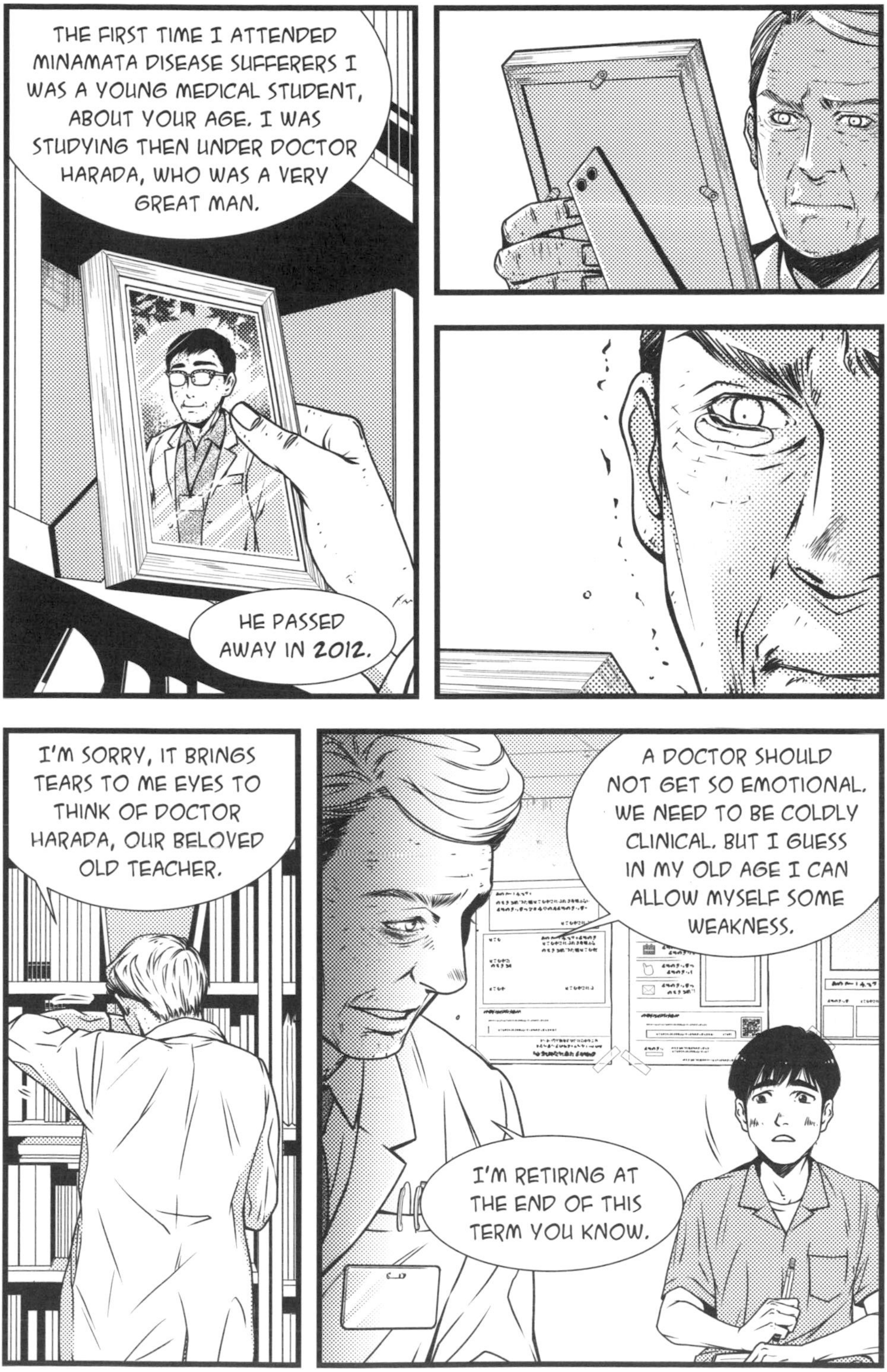
THE FIRST TIME I ATTENDED MINAMATA DISEASE SUFFERERS I WAS A YOUNG MEDICAL STUDENT, ABOUT YOUR AGE. I WAS STUDYING THEN UNDER DOCTOR HARADA, WHO WAS A VERY GREAT MAN.
HE PASSED AWAY IN 2012.
I'M SORRY, IT BRINGS TEARS TO ME EYES TO THINK OF DOCTOR HARADA, OUR BELOVED OLD TEACHER.
A DOCTOR SHOULD NOT GET SO EMOTIONAL. WE NEED TO BE COLDLY CLINICAL. BUT I GUESS IN MY OLD AGE I CAN ALLOW MYSELF SOME WEAKNESS.
I'M RETIRING AT THE END OF THIS TERM YOU KNOW.

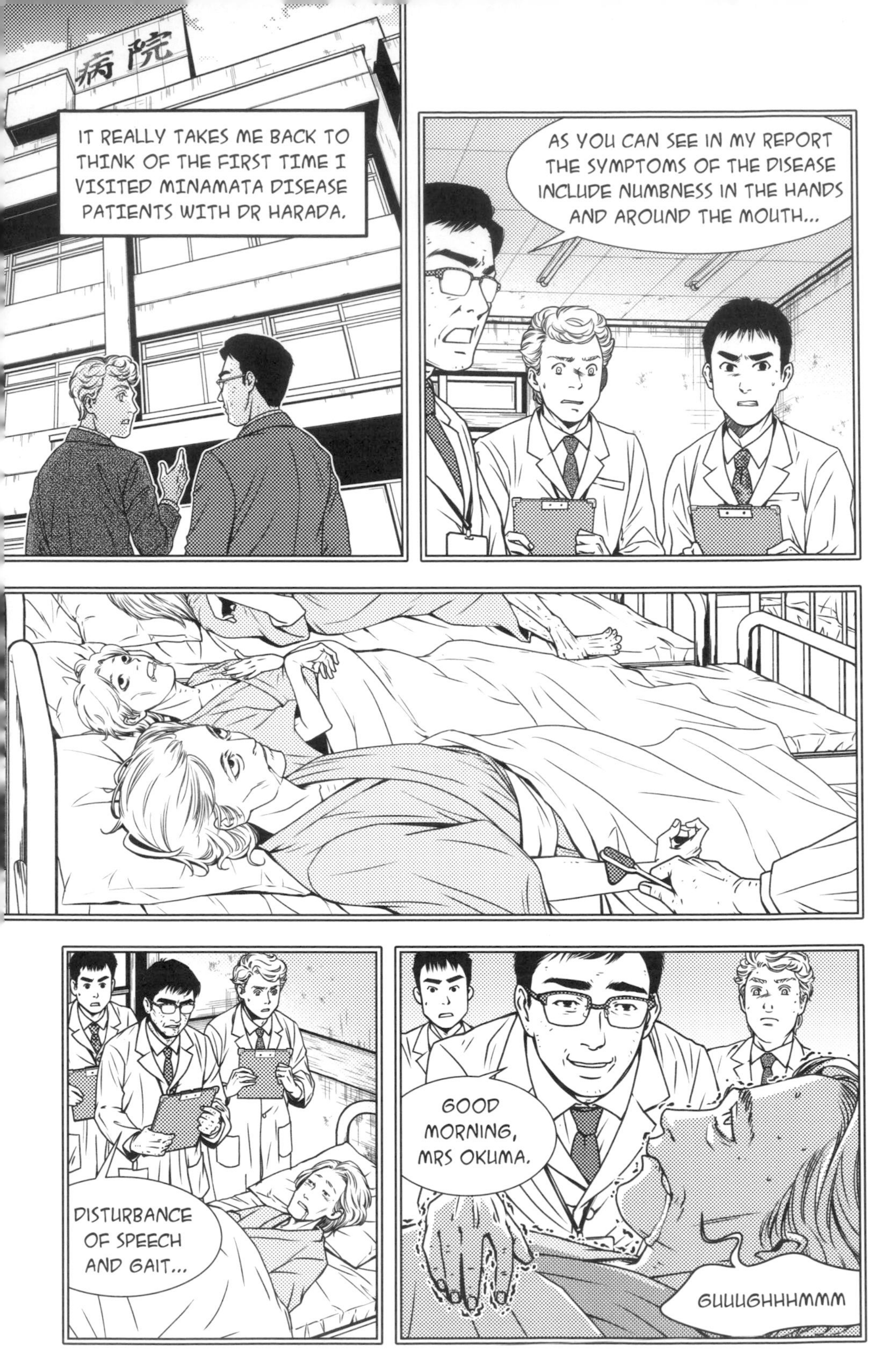
病院
IT REALLY TAKES ME BACK TO THINK OF THE FIRST TIME I VISITED MINAMATA DISEASE PATIENTS WITH DR HARADA.
AS YOU CAN SEE IN MY REPORT THE SYMPTOMS OF THE DISEASE INCLUDE NUMBNESS IN THE HANDS AND AROUND THE MOUTH...
DISTURBANCE OF SPEECH AND GAIT...
GOOD MORNING, MRS OKUMA.
GUUUGHHHMMM

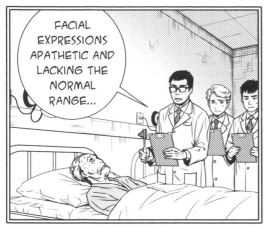

FACIAL EXPRESSIONS APATHETIC AND LACKING THE NORMAL RANGE...

AND THE FIELD OF VISION RESTRICTED TO STRAIGHT AHEAD. LEFT AND RIGHT SIDES ARE VERY WEAK.

IT BROKE MY HEART TO SEE THEM LIKE THIS, AND I FELT USELESS. THERE WAS LITTLE I COULD DO TO COMFORT THE FAMILIES AND IT SEEMED LIKE THERE WAS NEXT TO NOTHING WE COULD DO TO COMBAT THE DISEASE.

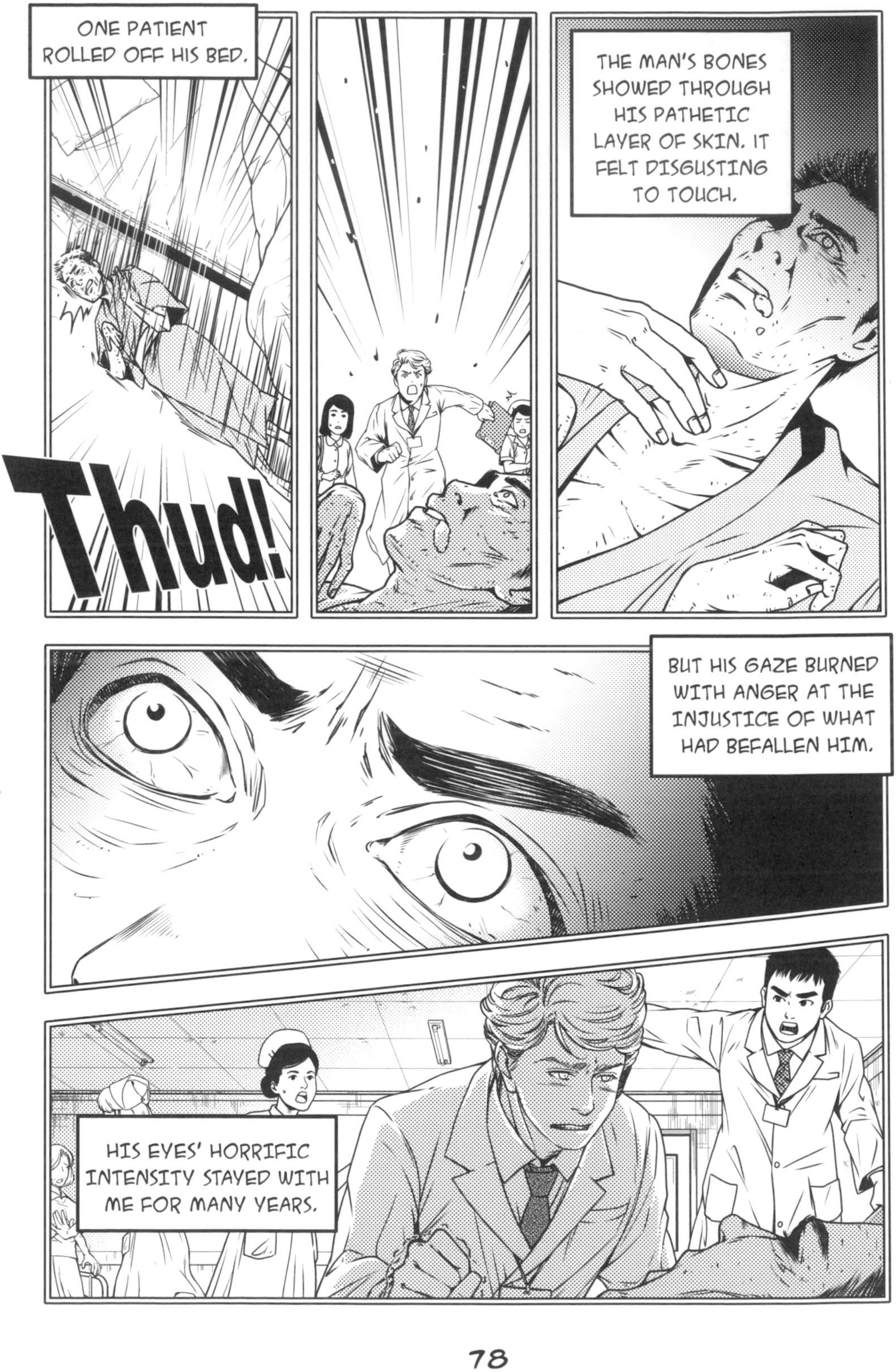
ONE PATIENT ROLLED OFF HIS BED.
Thud!
THE MAN'S BONES SHOWED THROUGH HIS PATHETIC LAYER OF SKIN. IT FELT DISGUSTING TO TOUCH.
BUT HIS GAZE BURNED WITH ANGER AT THE INJUSTICE OF WHAT HAD BEFALLEN HIM.
HIS EYES' HORRIFIC INTENSITY STAYED WITH ME FOR MANY YEARS.

THE POOR GIRL'S BODY WAS COVERED IN THE MOST DISGUSTING SORES. HER PARENTS LOOKED IN A DAZE, UTTERLY LOST.

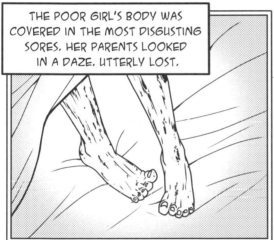

SHE DIED LATER THAT MONTH.

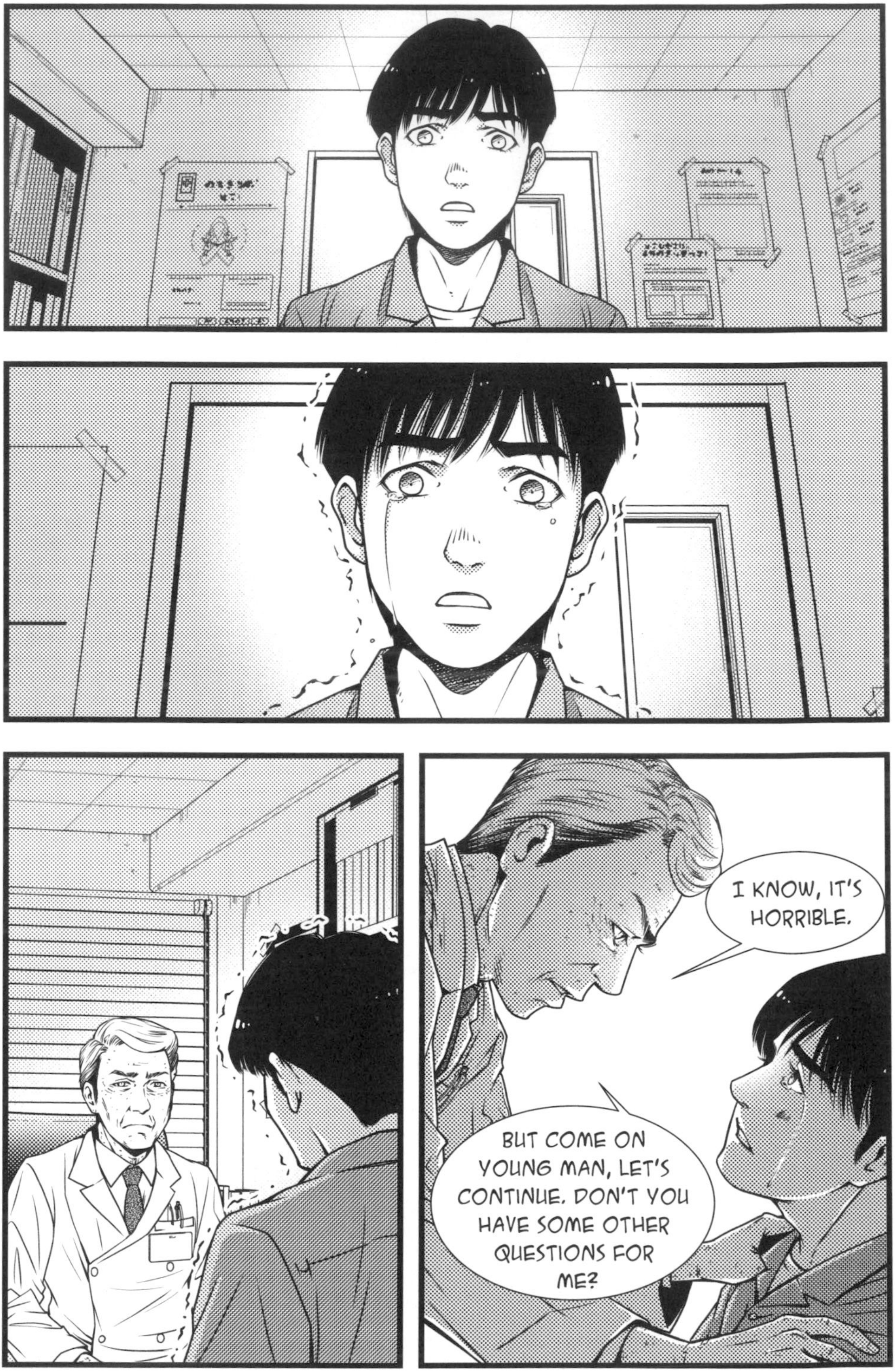
I KNOW, IT'S HORRIBLE.
BUT COME ON YOUNG MAN, LET'S CONTINUE. DON'T YOU HAVE SOME OTHER QUESTIONS FOR ME?

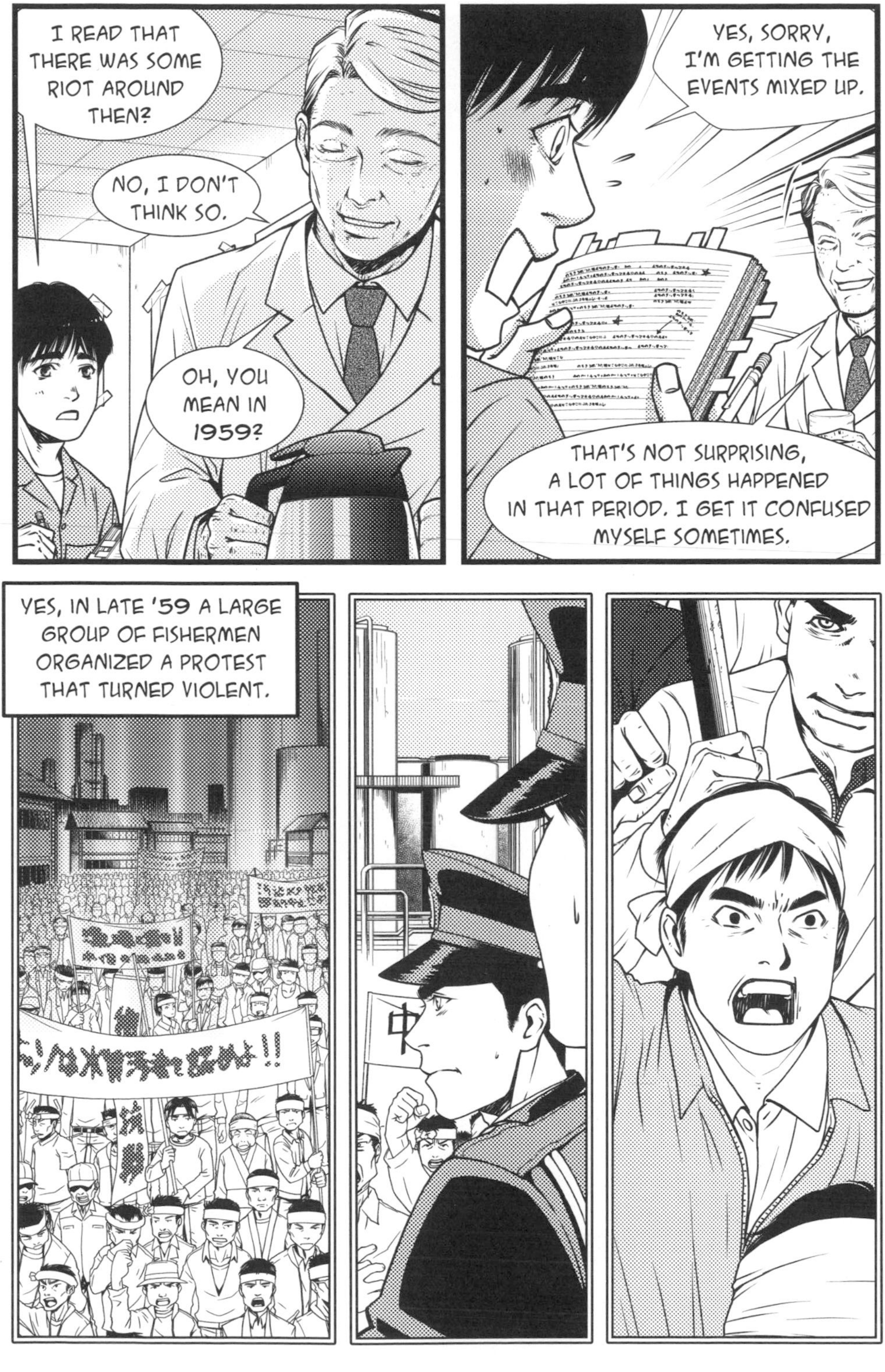
I READ THAT THERE WAS SOME RIOT AROUND THEN?
NO, I DON'T THINK SO.
OH, YOU MEAN IN 1959?
YES, SORRY, I'M GETTING THE EVENTS MIXED UP.
THAT'S NOT SURPRISING, A LOT OF THINGS HAPPENED IN THAT PERIOD. I GET IT CONFUSED MYSELF SOMETIMES.
YES, IN LATE '59 A LARGE GROUP OF FISHERMEN ORGANIZED A PROTEST THAT TURNED VIOLENT.

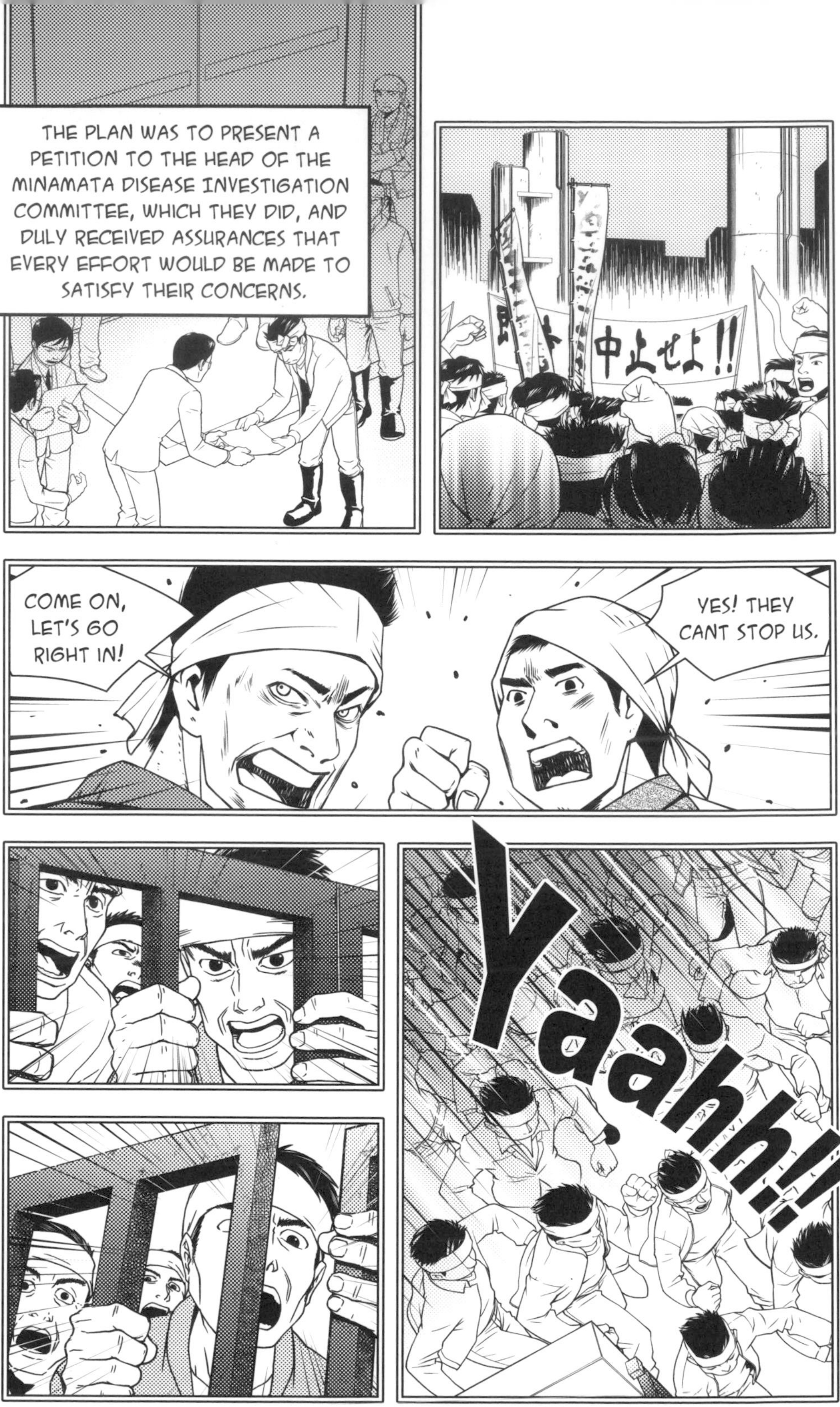
THE PLAN WAS TO PRESENT A PETITION TO THE HEAD OF THE MINAMATA DISEASE INVESTIGATION COMMITTEE, WHICH THEY DID, AND DULY RECEIVED ASSURANCES THAT EVERY EFFORT WOULD BE MADE TO SATISFY THEIR CONCERNS.
中止せよ!!
COME ON, LET'S GO RIGHT IN!
YES! THEY CANT STOP US.
Yaaahh!!

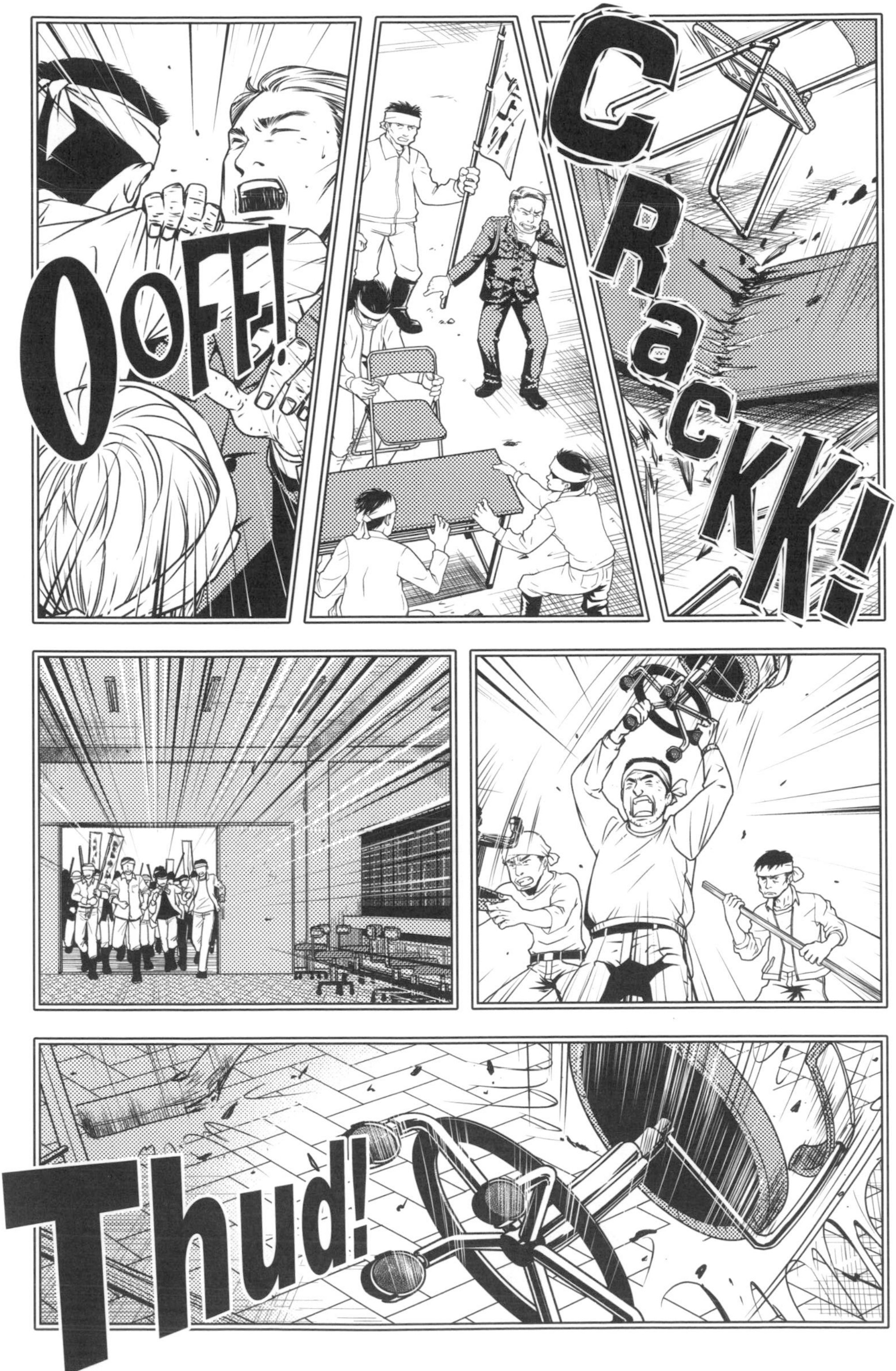
OOFF!
CRaCKK!
Thud!

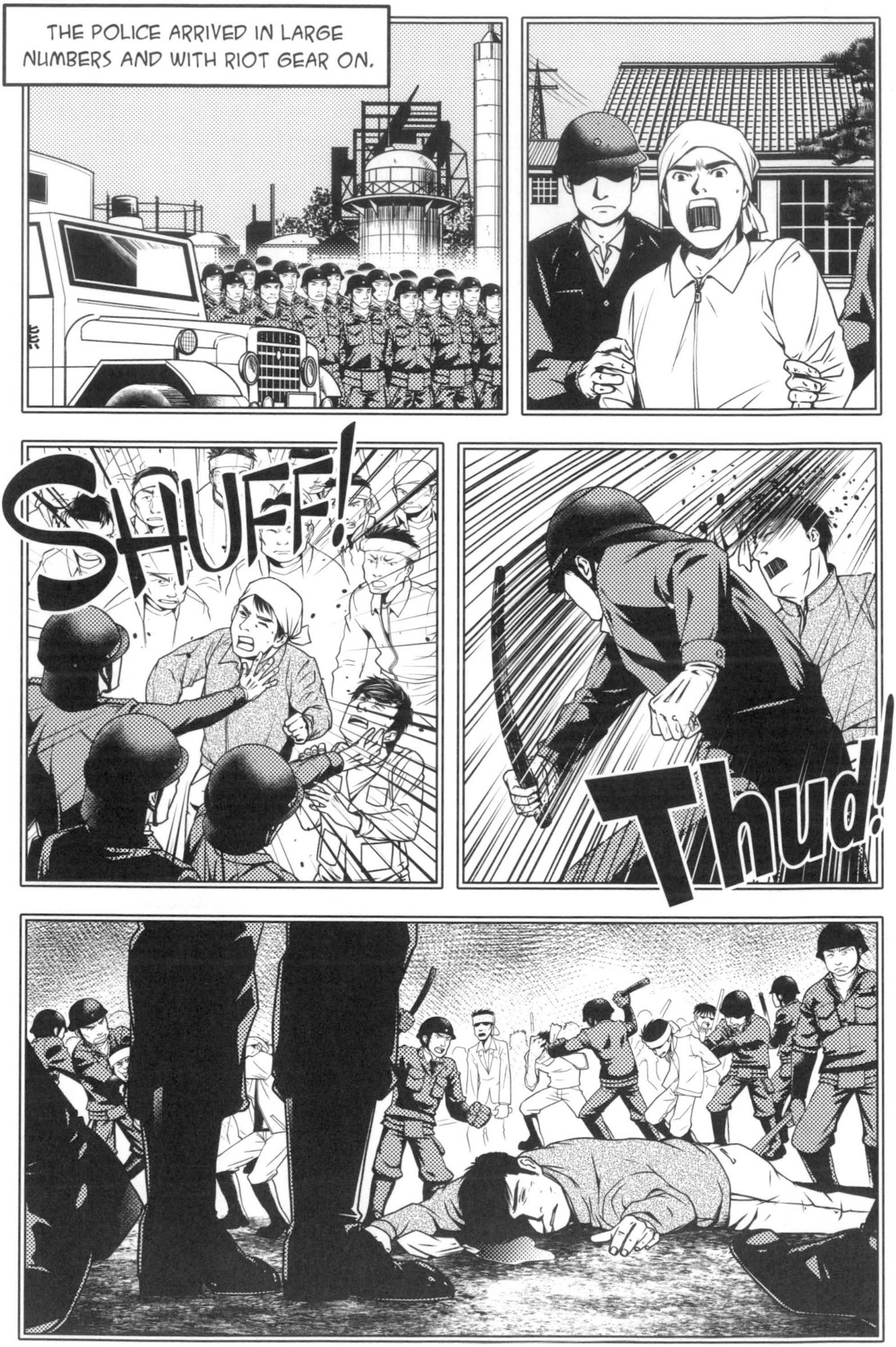
THE POLICE ARRIVED IN LARGE NUMBERS AND WITH RIOT GEAR ON.
SHUFF!
Thud!

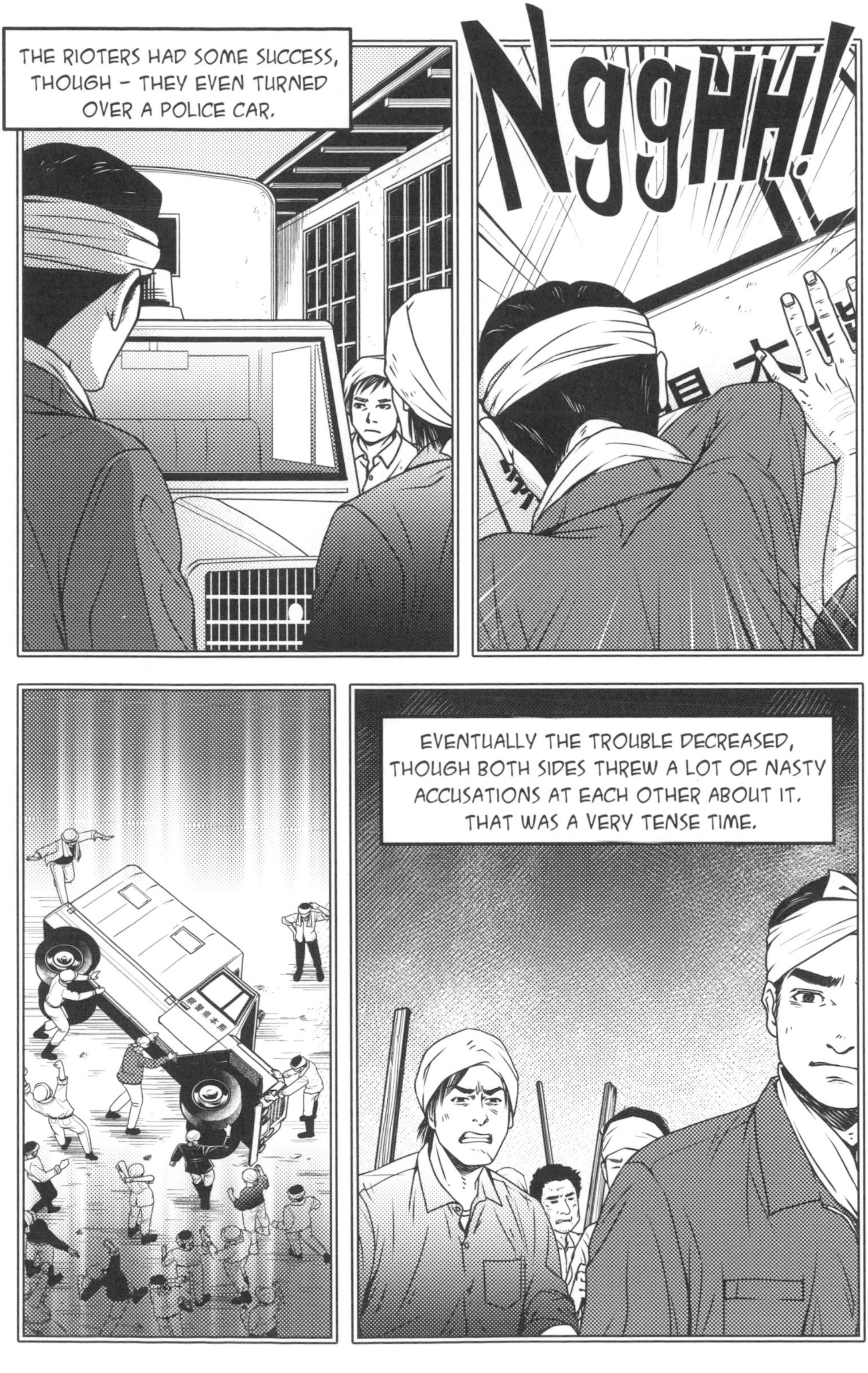
THE RIOTERS HAD SOME SUCCESS, THOUGH – THEY EVEN TURNED OVER A POLICE CAR.
NggHH!
EVENTUALLY THE TROUBLE DECREASED, THOUGH BOTH SIDES THREW A LOT OF NASTY ACCUSATIONS AT EACH OTHER ABOUT IT. THAT WAS A VERY TENSE TIME.

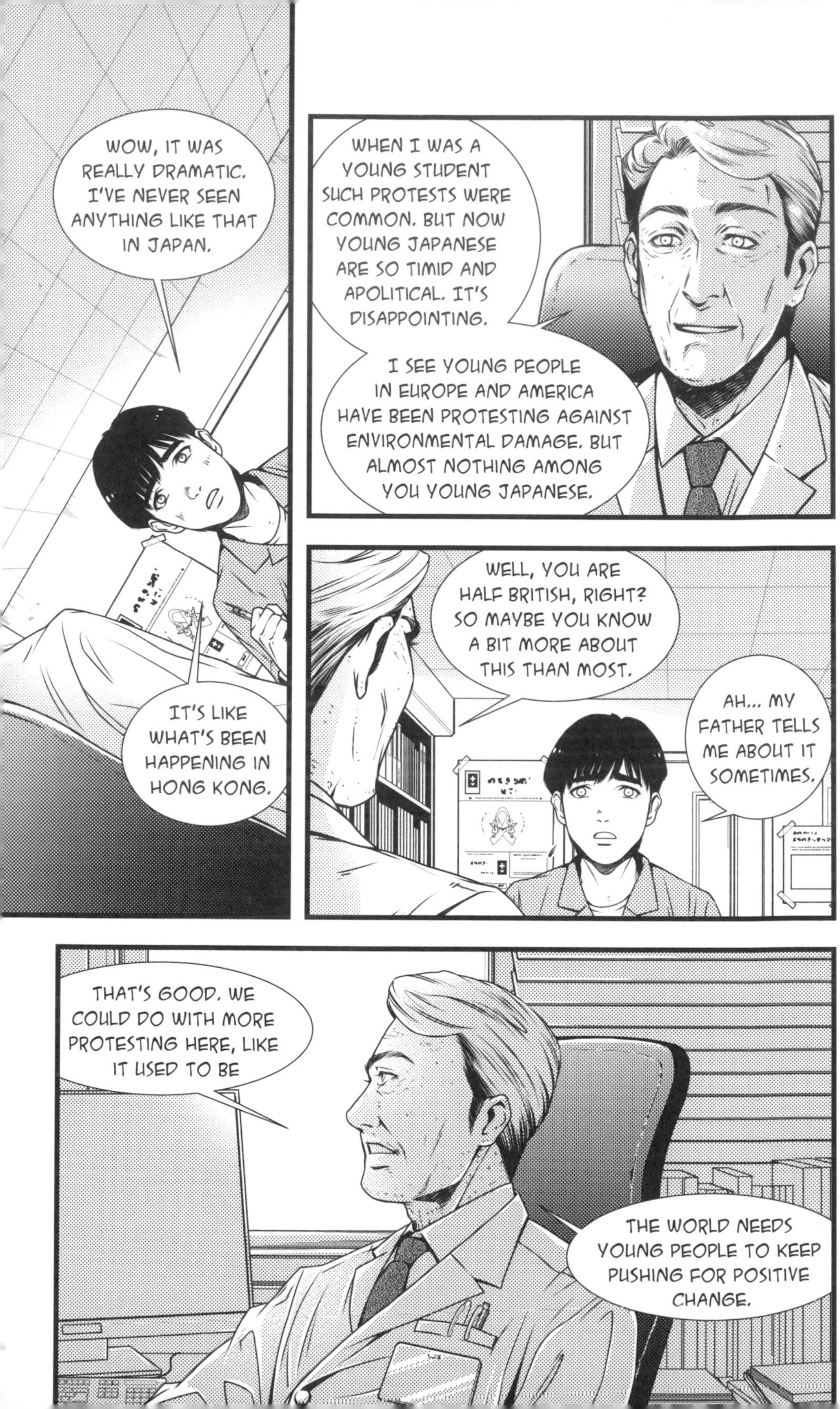
WOW, IT WAS REALLY DRAMATIC. I'VE NEVER SEEN ANYTHING LIKE THAT IN JAPAN.
IT'S LIKE WHAT'S BEEN HAPPENING IN HONG KONG.
WHEN I WAS A YOUNG STUDENT SUCH PROTESTS WERE COMMON. BUT NOW YOUNG JAPANESE ARE SO TIMID AND APOLITICAL. IT'S DISAPPOINTING.
I SEE YOUNG PEOPLE IN EUROPE AND AMERICA HAVE BEEN PROTESTING AGAINST ENVIRONMENTAL DAMAGE. BUT ALMOST NOTHING AMONG YOU YOUNG JAPANESE.
WELL, YOU ARE HALF BRITISH, RIGHT? SO MAYBE YOU KNOW A BIT MORE ABOUT THIS THAN MOST.
AH... MY FATHER TELLS ME ABOUT IT SOMETIMES.
THAT'S GOOD. WE COULD DO WITH MORE PROTESTING HERE, LIKE IT USED TO BE
THE WORLD NEEDS YOUNG PEOPLE TO KEEP PUSHING FOR POSITIVE CHANGE.

THE REPORT

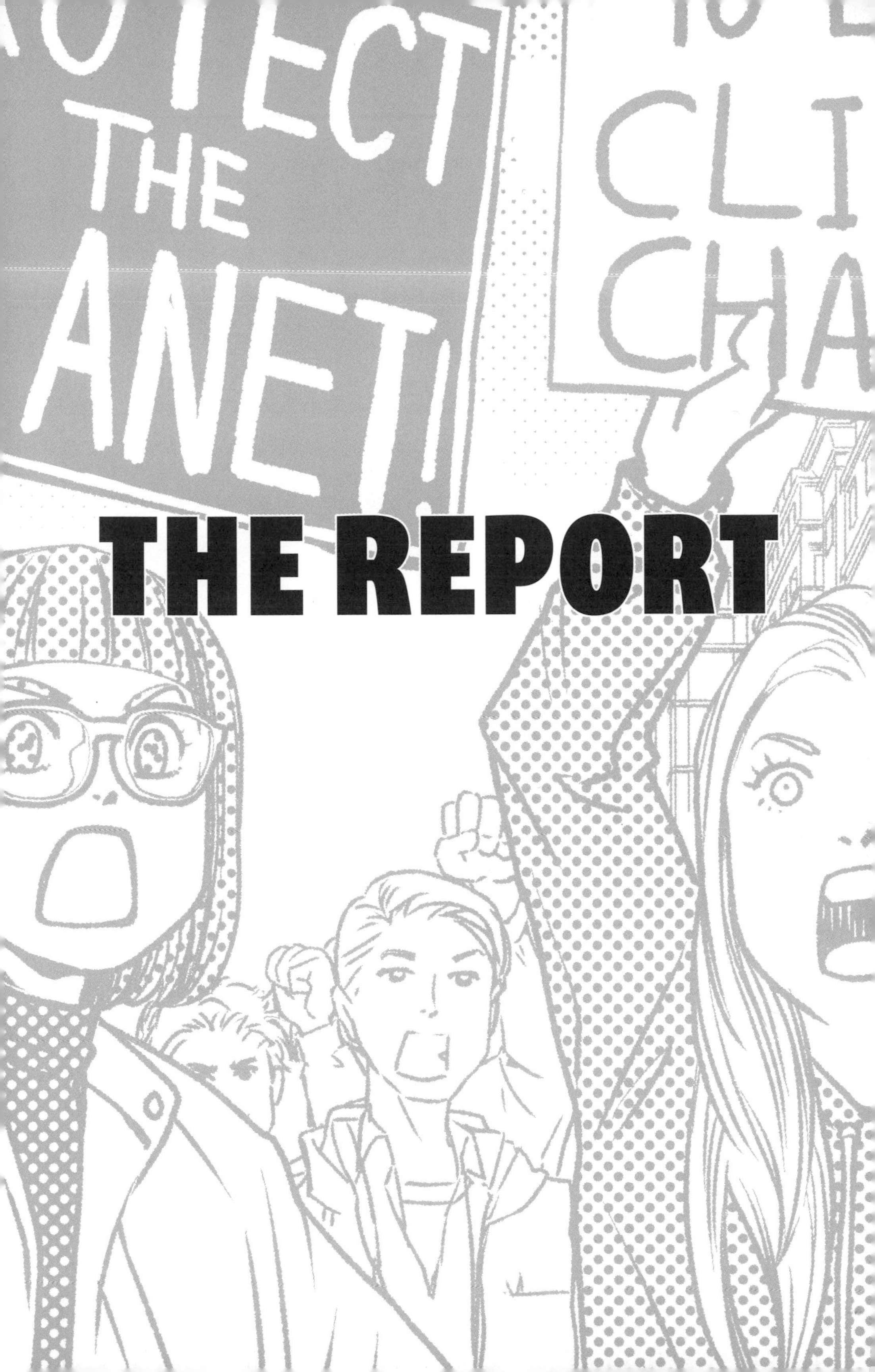
OTECT
THE
ANET!
CLI
CHA

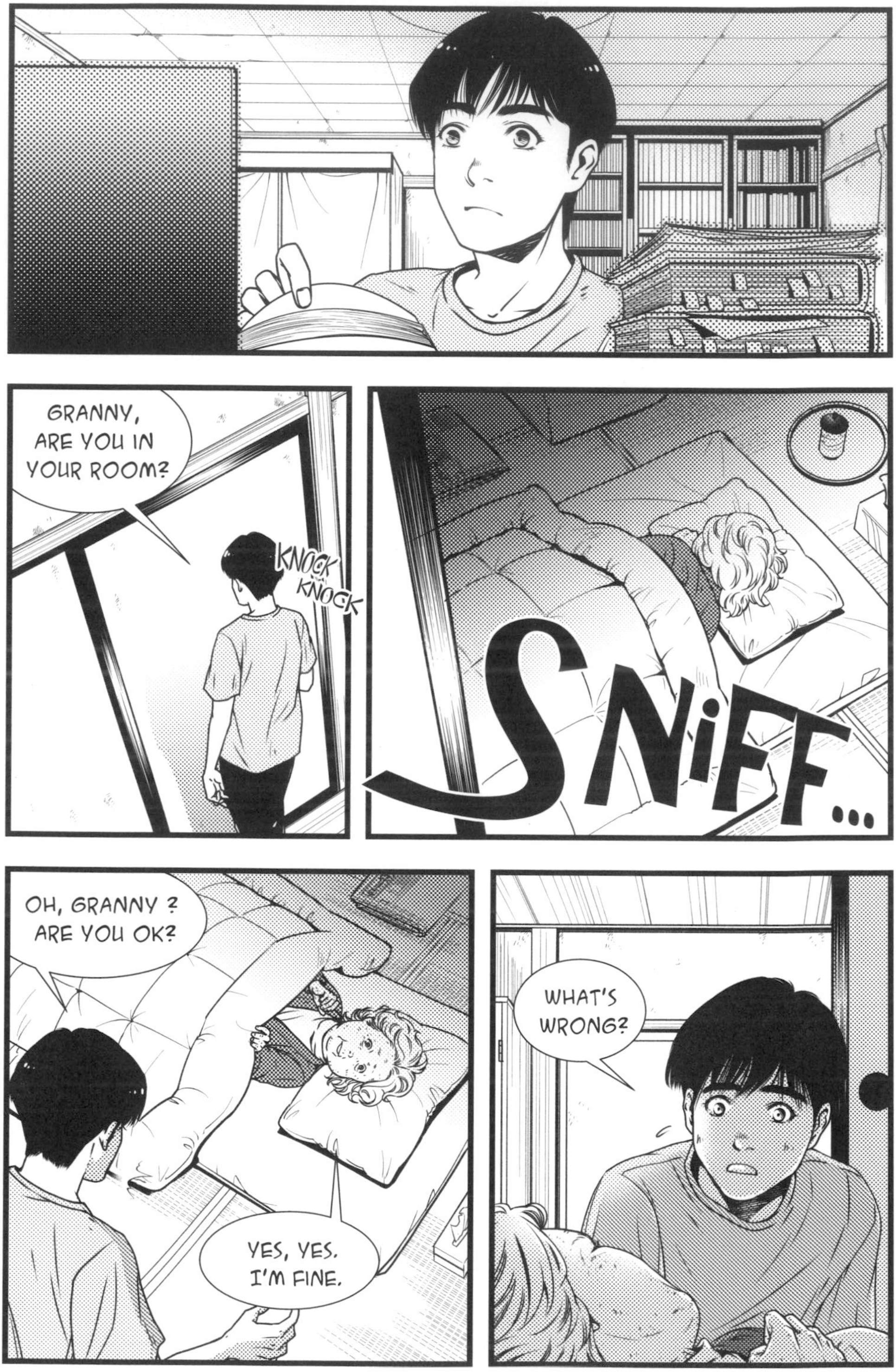
GRANNY, ARE YOU IN YOUR ROOM?
KNOCK KNOCK
SNIFF...
OH, GRANNY? ARE YOU OK?
YES, YES. I'M FINE.
WHAT'S WRONG?

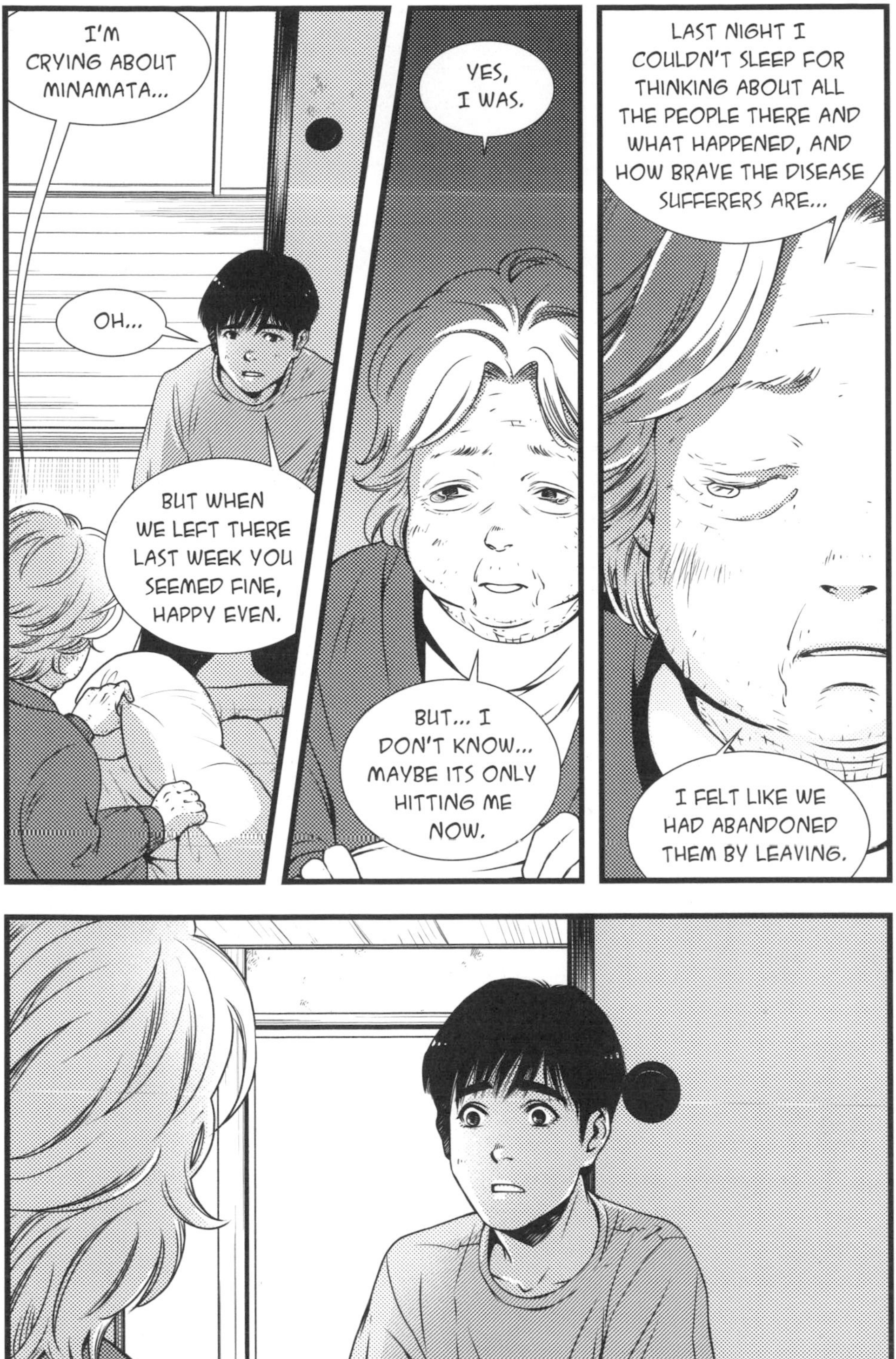
I'M CRYING ABOUT MINAMATA...
OH...
BUT WHEN WE LEFT THERE LAST WEEK YOU SEEMED FINE, HAPPY EVEN.
YES, I WAS.
BUT... I DON'T KNOW... MAYBE ITS ONLY HITTING ME NOW.
LAST NIGHT I COULDN'T SLEEP FOR THINKING ABOUT ALL THE PEOPLE THERE AND WHAT HAPPENED, AND HOW BRAVE THE DISEASE SUFFERERS ARE...
I FELT LIKE WE HAD ABANDONED THEM BY LEAVING.

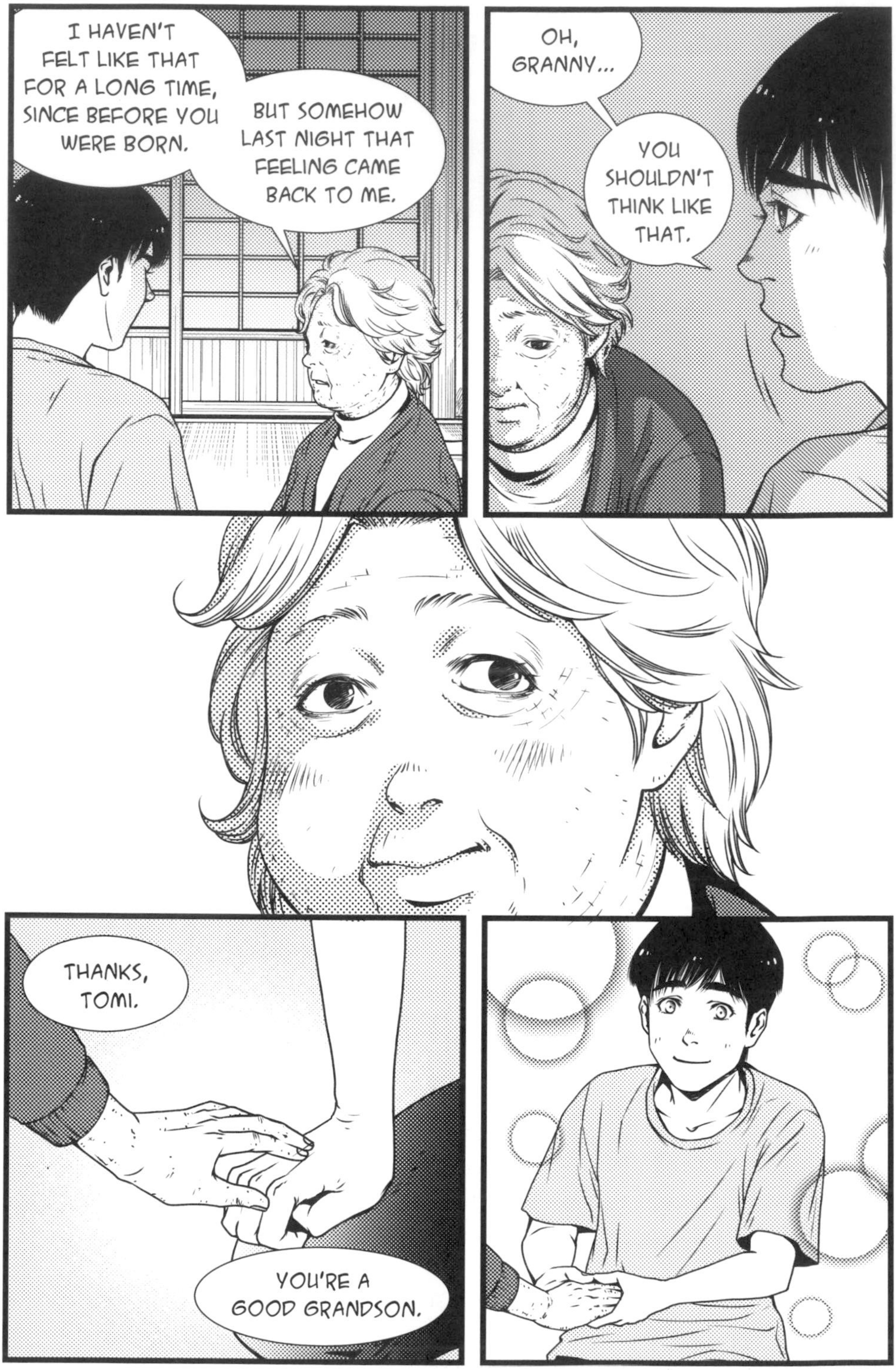
I HAVEN'T FELT LIKE THAT FOR A LONG TIME, SINCE BEFORE YOU WERE BORN.
BUT SOMEHOW LAST NIGHT THAT FEELING CAME BACK TO ME.
OH, GRANNY...
YOU SHOULDN'T THINK LIKE THAT.
THANKS, TOMI.
YOU'RE A GOOD GRANDSON.

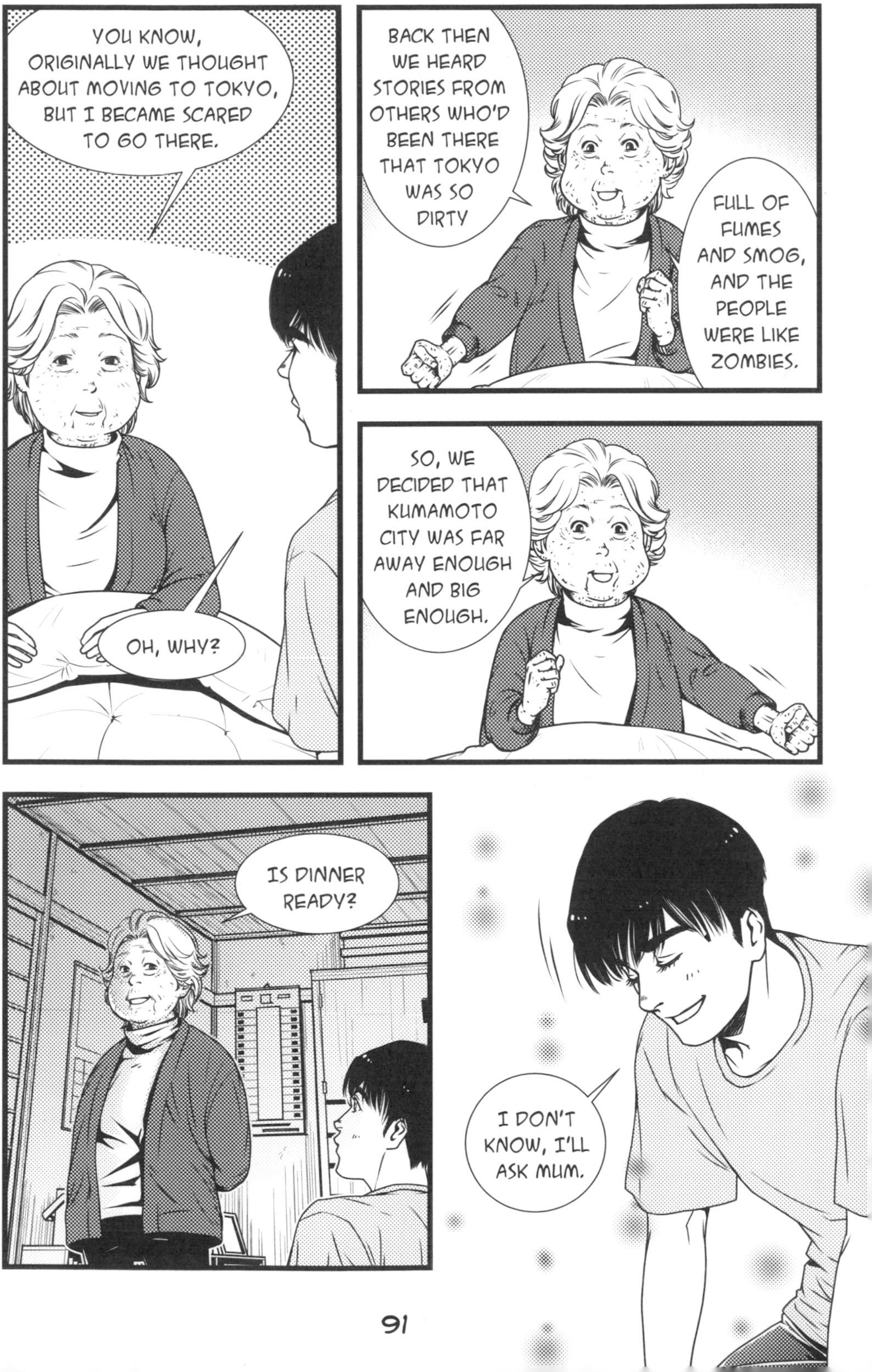
YOU KNOW, ORIGINALLY WE THOUGHT ABOUT MOVING TO TOKYO, BUT I BECAME SCARED TO GO THERE.
OH, WHY?
BACK THEN WE HEARD STORIES FROM OTHERS WHO'D BEEN THERE THAT TOKYO WAS SO DIRTY
FULL OF FUMES AND SMOG, AND THE PEOPLE WERE LIKE ZOMBIES.
SO, WE DECIDED THAT KUMAMOTO CITY WAS FAR AWAY ENOUGH AND BIG ENOUGH.
IS DINNER READY?
I DON'T KNOW, I'LL ASK MUM.

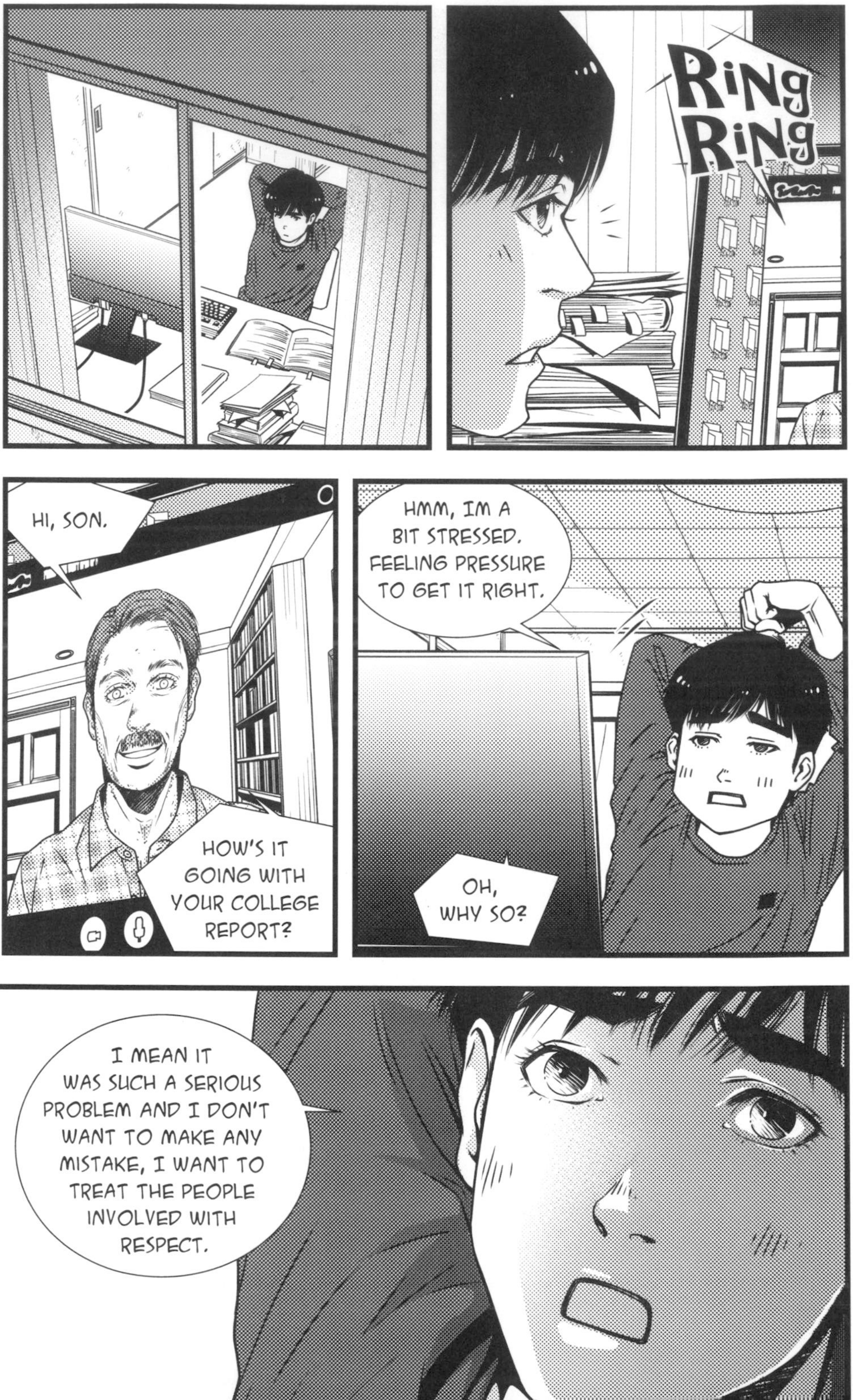
RING RING
HI, SON.
HOW'S IT GOING WITH YOUR COLLEGE REPORT?
HMM, IM A BIT STRESSED. FEELING PRESSURE TO GET IT RIGHT.
OH, WHY SO?
I MEAN IT WAS SUCH A SERIOUS PROBLEM AND I DON'T WANT TO MAKE ANY MISTAKE, I WANT TO TREAT THE PEOPLE INVOLVED WITH RESPECT.

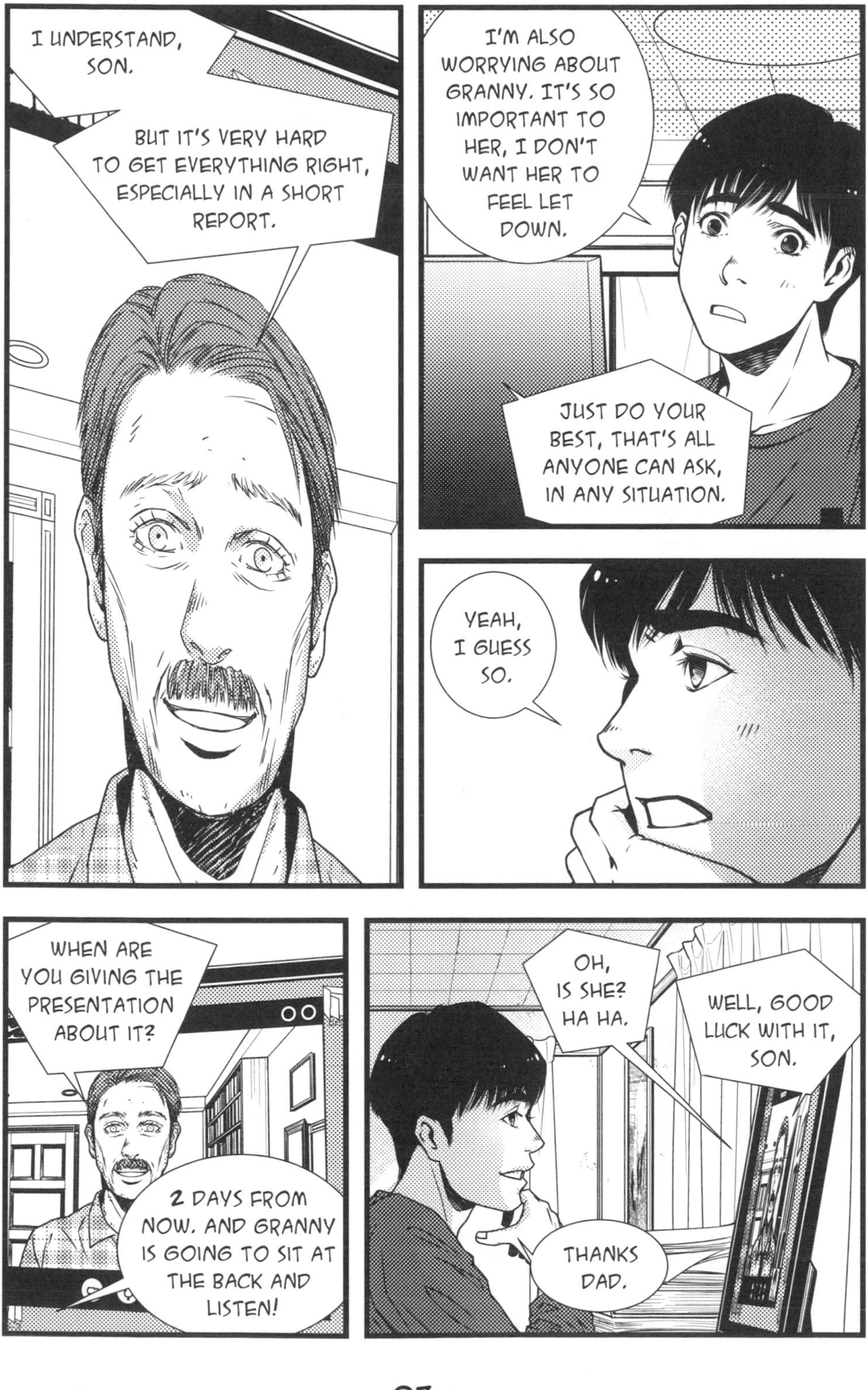
I UNDERSTAND, SON.
BUT IT'S VERY HARD TO GET EVERYTHING RIGHT, ESPECIALLY IN A SHORT REPORT.
I'M ALSO WORRYING ABOUT GRANNY. IT'S SO IMPORTANT TO HER, I DON'T WANT HER TO FEEL LET DOWN.
JUST DO YOUR BEST, THAT'S ALL ANYONE CAN ASK, IN ANY SITUATION.
YEAH, I GUESS SO.
WHEN ARE YOU GIVING THE PRESENTATION ABOUT IT?
2 DAYS FROM NOW. AND GRANNY IS GOING TO SIT AT THE BACK AND LISTEN!
OH, IS SHE? HA HA.
WELL, GOOD LUCK WITH IT, SON.
THANKS DAD.

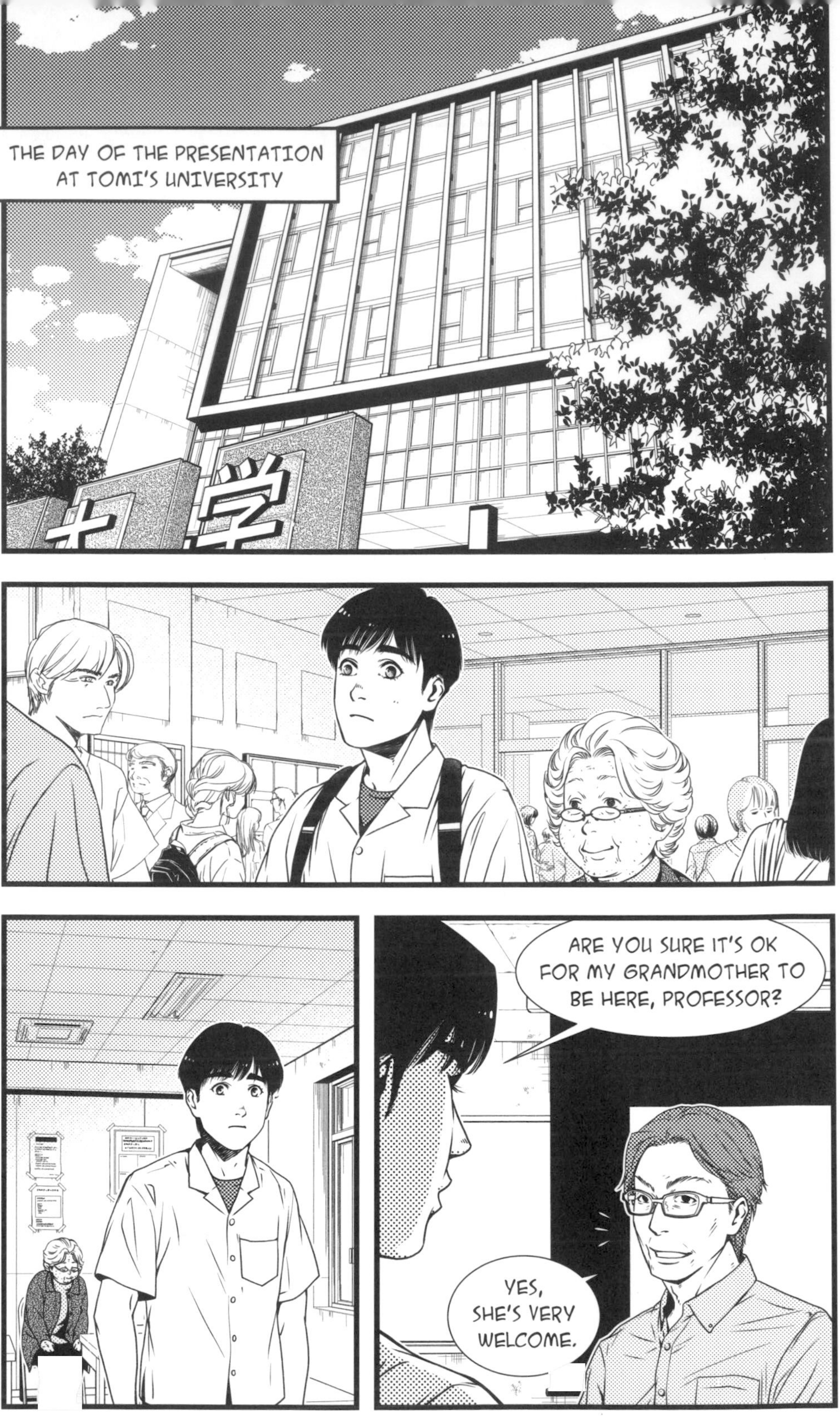
THE DAY OF THE PRESENTATION AT TOMI'S UNIVERSITY
ARE YOU SURE IT'S OK FOR MY GRANDMOTHER TO BE HERE, PROFESSOR?
YES, SHE'S VERY WELCOME.

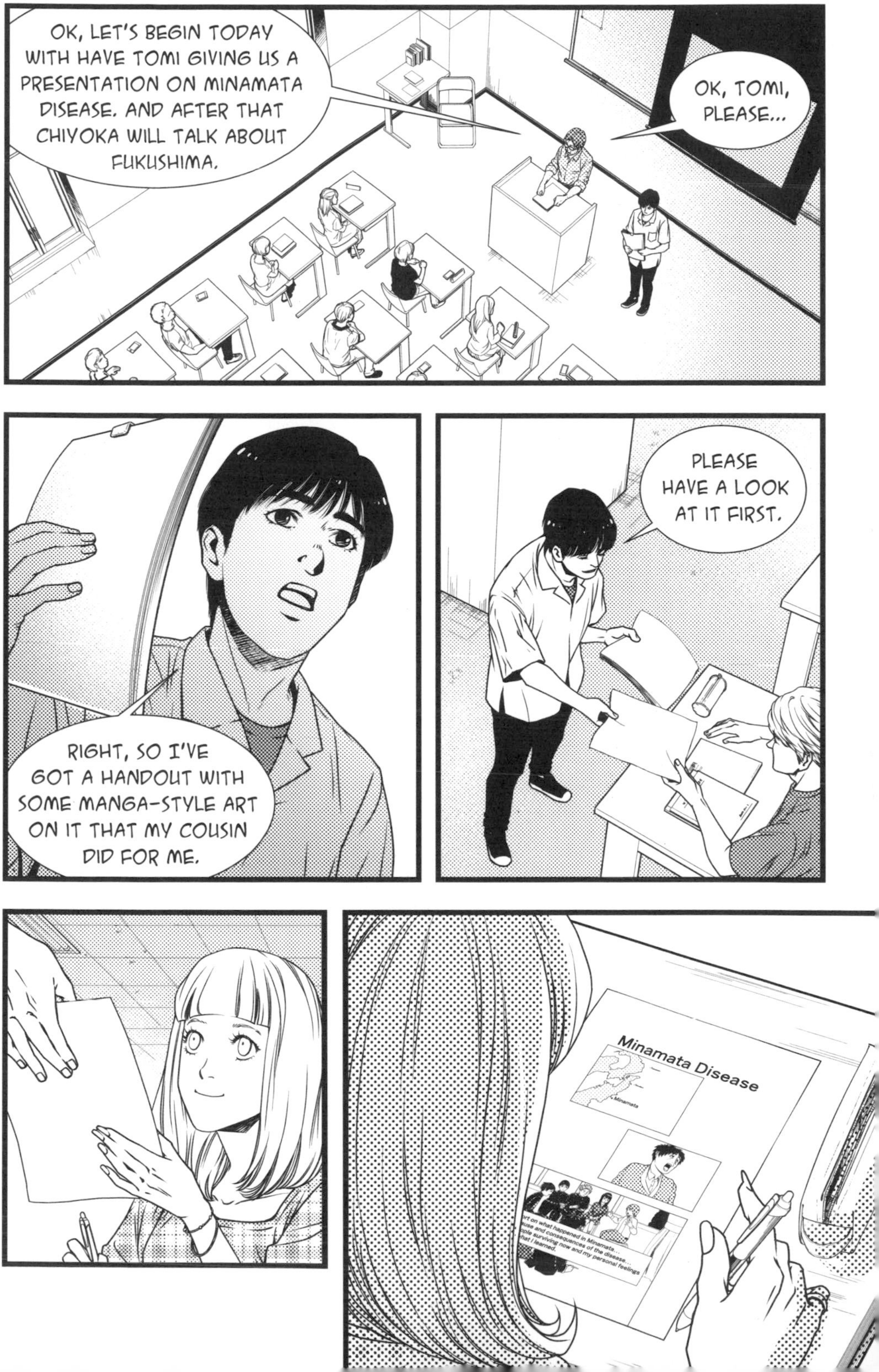
OK, LET'S BEGIN TODAY WITH HAVE TOMI GIVING US A PRESENTATION ON MINAMATA DISEASE. AND AFTER THAT CHIYOKA WILL TALK ABOUT FUKUSHIMA.
OK, TOMI, PLEASE...
RIGHT, SO I'VE GOT A HANDOUT WITH SOME MANGA-STYLE ART ON IT THAT MY COUSIN DID FOR ME.
PLEASE HAVE A LOOK AT IT FIRST.
Minamata Disease
Minamata

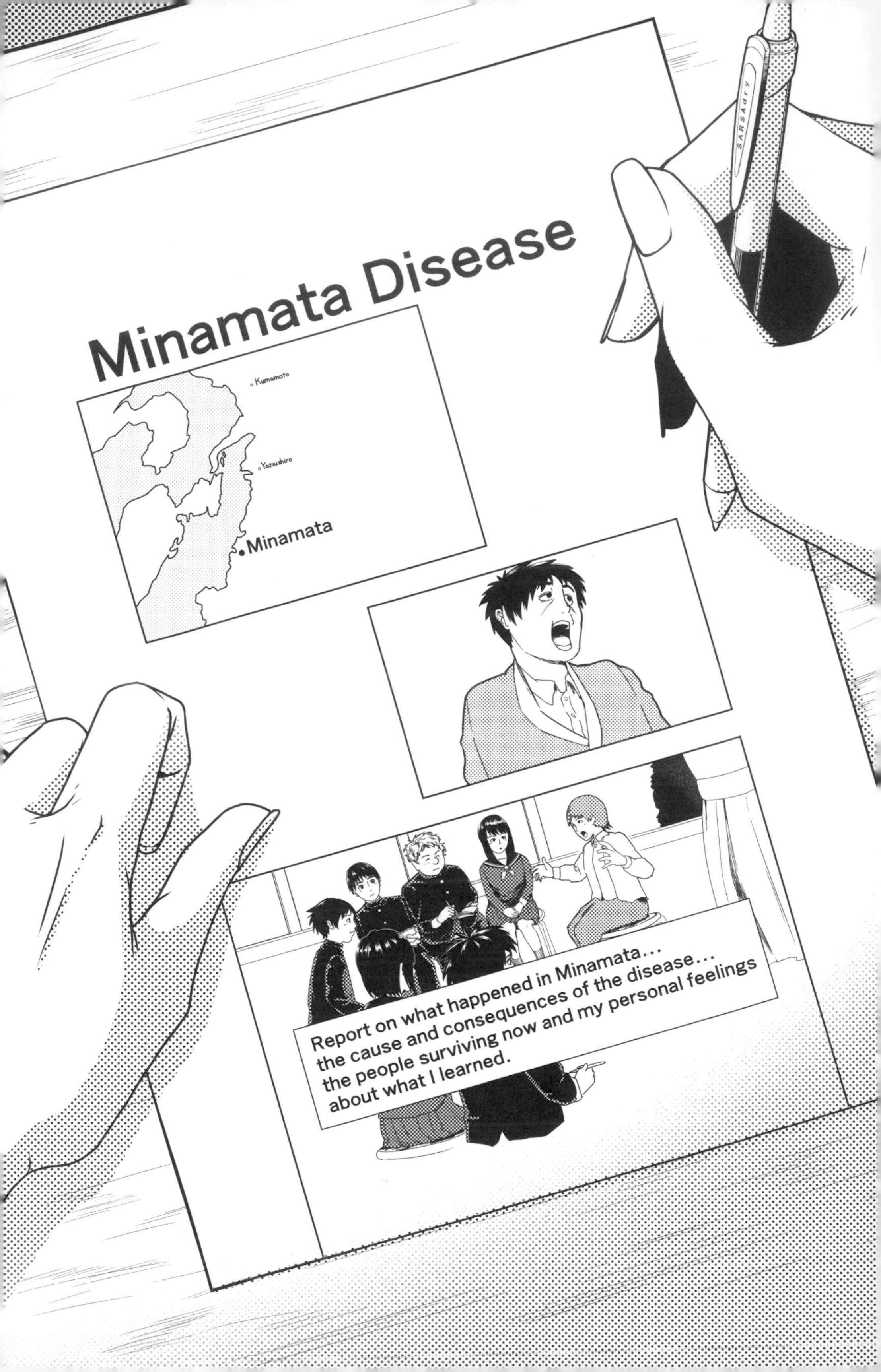
Minamata Disease
Kumamoto
Yatsushiro
Minamata
Report on what happened in Minamata…
the cause and consequences of the disease…
the people surviving now and my personal feelings
about what I learned.

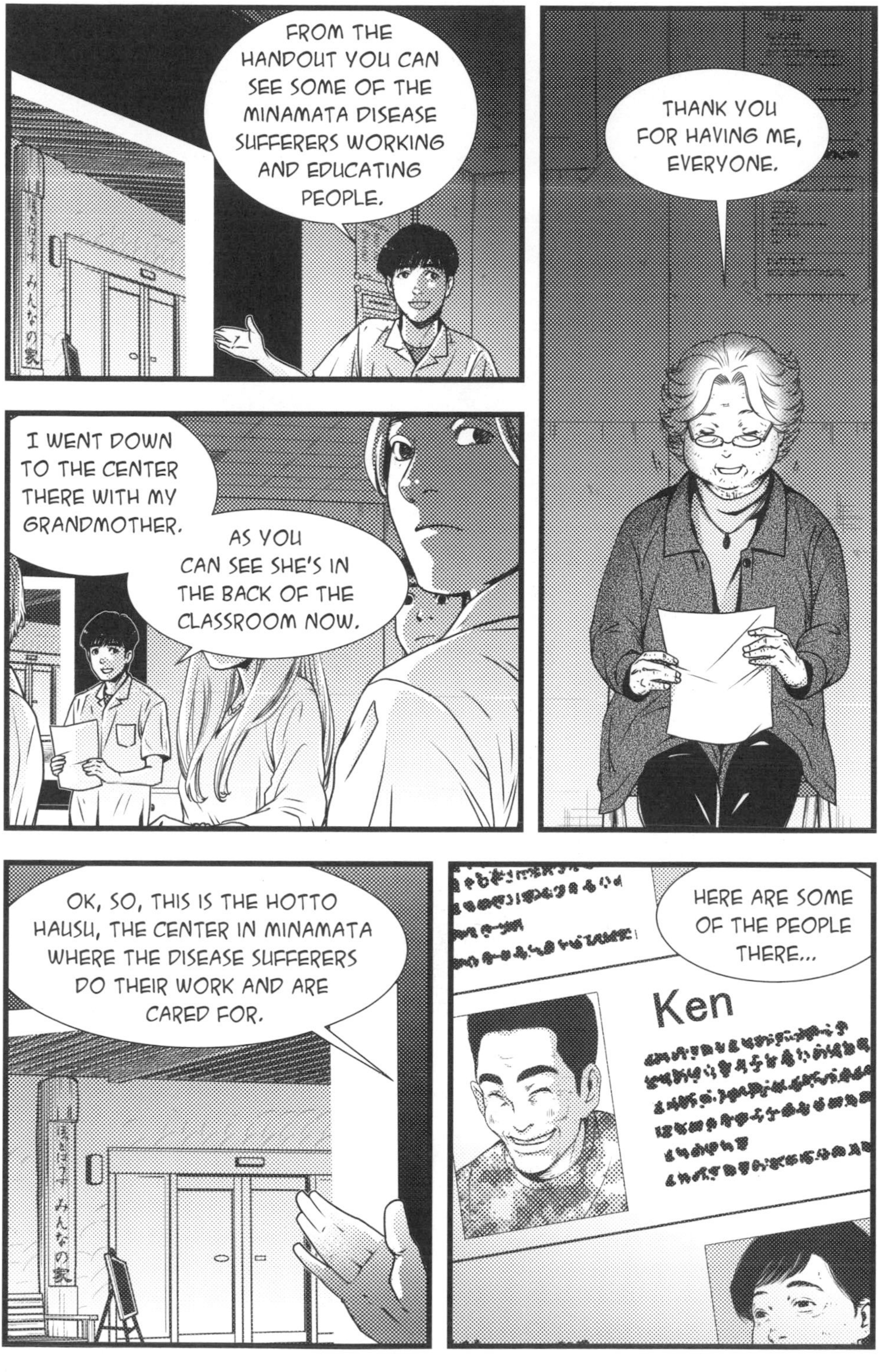
FROM THE HANDOUT YOU CAN SEE SOME OF THE MINAMATA DISEASE SUFFERERS WORKING AND EDUCATING PEOPLE.
I WENT DOWN TO THE CENTER THERE WITH MY GRANDMOTHER.
AS YOU CAN SEE SHE'S IN THE BACK OF THE CLASSROOM NOW.
THANK YOU FOR HAVING ME, EVERYONE.
OK, SO, THIS IS THE HOTTO HAUSU, THE CENTER IN MINAMATA WHERE THE DISEASE SUFFERERS DO THEIR WORK AND ARE CARED FOR.
みんなの家
HERE ARE SOME OF THE PEOPLE THERE...
Ken

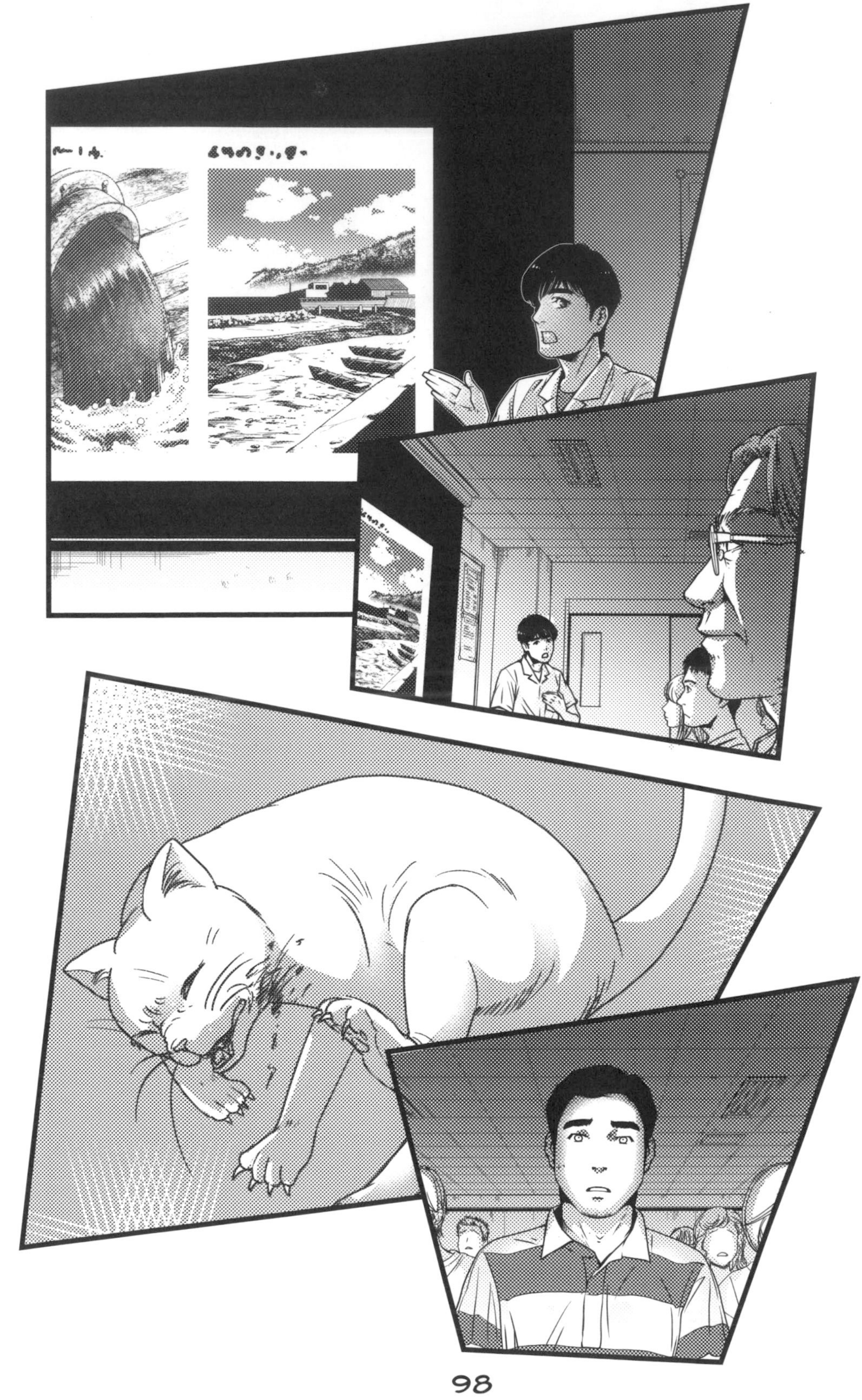

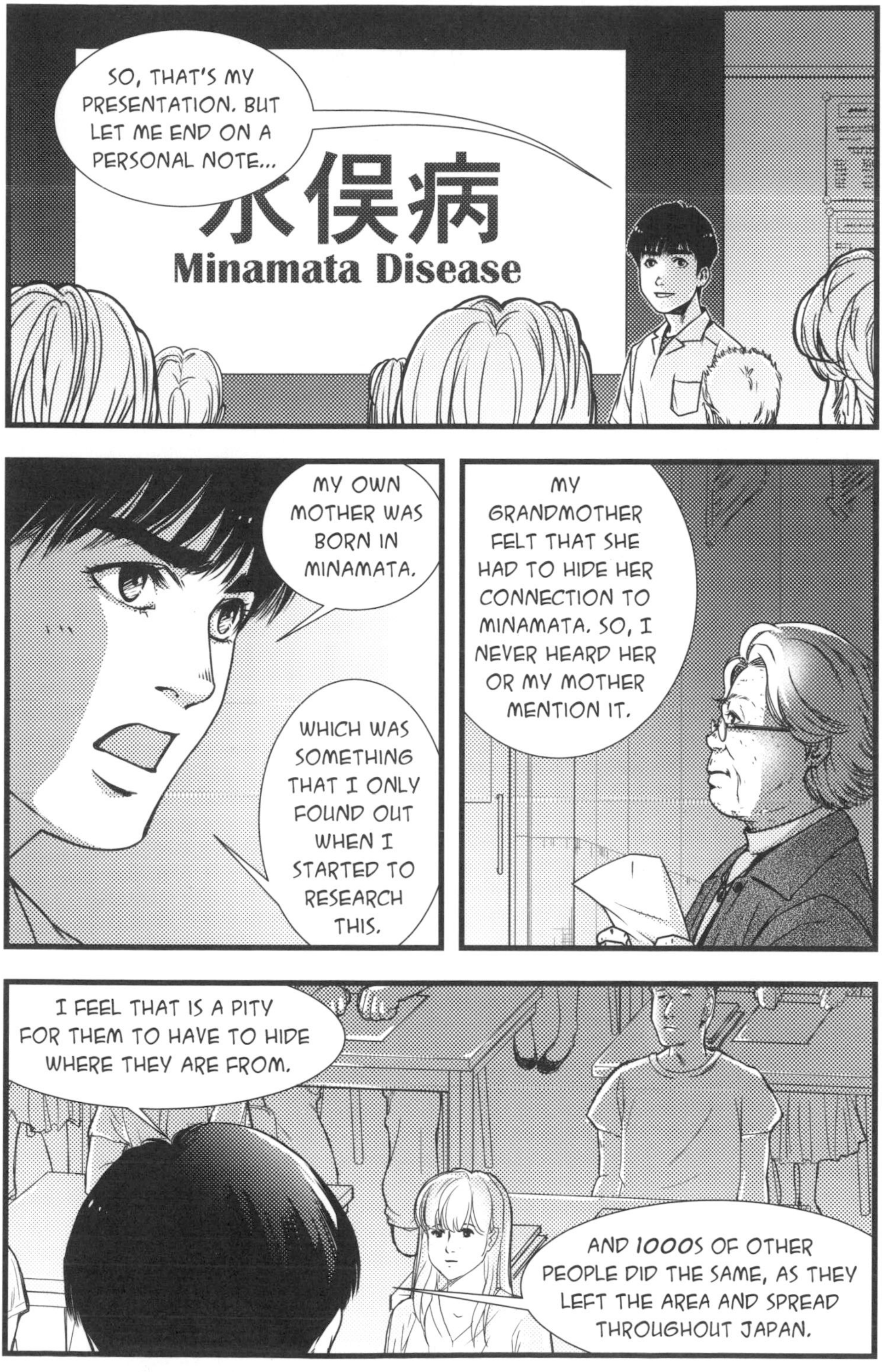
SO, THAT'S MY PRESENTATION. BUT LET ME END ON A PERSONAL NOTE...
Minamata Disease
MY OWN MOTHER WAS BORN IN MINAMATA.
WHICH WAS SOMETHING THAT I ONLY FOUND OUT WHEN I STARTED TO RESEARCH THIS.
MY GRANDMOTHER FELT THAT SHE HAD TO HIDE HER CONNECTION TO MINAMATA. SO, I NEVER HEARD HER OR MY MOTHER MENTION IT.
I FEEL THAT IS A PITY FOR THEM TO HAVE TO HIDE WHERE THEY ARE FROM.
AND 1000S OF OTHER PEOPLE DID THE SAME, AS THEY LEFT THE AREA AND SPREAD THROUGHOUT JAPAN.

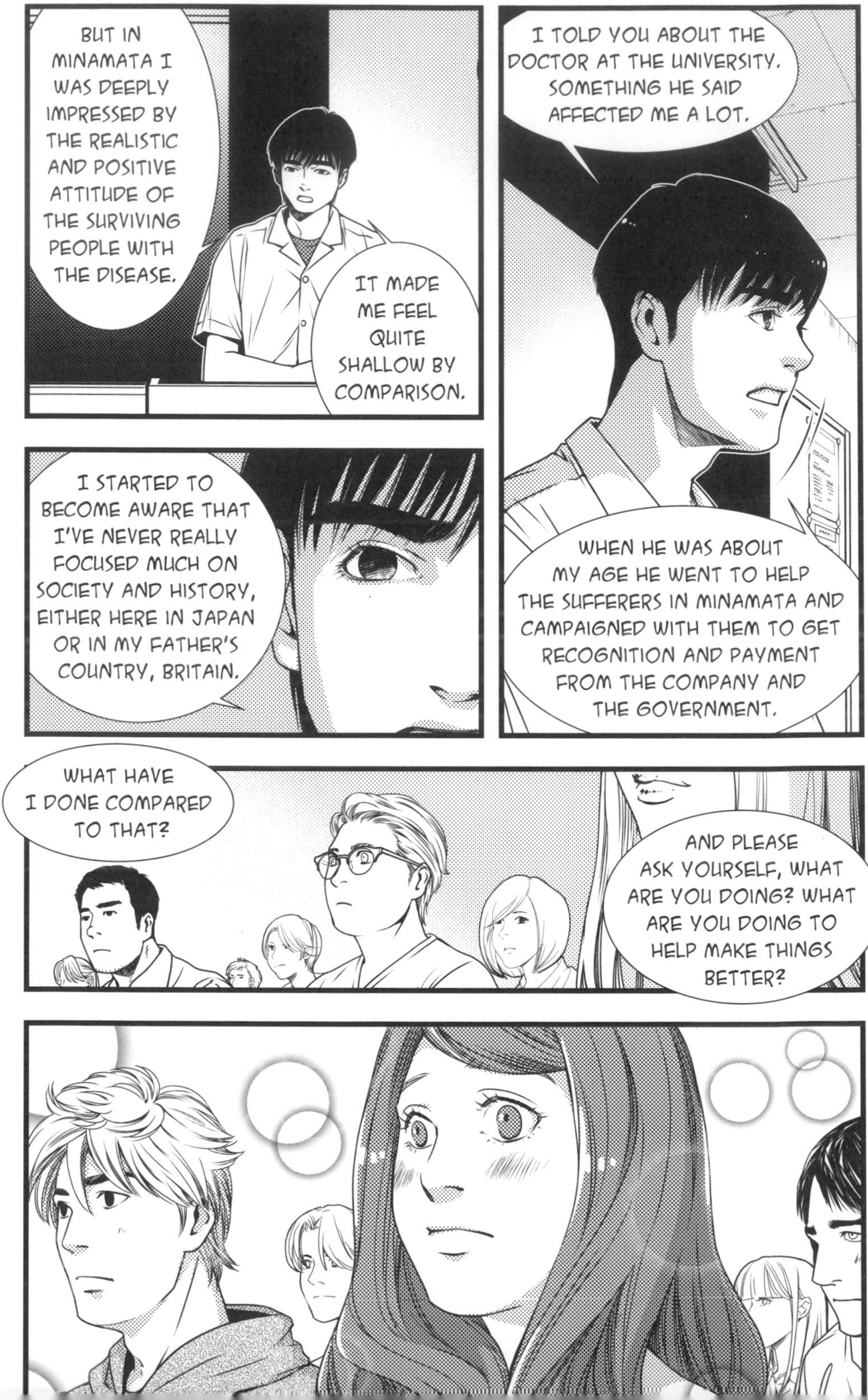
BUT IN MINAMATA I WAS DEEPLY IMPRESSED BY THE REALISTIC AND POSITIVE ATTITUDE OF THE SURVIVING PEOPLE WITH THE DISEASE.
IT MADE ME FEEL QUITE SHALLOW BY COMPARISON.
I TOLD YOU ABOUT THE DOCTOR AT THE UNIVERSITY. SOMETHING HE SAID AFFECTED ME A LOT.
I STARTED TO BECOME AWARE THAT I'VE NEVER REALLY FOCUSED MUCH ON SOCIETY AND HISTORY, EITHER HERE IN JAPAN OR IN MY FATHER'S COUNTRY, BRITAIN.
WHEN HE WAS ABOUT MY AGE HE WENT TO HELP THE SUFFERERS IN MINAMATA AND CAMPAIGNED WITH THEM TO GET RECOGNITION AND PAYMENT FROM THE COMPANY AND THE GOVERNMENT.
WHAT HAVE I DONE COMPARED TO THAT?
AND PLEASE ASK YOURSELF, WHAT ARE YOU DOING? WHAT ARE YOU DOING TO HELP MAKE THINGS BETTER?

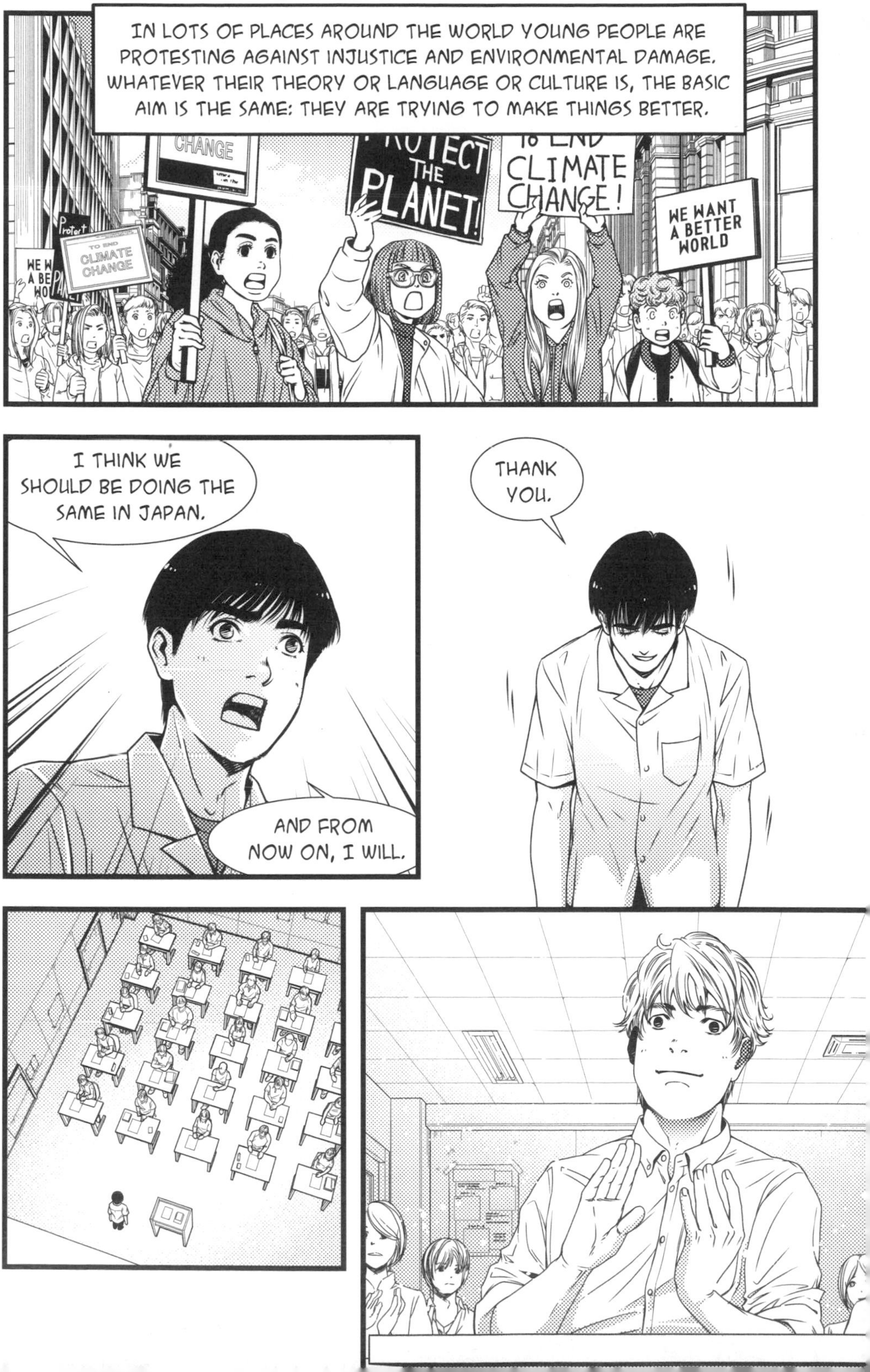
IN LOTS OF PLACES AROUND THE WORLD YOUNG PEOPLE ARE PROTESTING AGAINST INJUSTICE AND ENVIRONMENTAL DAMAGE. WHATEVER THEIR THEORY OR LANGUAGE OR CULTURE IS, THE BASIC AIM IS THE SAME: THEY ARE TRYING TO MAKE THINGS BETTER.
CHANGE
THE PLANET!
CLIMATE CHANGE!
WE WANT A BETTER WORLD
TO END CLIMATE CHANGE
I THINK WE SHOULD BE DOING THE SAME IN JAPAN.
AND FROM NOW ON, I WILL.
THANK YOU.

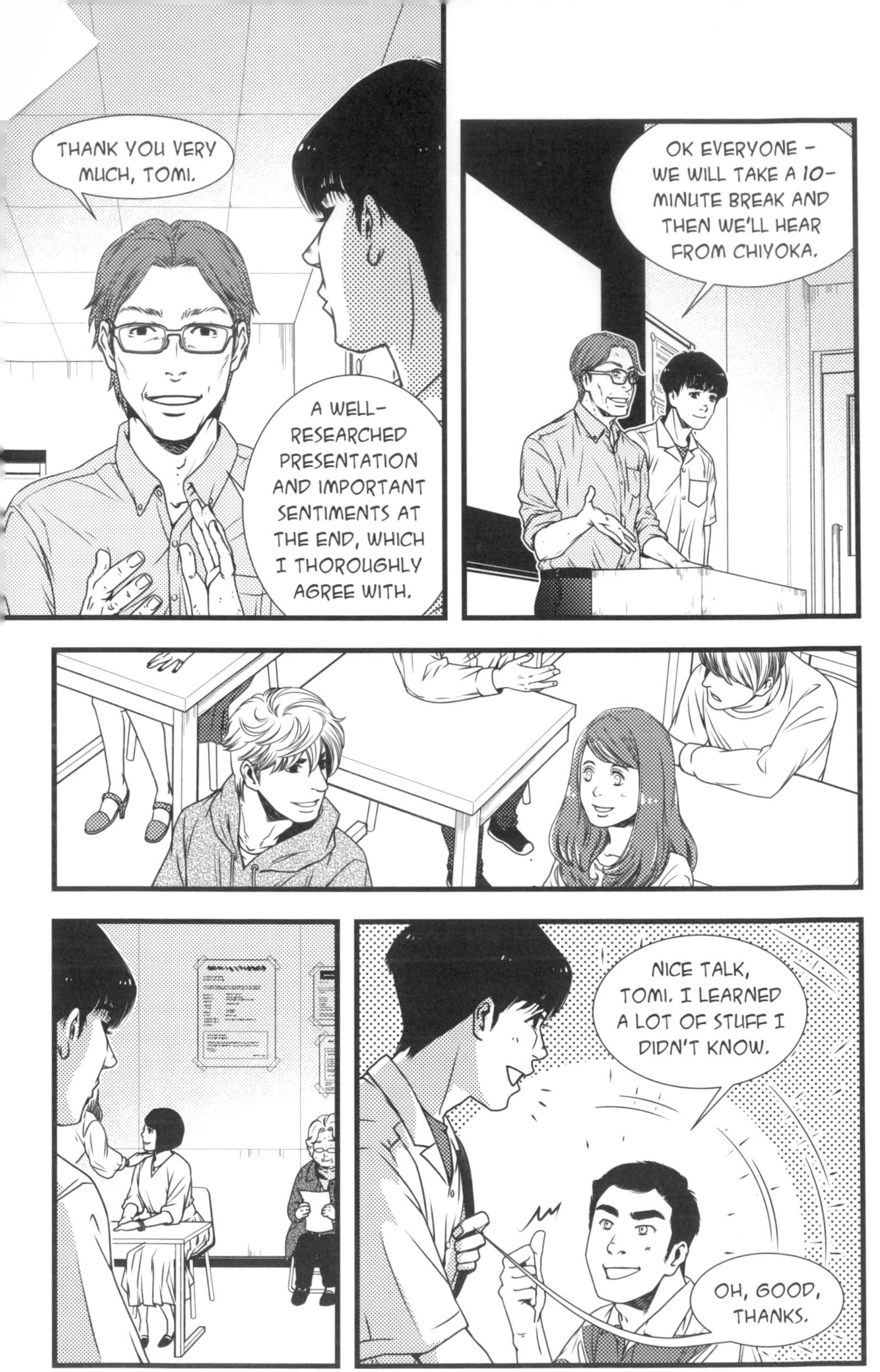
THANK YOU VERY MUCH, TOMI.
A WELL-RESEARCHED PRESENTATION AND IMPORTANT SENTIMENTS AT THE END, WHICH I THOROUGHLY AGREE WITH.
OK EVERYONE - WE WILL TAKE A 10-MINUTE BREAK AND THEN WE'LL HEAR FROM CHIYOKA.
NICE TALK, TOMI. I LEARNED A LOT OF STUFF I DIDN'T KNOW.
OH, GOOD, THANKS.

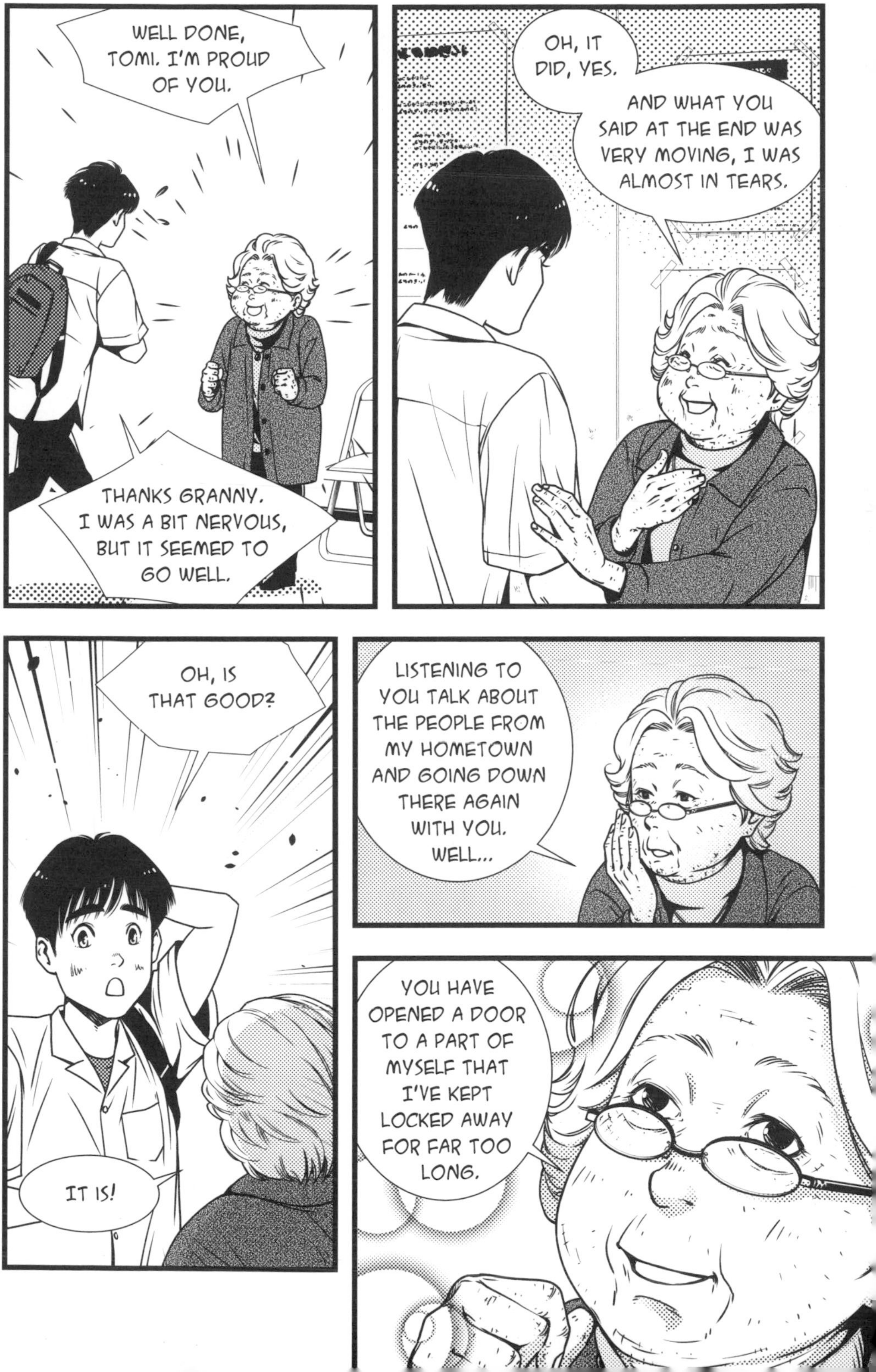
WELL DONE, TOMI. I'M PROUD OF YOU.
THANKS GRANNY. I WAS A BIT NERVOUS, BUT IT SEEMED TO GO WELL.
OH, IT DID, YES.
AND WHAT YOU SAID AT THE END WAS VERY MOVING, I WAS ALMOST IN TEARS.
OH, IS THAT GOOD?
IT IS!
LISTENING TO YOU TALK ABOUT THE PEOPLE FROM MY HOMETOWN AND GOING DOWN THERE AGAIN WITH YOU. WELL...
YOU HAVE OPENED A DOOR TO A PART OF MYSELF THAT I'VE KEPT LOCKED AWAY FOR FAR TOO LONG.

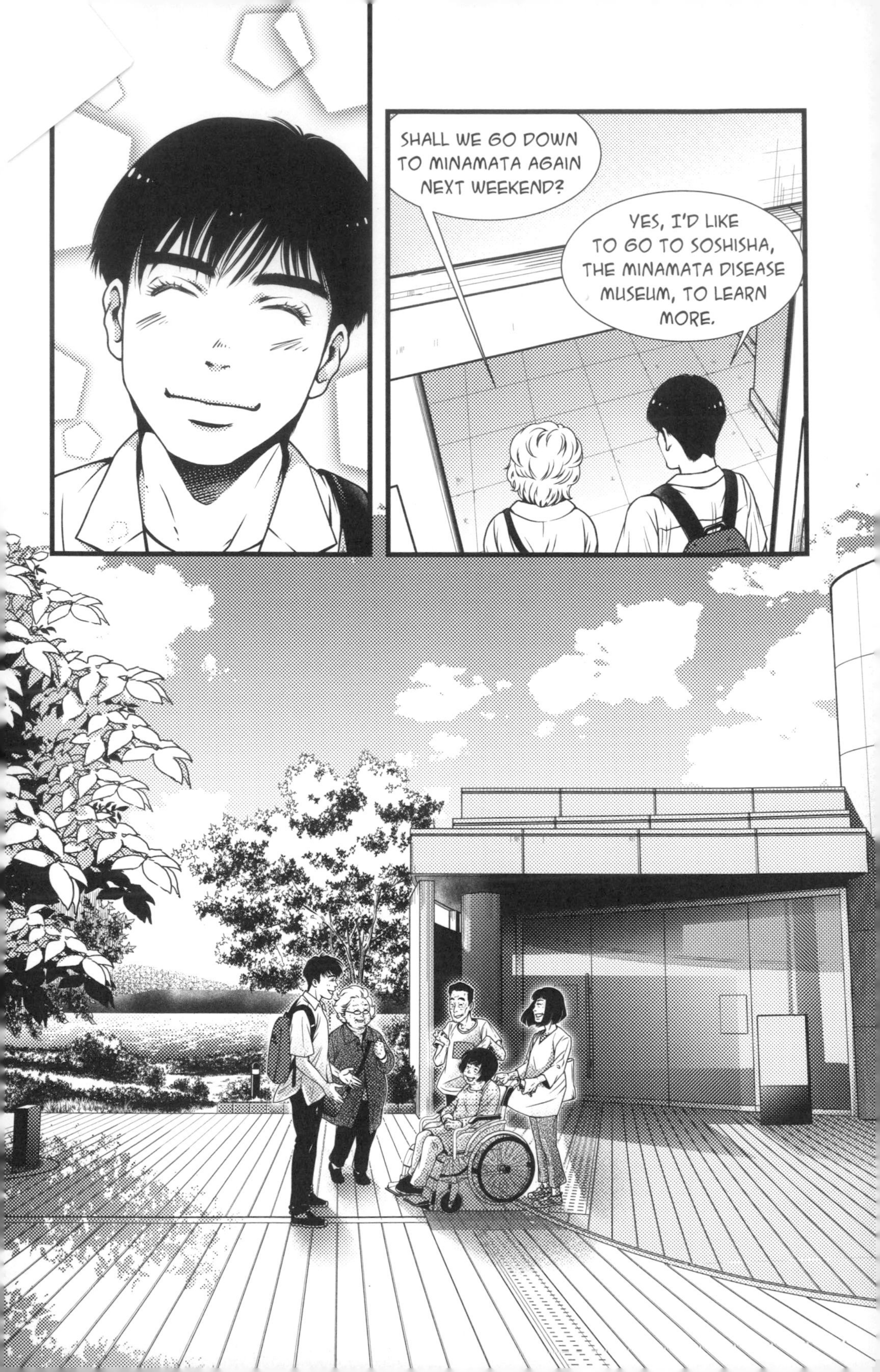
SHALL WE GO DOWN TO MINAMATA AGAIN NEXT WEEKEND?
YES, I'D LIKE TO GO TO SOSHISHA, THE MINAMATA DISEASE MUSEUM, TO LEARN MORE.

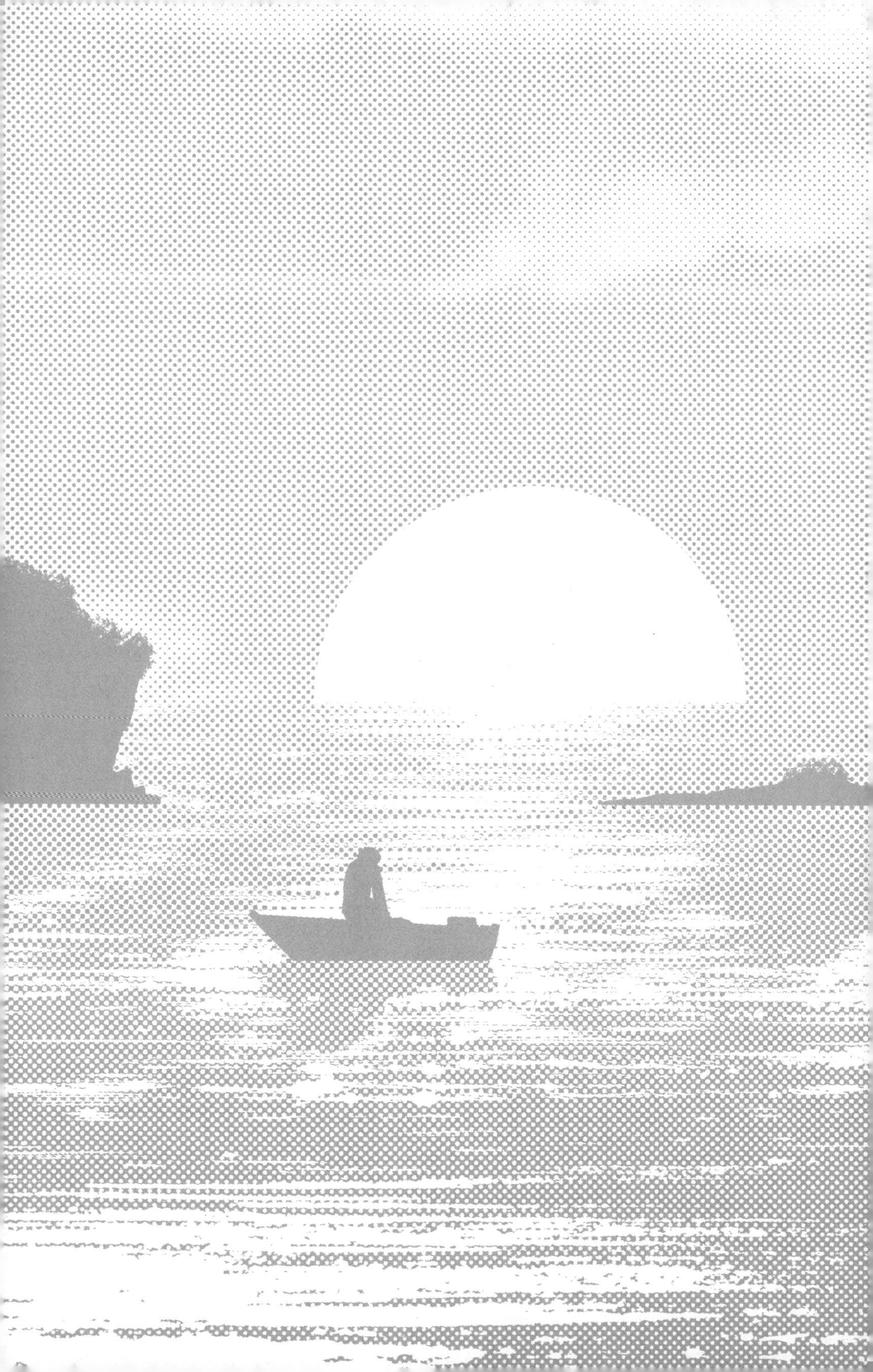

CHARACTERS IN PROFILE

These are the stories of some of the real people that the characters in this book are based upon.

Kenji Nagamoto was born in the Umedo area of Minamata in 1959. He was certified as a congenital Minamata disease patient in 1963. He gave a speech of behalf of bereaved families at the memorial service for Minamata disease victims in 2003 and 2012. When he was bullied in childhood due to his disease, looking at the cranes in Umedo Port cheered him up. He tells of his severe experiences with his poetic expressions and humor.

Yuji Kaneko was born in the Myojin area of Minamata in 1955. He was certified as a congenital Minamata disease patient in 1962. All of his family are also certified. When he was 40 he and other congenital patients founded Hotto Hausu as a workshop. His dream of getting a job finally came true after 20 years.

Kiyoko Kagata was born in the Tsukinoura area of Minamata in 1955. She was certified as a congenital Minamata disease patient in 1962. From the age of 7 to 25 she was in the Yunoko Hospital and Meisuien (a facility for Minamata disease patients), so she has no memory of living with her family. The isolation she felt at that time has not gone away. She tells people about the congenital patients who are not able to speak due to dysfunction cause by the disease. She is confined to a wheelchair but dearly wishes to push her fellow patients if she can ever walk again.

Kazumitsu Hannaga was born in another of the areas mentioned in this book, the Hachinokubo area of Minamata, in 1955. He was certified as a congenital Minamata disease patient in 1962. He has lived in the Yunoko Hospital and Meisuien since 1965. Because of his illness he has a speech disability; however, he takes photos to express himself. His photo book *Funeral Toruzo* was published in 1977. Before that he had a photo exhibition at an international convention held in Minamata. This became the starting point for the creation of Hotto Hausu. Now he goes there once or twice a week to spend time with his friends.

Takeko Kato was born in Fuchu, Tokyo, in 1950. In 1988–89 she joined a sit-in with uncertified patients in front of the Chisso factory in Minamata. In 1992 she moved to Minamata, where she actively supported congenital patients' daily lives and helped found the group "Cassiopeia." Later the group served as a starting point for the Hotto Hausu center, where she subsequently worked as director. Her life's work is disseminating the "treasures" that come from Minamata disease. She has gone to many places in this effort—anywhere that people are interested in listening.

FURTHER READING

George, Timothy. *Minamata: Pollution and the Struggle for Democracy in Postwar Japan*. Harvard University Asia Center, 2002.

———. "Fukushima in Light of Minamata." https://apjjf.org/2012/10/11/Timothy-S.-George/3715/article.html.

Ishimure, Michiko. *Paradise in the Sea of Sorrow*. University of Michigan Center for Japanese Studies, 2003.

Kuwabara, Shisei. *The Minamata Disaster* 水俣事件. Fujiwara Shoten, 2013.

Oiwa, Keibo. *Rowing the Eternal Sea*. Rowman and Littlefield, 2001.

Tsurumi, Kazuko. *The Adventure of Ideas*. https://www.howtodrawmanga.com/products/tsurumi.

Tsurumi, Kazuko, and Tom Gill. "New Lives: Some Case Studies of Minamata." https://apjjf.org/2014/12/34/Tom-Gill/4169/article.html.

Yoneyama, Shoko. "Life-world: Beyond Fukushima and Minamata." https://apjjf.org/2012/10/42/Shoko-YONEYAMA/3845/article.html.

ABOUT THE CREATORS

SEÁN MICHAEL WILSON is a comic book writer from Scotland. Working with various Japanese artists he has written a unique line of Japanese history/martial arts books, including *The Book of Five Rings*, *Yakuza Moon*, and *Black Ships*. In 2016 his book *The Faceless Ghost* was nominated for the prestigious Eisner Book Awards and received a medal in the 2016 Independent Publisher Book Awards. In 2017 his book with Akiko Shimojima, *Secrets of the Ninja*, won an International Manga Award from the Japanese government—he is the first British person to receive this award.

AKIKO SHIMOJIMA is a comic artist from Japan. Her comics have been published by several companies in Japan and other countries. Her book *Cold Mountain* was the winner of the China Comic and Animation Competition 2015 Best Overseas Comic award. She also teaches how to draw digital comics at a college in Tokyo.